GW00630501

About the Author

At the age of 34 and bored with his job as a civil servant, David saw a 10 minute clip on TV about a race across the Sahara Desert.

Two years later, and determined to have just one adventure in his lifetime, he found himself standing on the start line of the 11th Marathon des Sables.

At the age of 53 David is still having adventures and continues to race in some of the most extreme Ultra-distance races in the world.

David lives on the Isle of Wight with his wife Marilyn and is currently writing his second book.

And he is still bored with his job as a civil servant!

www.daveberridge.co.uk
http://facebook.com/pages/david-berridge/452379348162384

FARTLEKS AND FLATULENCE

One man's epic journey, from a rather comfortable settee,
to the Great Sahara Desert and beyond.

David Berridge has asserted his right under the copyright
and patents act 1988 to be indentified as the author
of this work.

Published in 2013 by Dave Berridge

daveberridge.co.uk

ISBN 978-0-9927341-0-7
Printed by crossprint.co.uk

*To my wife Marilyn, whose absolute support
made the whole thing possible.*

FARTLEKS AND FLATULENCE

One man's epic journey, from a rather comfortable settee,
to the Great Sahara Desert and beyond.

This book is written by me - an ordinary bloke who fancied having a bash. It sort of chronicles my feeble foray into the world of "Ultra-distance Running."

I'm not an athlete or even a very good runner, but I do possess a thirst for adventure, a willingness to have a go, and a love of travel.

My fears, mistakes, questions and "cock ups" are all here.

It's not a book full of training tips, nutritional advice, kit lists etc. It is however a comprehensive list of the races I have done, the things I've got away with and the things I haven't.

Unfortunately I write much like I run, with an amateurish enthusiasm, so please forgive me.

Why the rather odd title "Fartleks and Flatulence"? Well, they are both what I would consider accidental imperatives, essential but involuntary actions that occur when I run, particularly when I'm training.

Flatulence, one of those embarrassingly pleasant pastimes that I can indulge in whilst out running on my own, no volume control required and no one to either pass comment or judgement!

I don't know why it happens when I run or why at such an intensity, but it happens. I used to think that I was the only runner in the world suffering from such an affliction, but no apparently it's quite common, just one of the many perks of running, I suppose!

Fartleks or "speed play" would seem to imply that I am a serious athlete, but alas and to my eternal shame my so called 'fartlek' sessions always come about accidentally, being the worlds laziest trainer I normally just plod along, until that is, a dog chases me, a mountain biker passes me, it starts to rain or attractive female or two appear, another runner comes into view, a tractor tries to squeeze pass in a narrow country lane and I need to speed up for the sake of self-preservation, I need a wee or worse! Any number of reasons make me run faster but rest assured the 'fartleks', much like my flatulence, just seem to happen!

CONTENTS

THE MARATHON DES SABLES 1996

All men dream but not equally
Those who dream by night in the dusty recesses of their
minds wake in the day to find that all was vanity; but
the dreamers of the day are dangerous men, for they
may act their dream with open eyes, and make it possible.

                                                    T. E. Lawrence

What is it: The most famous and the original
                 Desert Stage Race

When: April

Where: Morocco

Distance: 240km (150 miles)

It is: A six day multi stage Desert race

See: Darbaroud.com

One Saturday morning in 1994, I was up early, and with a cup
of tea and half a dozen choccie bickies in hand, I plonked myself
down in front of the television to watch "Transworld Sport".
I finished my tea and was busy brushing away the crumbs
(trying desperately to hide the evidence) when a ten minute
piece came on about a foot race across the Sahara Desert, the
race was held annually and was called the "Marathon Des
Sables". It was a 210 kilometer running race across the Sahara
Desert, the people running were an odd mixture, elite type
racing snakes, young, old and middle aged, fast and slow, tall
and short, fat and thin. I was fascinated! I grabbed a video

tape from the mountain that was beside the television. "Dirty Dancing" that would do, I shoved it in and hit record.

Over the weekend I watched it a couple of times, amazed that any one could, or would, want to run across a desert.

The following weekend whilst reading the Telegraph I came across an article by Mike Calvin, a journalist covering that year's 'Marathon Des Sables' and in particular Dr Mike Stroud's participation. Dr Stroud had not long returned from his epic crossing of Antarctica with Ranulph Fiennes. I read the article and watched the video for the umpteenth time and decided to write to Mike Calvin to find out a bit more about the race. A few days later a letter from the Telegraph arrived along with the details of the UK organiser, Chris Lawrence. 'The best of Morocco' was the man to talk to, another letter and another reply - only this time from Chris Lawrence. He had kindly sent me an official video. I watched it and read the details of how to enter, 'how to enter'- I hadn't planned to do the bloody thing, doing the bloody thing was for other people!

Even if I did fancy having a bash, which I didn't, the reality was that I was 34 years old, had not run a step since I was at school, and I had hated running at school. Memories of the dreaded cross country runs, cold red legs, runny nose, humiliation and black plimsolls all came flooding back.

I hadn't got the money - £1800 was a lot. I hadn't got the time or indeed the knowledge to train, how far is 210kms, how does anyone train to run for seven days on the trot, carrying a rucksack and across the desert?

I wouldn't know how to navigate, what to take, what to wear or what to eat and I'd never flown. The list of why I couldn't was impressive and long and getting more impressive and longer by the minute.

I knew what I had to do: just watch the video again to confirm what I already knew, and as I was watching it for the 50th time my wife came in wearing that look, the look that only an exasperated wife can a give a husband. She sat down and I proceeded to waffle on about the 'Marathon Des Sables', sort of explaining that I would love to have a go whilst knowing it was completely ridiculous. She politely listened as only that same slightly exasperated wife can listen. As you can see my wife spends a lot of time being in a state of utter exasperation. I thought I was making a pretty good case when bloody Patrick Swayze and Jennifer Grey started faffing about on the television, the words "You've taped over my "Dirty Dancing" bought the whole thing to an abrupt end!

The more I thought about it the more I wanted to do it. And if I really wanted to do it I needed to commit myself. Could I find the money? It would be difficult but yes, just! Could I train? The race was a year away, plenty of time (I hoped) What sort of training? That was a difficult one, all I could do was run and walk as much as possible, whilst carrying a rucksack. Time off work, with enough notice it should be okay, If I did manage by some miracle or other to get myself on to the start line I WOULD have to finish!

After the 'Dirty Dancing' debacle had died down (I had promised to buy her the video) I plucked up the courage to ask, well not ask exactly, more suggest, that my running 143 miles across the Sahara Desert, and paying £1800 for the privilege would be a good idea. It was a tough sell but I got away with it (It was only after I had returned, that my wife said she only said yes because "I didn't think for one minute you were stupid enough to go through with it").

With my wife's 'blessing' it was time to get my arse in gear. Three things needed to be done - train for it, pay for it and complete it. Easy. First the money, I would start saving immediately. Second, the training, ah! Before I start training I'll have to buy some trainers: bollocks, I'll have to start saving when I next get paid.

In the mean time I'll just get out and run round the street, within 20 minutes I was back and trying to put the kettle on. I was bollocksed, couldn't talk and needed a cup of tea.

Watching the video again and trying to pick up some tips on running through the desert, I noticed that there was one hell of a lot of walking involved. That made me feel a bit better.

With the training all I could do was to be patient, increase my distance bit by bit, but not my speed, do plenty of hills and lots of 'speed marching' whilst carrying a pack containing the plastic milk containers filled with water, slowly increasing the weight. Buy a compass and practise walking on a bearing, whatever that means (fortunately the compass I bought had an idiots guide to using it). Only the year before an Italian runner had got lost and was not found for 10 days. When he was eventually found he was in Algeria!

Over the following months I steadily increased my mileage but with Christmas rapidly approaching and the race scheduled to take place in March, I wasn't ready, I wasn't anywhere near ready and I knew it. Yes, training had gone well and yes I could run/walk 10 to 15 miles a day for three or four days but it wasn't enough and I was very aware of it!

So my first major decision, well second if you count my entering the thing, I decided to not do the 1995 race but wait another year and enter the 11th 'Marathon Des Sables' in 1996.

Decision made, I let my wife know of my revised plan and was once again treated to that exasperated look.

With the training side of things going well and with time rapidly passing by, it was time to sort the logistics out, the funds were coming together, I might have to borrow a bit, but the funds would be in place. The time off work: I managed to get 10 days off and with swapping a couple of shifts, that was all sorted.

What gear? ie: rucksack, cooker, clothes, shoes and food etc etc. Off to the local outdoor shop, when I say the local outdoor shop, we live on the Isle of Wight, the choice of outdoor shops is somewhat limited - Milletts! So it was a trip to Portsmouth where I managed to find a rucksack a 35ltr Lowe Alpine 'Mountain Contour' jobby. I also managed to find a pair of trainers, I tried a pair on in what was supposed to be a 'Sports

Shop' when a spotty, bored-looking 12 year old shop assistant asked if I was going to run in them!!

Food: this was a tricky one. What type of food could I carry in a rucksack? The food had to be light, I had to carry 7 days worth plus an emergency supply! It had to give all the required nutrition for hard physical labour, be easy to prepare and not get spoiled whilst being carried in a rucksack and in the heat. I had got no idea, then I remembered the book I had just read by Ranulph Fiennes, 'Mind over matter', an account of his journey in Antarctica. In the list of sponsors at the back was the name of the company that had supplied all the nutritional requirements used during that expedition. I wondered if they might be able to help or advise. I wrote a letter explaining my predicament and luckily they had not only heard of the "Marathon Des Sables" but could supply me with all that I would need - problem solved.

They gave me a list of what was needed and more importantly why it was needed. I was impressed and after all, if they were good enough for Ranulph Fiennes they were good enough for me.

A few days later the postman arrived with my food parcel. He struggled up the garden path, his face and upper torso hidden behind a quite substantial package, or should I say 'crate' containing my 'essential' food! On opening the box I saw it contained 28 'power bars' (3 a day) and packets and sachets of God knows what. I reasoned that if this is what the 'experts' considered essential I was in trouble. I wouldn't be able to carry that amount, let alone all the other stuff I would need. In the end I decided on about two thirds of their total, of which I ended up eating less than half, and only one mouthful of the 28 power bars!

What to wear? I sound like my wife now! But, like everything else to do with this race, I had to get it right. The clothing needed to be cool (not as in trendy), not chafe, prevent sunburn and be comfortable. The clothing couldn't be heavy or bulky. I decided on the following; 2 Great Ormond Street t-shirts, Great Ormond Street was the hospital that I had decided to raise money for, 1 pair of coolmax shorts, 4 pairs of socks (I had to look after my feet, so decided to treat them with clean socks) 1 Helly Hansen thermal top, 1 Helly Hansen thermal leggings, 1 pair of training shoes, 1 pair of sponge flip-flops and 2 pairs of underpants.

Sleeping bag: with what little research I managed to do, I found out that at night the desert was freezing, so a good sleeping bag would be essential, but again it was which sleeping bag? I reasoned that the warm sleeping bags would be the big sleeping bags, however I had to squeeze mine into a rucksack and carry the thing!

Like everything else I hadn't got a clue, I didn't even know where to look. Back to Portsmouth and the shop where I had purchased my rucksack. Trying to look as if I knew what I was doing and exactly what I was looking for, I stumbled on Mountain Equipment's 'mountain marathon' (I didn't even know there was such a thing as a mountain marathon) at 750gms it was light, and it was down filled, down-filled = warmth!

Cooking, I don't even cook at home, so this would be a challenge. Luckily most of the meals were the 'just add hot water' type. Even I couldn't cock that up!

I was a little bit limited in my choice of cooker because most airlines don't allow fuel ie: gas, meths or petrol. So I would have to use solid fuel tablets: these hexamine blocks worked magnificently - I did practise a lot in the garden.

The training had gone well, I had remained injury-free and felt confident-ish. The thing was paid for and my place secured, kit was assembled, leave from work sorted, I had passed my medical and had flights organised. I was in effect 'good to go' (I think).

D Day

Friday 22nd March 1996. It was here, the day I had been dreading and looking forward to had arrived, and so had I, at Terminal 3, London's Heathrow airport. My first flight, I hadn't got a clue what I was doing but just bimbled my way through. I had a strange feeling I would be doing a lot of 'just bimbling my way through' over the next few days.

After completing my 'check in' I grabbed a coffee and a few quiet moments to contemplate what the hell I had done, and indeed was about to do. I was actually flying to Morocco to take part in what was billed as the 'Toughest Foot Race on Earth' running 143 miles across the Sahara Desert, what a plank!

I had nearly 3 hours before the flight: 3 hours to kill. I looked around and tried to see if I could spot any other like-minded individuals, I couldn't. Everyone else looked relatively normal. Surely the people that would be having a bash at the 'worlds toughest foot race' would be easy to spot? Strong, athletic-looking, a spring in the step, confident and cool, trained, toned and ready for the task in hand? Wrong. I didn't spot any of them because we were after all just average runners, dreamers and joggers, young, old and middle aged but we had got one thing in common we wanted to, no, needed to, take part in this, the maddest of adventures, the "Marathon Des Sables".

Touching down in the small desert town of Ouarzazate, the air was oppressive. The short walk down the aircraft steps had me sweating, the little airport was quite literally swamped with nearly 200 hundred athletes, and God knows how many race staff and tourists. The officials fortunately rose to the challenge and started the long laborious job of processing each and every one of us. There were pained expressions on the check in staff as they desperately tried to get to grips with the various languages:- English, Russian, German, Italian and Danish to name but a few.

After having my passport stamped I was taken to one side by a member of staff who was wearing an ill-fitting and grubby uniform: a small man who but for his position I would not have given a second glance. Behind him stood a sour-faced stern-looking individual who was dressed in plain clothes, strangely it was the plain-clothed individual who seemed more menacing. After placing my holdall and rucksack on the bench in front of them, the smaller uniformed man asked, well indicated, that he would like me to open them. It was at this point that I remembered placing seven packs of dehydrated food very neatly on the top of my kit - all the uniformed bloke saw was seven bags of white powder. The look on his face said it all. Whilst I had visions of the film 'Midnight Express' and 15 years in a Moroccan jail, and the inescapable fact that my life was now officially over, he called to the plain clothes bloke. He looked at the bags of white powder, they looked at each other and then they each looked at me. I smiled, well I think I smiled, it was definitely supposed to be a smile, I then explained or at least tried to explain that it was food, I was with the 'Marathon Des Sables'. I said 'Marathon Des Sables' using my very best French accent, I don't know why but I did. Thankfully and thanks in no small part to my impressive language skills, he understood, smiled and waved me through, the uniformed bloke looked crestfallen. I zipped the bag up and got the hell out of there.

I boarded one of the coaches that would be taking us to the hotel. It just so happened that I had boarded the wrong coach, the one that was last to leave. After 20 minutes waiting I was getting fidgety: after half an hour I was bored and fidgety and after an hour everyone was bored, fidgety, hot and fed up.

Eventually we were told what the hold-up was; apparently an Israeli athlete was having all sorts of problems getting through Customs. He did however manage to eventually get through.

The next problem was Helen Klein and her husband Norm. Helen is a bit of a legend in Ultra running circles, she holds numerous world records, she is also in her seventies. A truly remarkable women, who at the age of seventy five took part in the 'Eco Challenge' - one of the toughest adventure races on earth. Both she and her husband had apparently missed their connecting flight from New York and would not be competing in this year's race.

We finally arrived at our hotel late at night and I have to say it was far better than I was expecting. As luck would have it, our time here was to be short, we literally had a quick meal, were allocated rooms and were told to be ready to leave at six in the morning. We were to be taken to the airport and then on to the coaches for the 310 km trip to the start.

My roommate and as it would turn out, part time running partner, was a thirty-something rugby playing, Welsh policeman Alun, who in the next few days would impress everyone with his huge appetite, love for dehydrated food (which I thought tasted like wet sawdust!) and ability to outsnore anyone else.

The morning saw us up bright and early for breakfast. I decided to eat as much as I could as I knew that this would be the last proper food we would see for a while. After breakfast we were taken to the airport to meet the coaches. As was to become the norm we had a bit of hanging about to do. It did however give me the opportunity to meet the other runners and write a postcard or two. It was noticeable how hot it was even at eight o'clock in the morning.

The all day drive was long, hot and uncomfortable (that's twice I've moaned about the heat, and I'm in the Sahara Desert, plank!) It did however give me a chance to look at the terrain that we would have to cross over the next few days.

Stopping at a very scenic area for a lunch break we were handed packed lunches and people started taking pictures. The terrain was very beautiful but extremely harsh. Even though I had just arrived, I liked the place.

When we finally arrived, the kit bags were loaded on to 4x4 vehicles to be transported the mile or so to the camp, which we could see in the distance. I decided to carry my small rucksack and along with all the other runners proceeded to walk to the camp. The image of 190 people walking during the early evening across the desert was somewhat surreal. The elongated shadows cast by the setting sun, the strange colours and total silence combined with the dust that nearly 400 feet were kicking up made the whole scene other-worldly.

Arriving at the tents the little group of Brits that had walked more or less together made for an empty tent at the far end of the camp. Dropping my bag and claiming my little bit of floor I noticed that even after that short walk my back was soaking with sweat!

Eleven of us squeezed into the tent (the term tent would be somewhat generous). The floor was covered in carpet, the roof was a collection of sewn together hessian sacks, raised above the ground using several wooden poles, the walls, well, the walls didn't exist, it was roof and carpet.

It was now that I discovered my first major error:- the threadbare carpet covered the sharp stony ground, and in my stupidity, I thought the desert was sandy and consequently I wouldn't need a sleeping mat, mattress thingy. Wrong. It turns out that the desert is mainly small, sharp stones and rocks. Owing to that one stupid mistake I would miss out on a lot of vital sleep during the next few days.

It was interesting to watch little groups forming, various nationalities occupying 'their' tents which in turn became a little piece of Japan, America, Italy, France or whatever. We Brits were no different with our Union Jack proudly unfurled and gently flapping in the breeze.

The evening meal was to be in one of the large 'admin' tents and once again I felt obliged to eat as much as I could. This was helped by the fact that the food was really nice.

The following day it was up early - breakfast and administration. Every one of the 197 runners had to have their kit checked, checking to make sure we all had the right kit and the compulsory kit, ie: compass, anti-venom pump, sleeping bag, 2000 calories a day, cooker etc, etc. Once the staff were happy the whole lot was weighed, my pack weighed a little over 13kgs.

That done it was on to the medical tent, paper work was handed in, an ECG reading, letter from the Doctor stating that I was physically up to the challenge, blood group, heart rate, blood pressure reading, height, weight and inside leg measurement, well not quite but they were thorough!

When the Doctor asked me what preparation I had done to my feet I had to say none (I didn't know you could prepare your feet). He didn't say anything but he did give me a look, the look that said I know something you don't know, YET.

On returning to the tent I decided to sort my kit out: whilst packing at home I decided that the only things that I would take to Morocco were the absolute essentials, everything I had was therefore needed to get me through the race. Now that my pack weighed 13 kg it was different and like everyone else I was having a rethink. I packed and repacked, decided on one t-shirt and not two, got rid of some power bars and a pair of socks.

I tried the rucksack on and it really didn't feel that much different, but I felt better.

Looking around I noticed that some runners had huge packs, one Japanese lady's rucksack was so big that when she had it on it went above her head and below her bum.

I also noticed that the Japanese had brought everything with them: pots and pans, spare clothing even their own TV crew that filmed their every move. They were always smiling and always eating.

There was a lovely campfire atmosphere forming - everyone seemed happy and smiling. The various nationalities were mixing and chatting, singing, checking maps and eating. Members of the press were mingling and interviewing.

It was noticeable how quickly it got dark. Once it was dark there wasn't a lot to do and so most of us were tucked up in our sleeping bag by 19:00.

Lying there, discreetly picking my nose (the super fine dust, honest!) I was listening with great interest to the conversations that were going on around me, mainly reminiscing about past races: Ironman triathlons, Ultras and previous 'Marathon Des Sables'. Training tips and schedules were talked through and analysed, the horrendous desert conditions of previous years the blisters, rucksack rub (where the rucksack rubs the skin until raw patches form) sunburn, twisted this and twisted that.

I should have put my fingers in my ears and hummed pleasant tunes, but no, I had to listen and scare my self shitless!

I was now beginning to seriously think that my training was woefully inadequate and I had got my ambition mixed up with my very limited and as yet untested ability:- in short I was way out of my depth.

The questions were now coming thick and fast - would I manage to survive day one, and, if so, would I survive day two etc, etc? On top of that had I got enough food, would the heat be too much? (3 weeks ago I was out training in the snow!) and so it went on and on.

Trying to sleep on what was, quite literally, a rock hard floor, with my confidence severely shattered and nerves frayed, I lay there selfishly hoping that the others were having the same thoughts and worries but, judging by the impressive snoring that was coming from one end of the tent, it was plainly obvious that at least one of us was having a very good nights sleep - bastard! Though I didn't or, should I say, couldn't sleep dawn arrived much too quickly. It was here - the Day of Reckoning - race day had arrived.

Day 1

I was knackered before I started. Tired, dishevelled, dusty - looking around, bodies started to rise. Cookers were lit, teeth were cleaned and with toilet rolls in hand a steady procession of happy campers made their way to distant lands for their morning constitution. Likewise and with toilet roll in hand I marched off into the distance, yes the there were toilets: half a dozen canvas telephone box shaped objects. I tried, I really did, but the fact that I could not hold my breath long enough meant that I had to make alternative arrangements, hence the long walk that I was now making. There wasn't anything to hide behind because the whole area was snooker table flat. The only thing to do was to walk far enough away so that you were not recognisable.

After about half a mile I was confident enough. Mission accomplished, I made my way back and lit my stove for breakfast: porridge and coffee. I couldn't eat the porridge but I tried - small malteser size portions were forced down. A couple of cups of sweet black coffee, a handful of mixed fruit and nuts and a glucose sweet and I was good to go.

With less than an hour to go I started to get dressed and packed. The rucksack still weighed a ton and worse made a noise when I ran. I repacked and that seemed to do the trick - it wasn't lighter but it was quieter. With about half an hour to go people started to make their way over to the start line. The atmosphere was changing; camp staff and volunteers were buzzing around as were the helicopters high above us. Film crews and photographers were jostling for the best positions and runners were indulging in nervous, excited chatter.

I stood there amongst them all, quietly taking it all in. This was it - the culmination of 2 years hard work, months of training, planning and dreaming, I was here - actually on the start line of the '11th Marathon Des Sables', the race I had seen on the television early one Saturday morning whilst eating a handful of chocolate biscuits some 2 years ago.

The time was now 07:45, the race was scheduled to start at 08:00 - early enough we were told, to avoid the searing heat for some of the day.

With muscles warmed and stretched, packs tightened and adjusted and with the nervous chatter dying away, we were ready. However, the race organisers were not. We had been issued 1.5 litres water to get us to the first checkpoint some 9.5 kms away. However, an hour and a half later we were still on the start line.

It was 10:00 before we started and it was bloody hot. The start was a mad dash, everyone shot off at a great rate of knots: the relief of finally starting coupled with the buzz of cameras, helicopters and cheering supporters meant that we all set off too fast. Fortunately it didn't last, everyone settled down to a more sedate pace. I was running along slowly, runners passed me, I passed runners - a quick exchange of pleasantries and they were gone.

I reached the first checkpoint relatively comfortably and was pleased but fully aware that it was early days. I grabbed a bottle of water, had my ID card checked and was off within seconds. Leaving this first checkpoint it was noticeable how the atmosphere had changed. People were now looking very serious and had gone much quieter.

Most of the terrain encountered thus far was stony with the occasional minute sand dune, a few yards long and a few yards wide. However, these small dunes had highlighted a problem. I had worked out that my feet were likely to swell up in the heat, and the pounding that they would be taking, so had bought a pair of training shoes that were slightly bigger than my usual size, thus allowing for the swollen feet. However, I was getting sand in my shoes before my feet had swollen and now that sand was acting as an abrasive rubbing the skin on my feet, causing blisters. I had been running less than a day and already I had blisters.

Arriving at the last checkpoint of the day was a blessed relief. 25kms down: 185 to go!

The campsite was a hive of activity and efficiency - the staff accounting for all the runners, the medics working hard patching up blistered, battered, limping and dehydrated runners. Reporters and photographers were frantically filming the carnage.

The routine for this first night would not vary much during the course of the race; get in, find the tent, claim a space, try and eat then patch up the bits of feet that were blistered.

Dinner for this night consisted of dehydrated beef casserole, a handful of fruit and nuts, a few fruit pastilles and a cup of sweet black coffee. Throughout the night I drank as much of the water as I could, desperately trying to keep myself hydrated.

I had a good look at my feet - I was now the proud owner of three blisters, one on each heel and one on my small toe on my left foot. I cleaned them and put plasters on, crossed my fingers and hoped they wouldn't get any worse.

I lay back on my sleeping bag, too tired and too sore to move very much, watching camp life going on all around me. People hobbled and limped about, some with bandaged and dressed feet, one or two very relieved-looking stragglers crossed the finish line.

I was bloody uncomfortable lying on the stony ground. I put my t-shirt and warm clothes under my sleeping bag, hoping for a little bit more cushioning but I was still uncomfortable; it was going to be a long night. Tossing and turning I tried to sleep, my feet hurt, the ground was hard and uncomfortable. Alun was snoring for Wales and someone was farting. Looking at my watch and worried about oversleeping I noticed it was very nearly 20:00, it would be a longer night than I had thought.

Eventually the morning arrived, people started to get up. I lay there for as long as possible, trying to break wind as discreetly as I could, hoping against hope that no one would notice. The whole place looked like a bomb had gone off, bits of kit everywhere. The camp crew put on an impressive display of dexterity, they went to each tent, grabbed the poles (I don't mean the Polish athletes) that were holding up the roof and, with a quick flick of the wrist, the whole lot had been removed. Anyone still lying in their sleeping bag was suddenly sleeping out in the open.

Usual routine: cooker on for breakfast, teeth cleaned and toilet roll in hand - off for my morning constitution. Again I tried to find a little bit of privacy. However, on this occasion necessity dictated otherwise - it was literally now or never. Mission accomplished it was back to the tent and breakfast.

I was not in the least bit hungry but knew I would have to eat. I made some porridge and tried to eat but just retched instead of swallowed. Then I had a brainwave: mix in some chocolate powder to make a sort of chocolate porridge. Again I retched. I gave up - two cups of coffee, a couple of fruit pastilles and a glucose sweet and I was ready.

Day 2
ERG　Chibi-Touz

This morning's start was a little more sedate - people hobbled and limped over to the start line. Tatty, dirty kit, and the apprehensive looks gave the impression that we had been at it for days and not just at the one 25km stage!

Though my feet were very tender I had decided to run nonstop to the first checkpoint some 8km away. This was managed using a strange mixture of hobbling, waddling and shuffling. I collected water and was joined by Alun. The terrain was getting noticeably more sandy. I tried to remember what the 'road book' had said: something about CP 2 being at the end of the "dunes". I'm not the sharpest tool in the box, but even I could work out that before we reached CP 2 we would be going across some sand dunes.

We approached the dunes with a degree of trepidation: even from a distance they looked huge. On arriving, all was confirmed as the first one loomed high above us.

Clambering up the side, following the zigzagging path left by previous runners, my breathing became laboured, my heart rate had increased and my legs were like jelly. I was climbing slowly but had no choice but to decrease my speed. With my hands on my knees I pushed onward and upward. My lungs felt and tasted like they were bleeding. The heat reflecting off the sand was also another worry. As we got to the top all we could see up ahead was more and more dunes; an endless procession of dunes and runners.

Dropping down was a somewhat short relief because 1- you knew had to climb up again and 2 - the dip or depression that you ended up in was so bloody hot you actually wanted to start climbing again.

When we reached one dune summit we noticed one of our tent mates Alan just sitting, taking a breather. Alan had come storming past us earlier and had looked pretty impressive and, annoyingly, always seemed relaxed as if he were on holiday. We had a quick chat and moved off. I think we both thought that Alan was suffering but by the same token so was everyone else.

The dunes were tough, demoralising and extremely unforgiving. To reach the top sapped away what little strength you had and on reaching the top you saw nothing but more of the same: really soul destroying. It wouldn't take much to get disorientated and lost. It was only the fact that we could either see other runners or their footprints that we knew we were on the right track.

A little light relief came in the shape of a small teddy bear that Alun was carrying. It was the mascot for the charity he was raising money for - apparently this well travelled teddy had been all over the world and was now to have his picture taken on top of a Saharan sand dune. Moving on from the impromptu photo shoot and summiting our umpteenth dune we were rewarded with a magnificent sight: CP 2 - and what was even better was that it was out of the dunes. Arriving at this checkpoint we came across another one of our tent mates - Martese, a homeopathist from London. She was doing this race with her brother who, unfortunately due to illness, had to pull out earlier.

The three of us left the checkpoint together. The terrain was flat and stony. We walked a bit and ran a bit, My feet were now giving me real problems: they hurt when I put my weight on them and they hurt when I took my weight off them. I was glad of the company of my two companions and happily plodded along in their wake - without them I knew my day would have been that much longer.

We passed by a small village called 'Khemliya', very few people were about but the odd one or two that did see us looked at us as if we were quite mad: strange-looking, brightly-coloured, sunburnt, limping, rucksack-carrying mad people running through their village.

We were now travelling along on what appeared to be a dried up river bed. The firm flat ground was a welcome relief after the nightmare that had been the sand dunes.

On arriving at CP 3 I again noticed how tatty we all were: there were 4 runners having a rest at this checkpoint. They, like us, were dust-covered and sweat-streaked, bleary eyed and knackered. ID cards were checked, water collected and we were off. The campsite was just 7 km away, we were now moving along what appeared to be a track for wheeled vehicles, not quite a road. There were wheel marks where a driver had driven through while the track was waterlogged. The whole thing was rutted and had been baked solid by the sun. At the end of the track was a small climb part way up a Jebel (mountain) dropping down the other side and a short run along another small dried river bed. We found the campsite 'hidden' around a bend, I was beginning to realise that the organisers had a sadistic streak, always hiding the campsites.

After checking in and collecting our water rations we made our way over to the tent. Some of the runners were already there - they greeted us and congratulated us. I plonked myself down in a spare part of the tent and had a quiet five minutes, just reflecting on the day's running and watching the activities around the camp. It was beginning to resemble a war zone with casualties hobbling about. After unrolling my sleeping bag I heated the stove for a hot drink and some food. Whilst waiting for the water to boil I examined myself. I felt pretty good and unlike some others had not got rucksack burns. My legs felt good but my feet were now a complete disaster area - a real mess. They were sore and swollen, the blisters were weeping and the bits that weren't blistered soon would be. I washed them with my precious water, wiped them with wet wipes and tried in vain to avoid knocking them or get sand in the sore raw bits!

It was now 21:00, we were all in except for Alan - the guy we had last seen sitting on the dunes. We weren't the only ones, apparently a few people had seen him just 'sitting on the dunes'. We were getting a little concerned especially as it was now dark and it was with some reluctance that we approached the race marshals. They were immediately on the radios and were able to confirm that he had left the last checkpoint an hour and a half ago and was heading for the camp. I was impressed on two counts: 1 - they were able to pinpoint the exact location of a runner so quickly and 2 - Alan had not given up, even though Alun and I both thought he would. On returning to the tent we went via the 'daily progress board'. I had come in at 128th place and had taken 6 hours and 44 minutes to cover the 33 kms.

Some three hours later Alan limped into the tent. He looked to be in a bad way. He wore an agonised expression and looked like a man who had literally given everything to get here.

We helped him with his kit and a couple of runners prepared a meal for him and encouraged him to eat and drink. He was shattered and all he wanted to do was sleep. Eventually, he ate a little and drank a little. Looking at him I personally thought that the price he had paid to get here was too high.

It was now late and time for sleep. I was very tired, more so because of not having had a lot of sleep during the past two nights and unfortunately tonight was to be no different. The rock hard ground and the stupidity of not bringing a sleep mat was one thing, but my painful feet were giving me real grief. My badly blistered heels meant I couldn't let them touch the ground. The alternative was to sleep on my side and unfortunately we were so tightly packed together in the tent that we were quite literally inches away from one another. If I slept on my side I would be breathing over someone and someone would be breathing over me: not nice for either of us.

I decided to sleep on my back, and resting my sore heels inside the back of my trainers, afforded me a little relief.

Morning arrived just as I got to sleep or at least that's how it felt. Prising myself out of my sleeping bag I went through the morning ritual: stove on for coffee, fruit and nuts and a couple of glucose sweets, teeth cleaned, a stretch and pack. (Luckily for me I didn't need to make the long walk with toilet roll in hand, I really hoped I was constipated - it would save me a lot of time and energy!)

My feet were very sore and swollen and I had real trouble trying to get my shoes on - the 'popped' blisters had now left rolls of excess skin. I had to cut away this loose skin using the scissors on my swiss army knife Then and only then could I prise my shoes on. When I initially stood on them with my full weight the pain made me suck in air, clench my fists and shut my eyes - all in perfect unison (and they say men can't multi-task).

I looked over and saw that Alan was up and packing. He said that yesterday had "totally bollocksed" him, and those "fucking dunes" were by far the worst experience of his life! But that was yesterday - he felt better today and was going to continue.

Like for the rest of us the 210km distance was the last bit of the jigsaw, the getting here, time off work, raising the money, time away from home and the endless hours of training, and the fact most of us were raising money for charity made giving up just a little bit harder. I'm sure that most of the other runners were like me, in that this experience was a one off - you wouldn't get a second chance if you failed to finish. You failed, end of story.

Day 3 Taouz-Remlia

Standing at the start - on feet that now resembled water-filled balloons, trying to keep people keep away from them, lest they stand on or kick them. Not only would I scream like a baby, I would probably cry. No-one likes to see a grown man cry and of course being British it really would not do!

I was successful in keeping my feet safe but less successful in understanding what the organiser was saying about todays stage. He spoke for about 45 minutes. Luckily there was a translation into English, that went something like "it's going to be bloody hot today - keep you head covered and drink plenty of water". When we did finally get going it was a blessed relief. Running alongside Alun we quietly got on with it, talking just occasionally. We both just wanted to get today over and done with as quickly as possible.

After a while I noticed that Alun's pace was a little slower than usual. I plodded on in my usual way. Reaching the first checkpoint I turned around fully expecting Alun to be close by, but he wasn't and he had still not appeared when I was ready to leave I plodded on knowing he would catch me sooner or later.

Today was another hot one, the faster runners were now catching and overtaking me. I carried on in my own little world.

Up ahead I saw that we were about to enter a village, this village was called Jdaid. Running through the village and out the other side I was surprised to see a load of support crew and vehicles. I was obviously doing better than I thought: I wasn't expecting the next checkpoint to be so close. I downed most of the water I had and poured the rest over my head to cool down a bit. Approaching the vehicles I was horrified to see that it wasn't a checkpoint but a collection of photographers and film crew catching us leaving the little village. Bollocks - another cock-up to add to my ever expanding list of cock-ups: I now had no water and no idea how far the next checkpoint was. On leaving the 'phantom' checkpoint I was joined by another one of our tentmates: Charlie - a policewoman from Hampshire. We moved along together, the terrain alternating from stony one minute to sand the next. The sand was becoming more prevalent until, finally, we were into another set of dunes. Plodding along quietly, cursing the wretched dunes, I looked up ahead and wow!

The steepest wall of sand I have ever seen. The runners that were already trying to get to the top looked as if they were crawling on all fours. We started our slow ascent. I had started with the sand down at my feet, a couple of steps later it rose to my knees then hips and before very long it was a sand wall in front of my face. I now adopted the ever popular hands and feet technique. It was like trying to ascend the descending escalator.

I was not only worried about my ability to reach the top but having no water was also a major concern and on top of that there were photographers and film crew on the summit of the dune filming us. I was trying to look the part and failing miserably. Finally, after a huge effort I reached the top and looking down the other side could see the second checkpoint. We arrived at the checkpoint, collected our water and were off. I was very relieved to have the water and was lucky indeed that my stupidity had not become serious.

As we left the checkpoint a lot of interest was suddenly focused on what was going on behind us: someone had let off a flare. We had all been issued with flares for use in an emergency so some poor sod was obviously in the shit! There was nothing we could do and as all the race crew seem to have seen the flare we carried on.

Though the going was tough and the temperature was bloody hot - with a bit of company and the realisation that I had had a lucky escape with the water drinking fiasco, the miles sort of flew by and we arrived at the next checkpoint pretty quickly. Whilst here I asked how hot it was and was told 124 degrees. There was now just 9kms to the campsite but between us and the finish were some small dunes. They were luckily not the monsters we had so far encountered. Just constant, one after the other. Moving through the dunes we came across a herd of black camels. They appeared to be wild with no one around except for us lunatics. I attempted to take some pictures whilst on the move. I didn't stop because I knew I would never be able to get going again.

As we got to the top of yet another dune we spotted a landcruiser 4x4 vehicle parked some way off. As we got closer we could see a runner sitting in its shade, obviously suffering with heat. The driver was giving him water which meant that the runner was now out of the race! What made it so sad was the fact that you could see the campsite up ahead: so near and yet so far.

We eventually reached the campsite half an hour later, one of our tent mates saw us come in and guided us over to the tent. We also found out that the person who had let off the flare was Alan, one set of dunes too many.

Usual routine; grab a space and get sorted. I was knackered, my feet hurt even more and looking at the state of them I realised that I had collected a couple more blisters. My heels had been replaced by blisters and my toes were also under attack: three on one foot and two on the other. The days were getting progressively longer. Day 1 had been 25km, day 2 33km, today 39km and tomorrow a whopping 76km.

It was interesting to watch the runners deteriorate, myself included. Runners that had previously looked so impressive were now slowing down and looking tatty, runners had given up and runners had been pulled out. The medics could pull any runner from the race. If they thought that to continue would put the runner at risk, they were pulled. We all looked and smelled awful - covered in dust and smeared with sweat stains.

I can't comment on the other tents but the runners that had been pulled out or had decided not to continue were really generous and supportive to those of us left: things like guiding us to the tent when we crossed the finish line, carrying our pack over and, because they were now being fed by the organisers, they split whatever goodies they had amongst us and smuggled in bits of bread and the occasional orange. Just because they were no longer running didn't mean they were no longer part of the team - they were!

With tomorrow's 76km monster looming, I went all out to prepare. I scrounged a couple of bits of cardboard to use as a mattress, tried to eat as much as my stomach would allow and tried to sort my feet out. My feet were in a desperate state: blisters on blisters, blisters overlapping blisters, blood blisters, popped blisters, blisters instead of heels. Blisters were on my toes, on the soles of my feet and under my toenails. I had to admit defeat and wandered over to the medical tent. It was like entering a battlefield hospital: bodies everywhere, some were under foil blankets, some were on intravenous drips but most were lying on their backs with one foot or other on a medics lap having their feet amputated. Well, by the expression on their faces that's what you would have thought they were doing.

There were two people in front of me and as I looked around I could see that one or two of the male medics were enjoying the slicing and dicing. I really hoped I got a sympathetic gentle female nurse.

I was lucky. A young nurse called me over, I placed myself at her mercy. I didn't have to explain the problem - she just told me to lie down and put my feet on her lap. She smiled sweetly, cleaned my feet and proceeded to amputate. Her skill with a scalpel was impressive, she sliced and cut away any loose skin taking it right back to new and as yet unblistered bits. After about half an hour she had finished cutting, then the 'coup de grace' IODINE, WOW!! She dressed the wounds and I hobbled off, trying to look all macho with feet covered in dressings, waddling like a duck and wearing yellow sponge flip-flops.

Lying back on my sleeping bag, I tried to focus on the enormity of tomorrow's 76km. The previous two days combined didn't make 76km, I had struggled with each of those as individual days. The upside was that if you survived tomorrow the chances were high that you would survive the whole race. With just the two days left (even though the very next day was the second longest day) you would surely make it!

Day 4

In the morning I was awake early but decided to treat myself to a bit of lie-in. I lay there watching the camp getting organised, had some breakfast and got up.

I packed up and noticed my rucksack didn't seem any lighter than when I started. Trying to put my shoes on, it would have been easier and quicker to do a Rubiks cube, I tried every possible combination but try as I might I couldn't get my feet in my shoes. I started to remove bits of dressing. I removed as much as I dared, but still I couldn't get them on. Then I had a brain wave - remove the insoles. Eureka - it worked! I had shoes on my feet but no cushioning, can't have everything I suppose.

I made my way over to the starting line and the atmosphere was a little sombre: more like a dentist's waiting room than a start line. I think everyone was aware that today was the day, the big one, the day that counted. If you survived today your chances were pretty good. However, if you didn't survive it had all been for nothing, so much was at stake.

After starting, I instantly got into a nice steady pace and decided that no matter what, I would run to the first two checkpoints: a total distance of 26 km. Then - well - then I would have to play it by ear.

After 9.5km we entered the village of Er Remelia and unusually there were spectators. The people seemed curious - normally they would be shy and reserved, but a quick smile and a "bonjour" or two usually resulted in a smile being returned, especially from the children.

On reaching CP 2 I was joined by another British runner from our tent called Dave. We ran together for a short while but he was much faster than me and ran on ahead. I preferred running on my own going at my own pace, in a world of my own, not having the worry of trying to keep up or slow down to someone else's pace.

Since leaving CP 2, my already slow pace had somewhat

decreased, and, again, my feet were giving me real problems. I could feel every rock and stone underfoot and with the insoles removed, the little bit of cushioning that I did have was gone, every single step hurt. There was no respite.

The flat rock and stony ground finally gave way to sand - very nice soft sand. However, the price paid for the soft sand was that the sand led up through a pass - it was a steady climb. On reaching the top I could see runners snaking far into the distance. The column of runners were all heading in the same direction and seemed to be making for a mound-like object in the middle of what appeared to be a dried up lake. This mound looked as if it could have been an island when the 'lake' had had water.

I studied the mound hard as I started my descent and could see that it was indeed a checkpoint. I reasoned that I would be there in about 20 minutes to half an hour - wrong! 45 minutes later I was still trying to get to it. It eventually took me 1 hour 45 minutes to reach it.

The ability to judge distance in the desert was a skill I had yet to master. Arriving at the foot of the mound was a blessed relief. Unfortunately the actual checkpoint was on the top. It wasn't a particularly high mound but it was particularly steep. It also required a lot of huffing, puffing and swearing to reach the top. On reaching the top I noticed there was not a lot of room and certainly nowhere to sit down. However, I was told that there was a place down on the other side. I walked over and saw a bigger tent full of dead, decaying bodies all trying to have a bit of a breather out of the sun.

Unfortunately, it was full to overflowing, so I had to sit outside. I thought I would check on my feet and instantly wished I hadn't:- they looked awful, felt awful and, by golly they smelt awful. Open, weeping and raw, pus, blood and sand mixed together with bits of dressing and loose skin made for an interesting spectacle. I attempted to re-stick the dressing and brush away the sand but it was really just a token gesture - not really making a blind bit of difference. I put the whole

horrible mess back together then had something to eat and
drink. It was now late afternoon and would soon be getting
dark. I got out my head torch and a long sleeve top, ready for
the oncoming night, then hobbled off into the setting sun.

For some reason I felt pretty good and was surprised to be
catching people. I knew it wouldn't last so decided to make
the best of it. At a little after 20:00 hours I spotted the next
checkpoint. On arriving I saw that there was plenty of room
for a sit down and decided to have a decent break. This was
made all the better when I was offered some mint tea. I
gratefully accepted - it was very sweet, very refreshing and
a real treat for my now redundant taste buds. I handed
them my empty glass and was offered another one and then
another. Apparently 3 cups of tea meant that you were a
friend. This checkpoint was now officially my favourite - the
trouble was prising my carcass away:- it was dark, I was
comfortable but knew if I didn't get my arse in gear soon I
could well be here until the morning. It was with the greatest
reluctance that I left and hobbled my way back into the race.
I had been there for 45 minutes.

To pay for my tea and laziness I decide to do a bit of running.
Looking at my watch I decided to run for 45 minutes, the 45
minutes that I had spent languishing at the 5 star checkpoint
had to be paid for somehow. As I ran I caught and passed a
'runner' then continuing on I could see another one. Though
my 45 minutes were up I decided to carry on until I caught
them. I did. I started walking again - eventually I came
across the last checkpoint before the finish. This checkpoint
had loads of room and was kitted out to accommodate the
runners that decided to have a sleep: it was tempting but I
decided to get out asap, spending less than 5 minutes there.

Moving on, I could see a couple of runners moving slowly.
When I eventually caught up with them I realised it was a
couple of blokes from the tent - Nick and Charlie. We teamed
up for a short while, until Charlie who was moving along
quite well decided to push on, leaving me and Nick. We were

both knackered but were happy to get on and finish this stage together. It was now late, getting on for 23:30, and we started talking all sorts of bollocks, the sort of bollocks that blokes come out with when the situation is desperate.

As we were both waffling away the time, and the distance, we both noticed something up ahead - a shadowy figure just in front of us. The waffling stopped and the ears and eyes strained to make sense of what it was. Then, suddenly and without warning the whole place was lit up! The sudden brightness made me lose my balance - I wobbled and stumbled a couple of steps and then heard voices in my head. What the *&^%$ was going on? Then my befuddled brain worked out what was happening - I realised that it was a film crew eager to catch out unsuspecting weary runners. We both politely declined the offer of an interview (at that moment I would have struggled to tell them my full name and date of birth). They understood and switched the lights off. My carefully built up night vision was now non-existent and I moved with unsure jerky movements, unsure of where to place my feet!

We continued along and noticed that the terrain was becoming very rocky and the green glowing snapsticks were becoming more numerous. Turning a corner to our right and following the line of lights took us right into the campsite and the finish line. We had done it. In a little over 16 hours we had completed the long stage day.

We crossed the line together, congratulated ourselves with a very manly pat on the back or two, then BANG Nick collapsed. The staff on the finish line called the medics over, Nick was taken to the medical tent, put on intravenous drips and wrapped in foil blankets. He looked bloody awful and yet not five minutes ago we were talking bollocks! I was happy he was getting sorted out and was in safe hands but I was knackered and in pain, needed something to eat and drink as I was of no use to any one just standing around the medical tent. I made my way over to our tent. A few people were awake including Charlie who inquired about Nick but some lucky sods were sound asleep and had obviously been here for hours. A quick bite to eat and bed time. A little over four hours later and the camp was awake. Today was a day off, well, it was for those of us lucky enough to have finished.

Looking around I noticed that some of the tent were still out there but stragglers were still coming in in dribs and drabs. The loud clapping and cheering when someone crossed the finish line gave us ample warning that another runner had arrived.

I sat there watching camp life, had a cup of coffee and something to eat then made my way over to the medical tent for more surgery and a little sympathy. Unfortunately, they had completely run out of sympathy and weren't expecting any anytime soon!

On my return to the tent I saw that three people had arrived:- two girls and Alun. It was good to see them but they did not look happy. On entering the tent I immediately detected an atmosphere, my 'atmosphere-detecting abilities' are acute and have been honed and finely-tuned over many years of getting myself in the doghouse at home! The two girls seemed furious - something or somebody had upset them - maybe they had upset each other. I desperately wanted to know but to broach the subject would require a degree of tact and diplomacy - skills that I didn't possess. Two very angry, tired females was something that most sensible men would be frightened of and I'm ashamed to say that my courage deserted me. I lay on my sleeping bag pretending that all was well. Eventually, however, and once they had calmed down a little (it takes a lot of effort to be that angry, effort that was for now in short supply) the whole story came out. Apparently it was all to do with the Italians, or should I say one Italian in particular. This one Italian had been in a desperate state, hardly moving, constantly stopping and sitting down and was generally in a bad way. The girls came across him, gave him some water and little bits of food, talked him into continuing when he had been so adamant that he would have to give up. They walked with him and encouraged him to keep going.

However, a couple of hundred yards away before finishing line, the Italian machismo, ego or pride kicked in. He just could not be seen to have been helped by the girls so he ran off trying to reach the finish before them. They were furious and the red mist descended. They gave chase, caught him and beat him - to the line that is. It was the ingratitude and downright cheek of the Italian that had so angered the girls.

Later on during the day Nick came over to the tent - he looked a lot better than when I had last seen him. However, he was out of the race, couldn't remember collapsing and was more embarrassed than annoyed. He looked thoroughly dejected but vowed to return.

It's a strange mixture of emotions when someone who, for whatever reason, is unable or unwilling to finish - as the girls had demonstrated - you would do whatever you could to help someone keep going, be it a dose of encouragement or more practical help. However, the moment the decision is made you secretly think to yourself, yes, another one down. A guilty thought that no one will ever admit to but a thought that 90% of us shared. It's not meant to be malicious, cruel or nasty - it is just a relief to know that you are not the only one suffering, regretting or crying your way round. Others are as well - only, you have for whatever reason, be it luck or stupidity, managed to hold on for just a little bit longer.

With Nick now out of the race it brought the total of non-finishers in our tent to 4. With still two days to go I wondered if there would be any more casualties. I hoped not - could I hold on? Physically it would be touch and go, but with a little bit of luck and a large dose of bloody-mindedness I might (fingers crossed) just make it.

Stage 5
Amjerane- Ifert

Though I had been lucky enough to have so far survived, and by survived I do mean SURVIVED, I was under no illusion that today was going to be tough.

At 42km it was the second longest stage, virtually a marathon. Any normal marathon runner would have been tapering off (gradually reducing their running prior to marathon day). Not us - from day one we had slowly been increasing our running prior to marathon day.

It was my total ignorance regarding training that was now a blessing - had I known that you were supposed to decrease and not increase the mileage I might have been a little concerned. I wasn't - all I knew that today wasn't as long as yesterday and after this stage we only had one even shorter day, left, just 18kms.

Walking over to the start line, we must have looked, like the zombies in Michael Jacksons 'Thriller' video. We hobbled, waddled, limped and dragged ourselves forward. We were a group of tatty, decomposing bodies that blindly moved forward.

With yesterday's rest day you would think that I would be fairly rested and fresh - wrong. My rucksack still felt as heavy as it did on day one, my feet were still in a desperate state and rigor mortis had set in from a day of inactivity. I was stiff and sore.

As the countdown began, I needed to formulate a game plan. How the hell was I going to survive today? I got away with it yesterday but my luck would have to end soon. I just had to get to the end, in theory a very simple task:- keep moving forward no matter what happens, just keep moving!

Three, two, one and we were off - shuffling along I soon found a nice steady, if somewhat slow pace and as the mass of runners thinned out, I looked ahead and spotted a runner with an orange-coloured rucksack, and that was it - my master plan, no matter what happened I would keep the orange rucksack in sight. I locked on to the rucksack. I didn't know or care who was carrying the thing, male, female, old or young. All I knew was that the rucksack would pull me along. Like the worst kind of stalker, I followed, altered my pace and concentrated my very limited efforts on the orange rucksack. Nothing but nothing would stop me following that rucksack, it would always be in sight.

I followed it to CP 1 - it left as I arrived. Minutes later I left the checkpoint and continued my now quite obsessive stalking. Nothing else mattered, the pace wasn't fast but it was constant and I needed that constant pace.

I followed it to CP 2, collected water, took a rough bearing (the 'road book' gave the direction to follow as 220 degrees). I roughly set the compass accordingly and left the checkpoint, then bugger me if the orange rucksack didn't disappear in the opposite direction. Now I was confused, worried, and worse:- I had to make a decision. Do I follow the rucksack or do I follow the compass? I weighed everything up - the rucksack had so far not put a foot wrong, but there is an old saying that you should 'trust' your compass. I also knew that when navigating you should not just blindly follow the person in front and then just as panic had started to make an appearance the rucksack altered course, which was fortunately the 220 degrees course.

Lesson learned, I followed on, still keeping one eye on the rucksack, and the other on the compass. Moving along, with thoughts of finishing, coca cola and ice cream running around my head, I suddenly realised that I was on a very steep incline and was breathing hard. Once I reached the top, I looked down on to was a very nasty-looking and steep descent. I would need to watch every footstep - the trouble with descending was that it hurt my feet more than they already hurt.

Once at the bottom it was just a short distance into a village and, like all the villages so far the kids came out to 'inspect' us, one or two deciding to run along with us, laughing and chatting away thinking it was great fun running with, and beating, the so called athletes. At one end of the village was a well that a couple of runners were using and it looked like a bloody good idea. I reached the well and lowered the bucket - the water was wonderfully cold. I poured the lot over me, then I felt extremely guilty about wasting the precious water.

Moving on I realised that my faffing about meant that I had lost sight of the orange rucksack.

Moving through the village I was struck by how lush and very green it was, with crops growing and water-filled irrigation ditches running this way and that. There were even birds flitting from one tree to another - a little green island in the harsh and barren landscape from which we had just emerged.

It was now extremely hot, the hottest day so far. Trying to find my way out of the village wasn't easy, there were three groups of runners that I could see, one group were going one way, the second group were going the other way and the third group were sitting by an irrigation ditch cooling off. Again I had to make a decision:- eeny, meeny, miney, mo!

It was very, very tempting to stop and dangle my swollen, sweaty, sore feet in the cold water - the trouble with that would be that I would be there for hours, unwilling or unable to get started again. As I was making a decision I took my hat, off submerged it in the cold water and watched as the group that had been cooling off moved off. I decided that they were the sensible ones and followed them.

CP 3 came and went, a curious thing about checkpoints was that each time I left one I spent all my time and energy trying to reach the next one. As I struggled along it was the thought of reaching the next checkpoint that kept me going, kept me motivated. It was the reward I craved and yet as soon as I got to a checkpoint I wanted to leave and was annoyed if anything delayed my departure. I wanted to get there but didn't want to be there.

As the day wore on so did my fatigue. I was getting slower: quite an achievement considering I was already going bloody slow. The distance I had already covered, the heat, lack of sleep and inability to eat properly were now taking their toll. I was now like an automaton, programmed to do nothing except move forward.

This day had been my toughest, I was hanging on by the skin of my teeth. Up ahead I saw a couple of runners and beyond them what appeared to be derelict stone buildings. I really hoped the this was the campsite, it wasn't, but I could see it up ahead maybe a mile, mile and a half away. Normally, I would try and speed up but my speeding up days had long since gone. It took me another 50 minutes before I arrived, I was now beyond knackered, so much so that when I collected my water I was shaking. I made my way over to the nearest tent. I didn't care that it wasn't the right tent, it was a tent and it would have to do. Fortunately for me a guy from our tent, called Tony, came over and not only led me to the right tent but also carried my rucksack:- the bloke was a hero. Though he was out of the race he had been watching the runners coming in and realised that I was struggling (I must have looked a right mess), so came over to help. On getting to the tent I was lucky to find a space at one end thus affording me just a little more space.

Tomorrow was the last day, a short 18km (a little over 10 miles). After a cup of coffee and a few sweets, I felt better, and decided to sort through my kit, throwing away anything that was no longer required. It was mostly packets of food and drink. I was shocked by how much I had left over, the implication being that I had eaten nowhere near enough. I was loathe to throw perfectly good (if not horrible tasting) food away, so decided to have a feast. I got the cooker going - this evening's chef's special was casserole, two CupaSoups and a rice pudding, washed down with sports drink, hot chocolate and a very sweet coffee. Fed and watered it was time to visit the medics tent. This would - I hoped - be the last time, it certainly turned out to be the longest time. The poor old medic cleaned, cut, dabbed and sliced, patched and prodded my oh so tender stumps. I was clenching my teeth and buttocks, whilst trying to stifle the little high pitched and involuntary yelps. Whilst hobbling my way back to the tent two things crossed my mind:- one: had I done any permanent damage to my feet? All the toes, a large percentage of the soles and both heels were blistered. They had been blistered and re-blistered and of the ten toenails I had started with, only three remained, the second thought that crossed my mind was, how the hell am I going to get my shoes on?

Getting back to the tent, I noticed someone had moved in next to me. It was Alun the worlds greatest snorer. The tent had an altogether more relaxed and lively atmosphere:- we all knew that this was the last night together, and consequently spent most of the evening swapping stories. These stories I'm sure will take on a life of their own when we get back home - the hills will be steeper, the packs heavier, the dunes higher and the heat hotter but for now the stories were real and didn't need exaggerating.

The Last Day

Even though I was sleeping next to the worlds greatest snorer, I had the best night's sleep so far. Was I that tired, or was I safe in the knowledge that I had all but completed the 'Marathon des Sables'?

This morning was a totally different atmosphere, not only because it was the last day but because of the guest runners. The race organisers had 'invited' people to take part in the last day - consequently the field of runners had practically doubled. They looked very out of place:- they were clean, smelled nice and walked properly. Once we were all lined up and the countdown began, they did seem to get a little apprehensive - maybe they thought they would end up looking like and smelling like us. Once we got going the bulk of them shot off - they probably weren't fast runners but they were fresh runners and that counted for a lot.

The terrain today was more urbanised, buildings and people

were more prevalent, tracks more defined. This made the going easier than it had been but my feet dictated my speed.

I hobbled along and approached the town of Tazzerin. Entering the town, and expecting a hero's welcome, I was disappointed most people didn't even notice. Some clapped and some looked annoyed that we were disrupting the routine of the place. I was now desperate to finish, hanging on by a thread, willing the finish line to appear and then I saw the wonderful 1km to go marker. I tried to speed up but failed, then the two girls from the tent appeared and with the finish line in sight we grabbed each others hands and ran. I wanted to, no I needed to, reach that finish line. I wanted the excruciating pain to end. Two years it had taken me to get to the finish line:- two years, a small fortune, blood, sweat and God knows how many layers of skin.

And then the shouting and the clapping intensified as we got closer and then suddenly it was done, we had finished! Patrick Bauer put a medal around my neck and that was that. It was over, my two year dream had come to a very abrupt end!

Home

Flying home I ate and I ate. I had lost 16 pounds in weight, my feet were so swollen that I had to cut the leg of my trousers just to get them over my feet.

It took me many days to recover.

Had it been worth it? The cost, the pain, the time and the effort, the answer I'm afraid was yes. Would I do it again? No. Would I recommend it to a friend? Yes!

But having said that I had learned a lot about myself, I had not once thought that I would not finish. Not once did I think about giving up and stopping, I had loved it, the challenge the people the whole atmosphere.

What next?

*Day 1
Still fresh
enough to
pose, note
the "Tubi
Gripped"
Gaiters!*

The calm before the storm, those on the truck were the DNFs

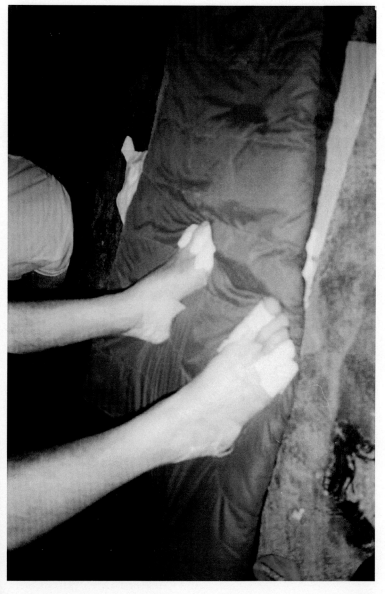

They weren't too bad here!

*After a
hard day's
work!*

HIMALAYAN 100 MILE STAGE RACE

What is it:	A 100 mile 5 stage footrace
When:	October / November
Where:	Sikkim, Indian Himalayas
Distance:	100 miles (161km)
It is:	A stunningly beautiful, friendly and tough race
See:	himalayan.com

6/11/98

Day 1

Sitting at Terminal 3 of London's Heathrow Airport with hours to kill, negative thoughts began to appear:- thoughts like: have I trained enough, did I taper too early, will I cope with the terrain, the altitude, will get I get ill, I could be at home, have I got the right kit, why the *&^%$ do I have the need to do these things?

When I do these things I get apprehensive, my confidence nosedives, my wallet gets emptied and my stress levels increase. Then, just to make matters worse, I remember, with absolute clarity, the pain and the suffering that was the 'Marathon des Sables'.

Why, why do I need to do these things? Extreme pain is certain, the possibility for humiliation and failure is high and yet here I am, once again!

What is it about Departure lounges that induce stress and misery? Sitting and people-watching I notice that not one person seemed happy, everyone seems confused, stressed and anxious, not one happy face, even the kids seem afflicted. Ah well - I'll have a cup of coffee and a piece of cake. That will cheer me up and take my mind off things! Wrong - more depressed, the cup of coffee cost £1.40.

Why do people need so much hand luggage (my kit for a week doesn't amount to as much as some people's hand luggage). Now I start to think I haven't got enough and I may have forgotten something.

Boarding the plane is a blessed relief, no more worrying about things I may or may not have forgotten, no more shall I "chicken out?" thoughts, no more worrying about training, its too late. I'm now committed, I'm on my way to run 100 miles in the Himalayas.

Disaster at 30,000ft one of the cabin crew spilt a jug of orange juice over my brand new cd player. He was very apologetic and slightly embarrassed. I tested the thing and it worked - he was so sorry that he gave me a bottle of champagne.

After landing at Delhi, it was a quick trip to the "Bureau de Change" to get £50 of rupees.

Then on to find the Himalayan 100 mile rep. It was here that I would get a first look at my fellow runners - like the 'Marathon des Sables' it was a complete mixed bag:- some serious looking athletes, every age accounted for, from the twenty-somethings to the sixty-somethings. After we were all assembled it was off to the hotel. We stayed for an hour which was just long enough for me to find my room.

We arrived at 07:00 and left at 08:00, back to the airport and then onto an internal flight to Bagdogra. Whilst waiting I decided to have a cup of coffee and was royally ripped off. I paid 100 rupees for a cup of coffee - at Bagdogra I bought a bottle of water and a Pepsi for 35 Rupees!

7/11/98

Day 2

At Bagdogra we transferred to small coaches or large minibuses for the long and very interesting drive to Mirik - the race start.

The scenery was stunning and the driver's skill was something truly to behold. Very steep narrow climbs with extremely tight switchbacks, the roads were so narrow that the drivers employed a 'mate' - a small boy whose job it was to hang outside the vehicle and tell the driver how close to the edge he was. This was bad enough when the 'mate' was using both arms to indicate 3 or 4 feet but it got serious when all he needed was his index finger and thumb to indicate 3 or 4 inches!

I desperately tried to look relaxed and unconcerned. However, my sweaty brow, white knuckles and nervous twitch that had suddenly developed might well have given the game away. To disguise my fear I looked out and I looked down into the precipice: a stupid thing to do as I spotted a lorry that had not quite made it. It was a crushed and crumpled heap of scrap metal. It was probably 400 to 500ft below and it still hadn't reached the bottom.

We eventually arrived at the small town of Mirik. In the hotel a wonderful meal had been laid on. I ate what I could but I was knackered and was ready for bed.

8/11/98

Day 3

I woke early and saw the place in daylight, it was absolutely breathtaking. Even though the hotel had seen better days the area was beautiful, we were perched right beside a lake, lush and beautiful.

I had a shower and that brought me back to reality. A cold, no, ice cold shower was very invigorating. Down to breakfast and then a leisurely walk around town.

The people seem very shy and very curious. A quick smile is usually returned and then one of those please, not me, moments. I could see someone out of the corner of my eye - the village idiot - he made a beeline for me and started waffling away. I tried my foolproof smile and nod technique, it didn't work. He kept on following me, getting louder and more animated. Then a hero made an appearance and ushered him along. He was apparently the local drunk and even at this early hour was slightly worse for wear.

After a small lunch a group of us decided to go for a little run around the lake. It was only 3:5 km and would stretch the legs out.

The little run very nearly ended in disaster:- I went arse over apex catching an unseen root (too busy talking bollocks). I tripped and was lucky indeed not to have injured myself - I looked and felt like a pillock but at least I was an uninjured pillock.

I got back to the hotel and realised I had been lucky, having got away with just a couple of grazes. After dinner we watched a video or should I say the horror film that was last year's race.

It looked - to put it mildly - a challenging course:- runners were bent double, faces showing pain and effort, looking like the figure in the Edvard Munch painting 'The Scream', degrees of despair and suffering in equal measure.

Today the Americans arrive and the luxury of having a room to myself comes to an end.

During the evening we were given a race briefing, a very long race briefing. This was followed by the dreaded "has anyone got any questions?" True to form, the British contingent, with their 'que sera, sera' attitude sat quietly, wanting to get stuck into the dinner that was ready in the next room. The Americans however had other ideas and proceeded to ask the most ridiculously mundane questions. I'm sure they had a bet amongst themselves to see who could ask the most irrelevant question.

Eventually they ran out of things to ask and we were allowed to get something to eat.

After dinner we were treated to an impromptu show by all the race staff - singing and dancing. All the runners were asked to get up and do a bit. I politely declined as I was a far better spectator than I was a singer or dancer. My wife - who has been witness to my determined efforts at both - has threatened to divorce me if I should ever attempt to sing in public. The same threat would have been forthcoming with regard to my dancing had she not been laughing so much!

9/11/98
Day 4

Though today was billed as a day off, it was in fact a trip to Darjeeling some 35km away and once again it was another 'interesting' 2.5 hour drive - interesting only in that the sheer drops and close to the edge driving meant even the strongest atheist would have said a sneaky prayer.

After arriving we were free to do as we saw fit - a bit of shopping. I needed a warm hat and a couple of postcards - if I don't send postcards I'll be in the doghouse. Walking along the streets I was approached by a man who asked if I would like to buy some marijuana - I politely declined. One group saw a dog eating a dead cat!

There was a little train that made the short trip up to the War Memorial. Three of us decided to make the trip as it was only 5km away. Whilst on the train I needed a wee so went into the WC and was somewhat surprised to see that the toilet was actually a hole cut in the floor, with the track passing a few inches below. At that point I was glad I only needed a wee!

On the drive back to Mirik we had to pull over:- one of the runners did not feel well, and the moment he got off the bus, he puked. It was an impressive display of multi-coloured projectile vomiting and at that moment I'm sure we all had the same selfish thoughts:- not the sympathetic, ah, poor old soul, I hope it's nothing serious and that he gets well soon, but rather, I hope I don't get it, I don't want to be ill etc.

Back at the hotel, it was a final briefing and it was now that I realised I had made a major cock-up:- I had no running kit, as per usual I wasn't listening to the very detailed instructions and missed the bit about "pack everything EXCEPT your running kit" I just packed everything and those bags were now on the way to the first night's camp!

10/11/98
Day 5
Race Day: 24 miles   Mannybayang-Sandakphu

Standing on the start line in my hastily cobbled together running kit, a purple t-shirt, a pair of Ron Hill tracksters, and a woolly pair of red socks - fortunately I had been wearing my trainers when I had packed everything else. I felt a bit silly and I probably looked even sillier.

We lined up and the nervous banter quietened down. Mr Pandy, the Race Director was speaking. Fortunately it was a mercifully short speech. However he handed over to a Holy man who proceeded to bless the race and each of us taking part and then each of us were presented with a yellow prayer shawl which was carefully draped over our shoulders. It was quite a touching moment.

The countdown began and the heart rate increased - three, two, one and we were off.

Gently running through the small town of Mannybayang whilst carefully negotiating our way though the narrow streets. Streets that were made narrower by the large number of spectators that had gathered.

I would like to think that the spectators had come to marvel at our undoubted athletic prowess but the expressions of bewilderment and concern gave them away. They thought we were barking mad:- who in their right mind would want to RUN around the foothills of the Himalayas!?

The first three to four miles weren't too challenging, almost pleasant and dare I say enjoyable but then we turned left and the climbing began.

I don't mind running uphill:- in fact I'm one of those odd characters who actually enjoys running uphill. The hill was steep and constant, I was enjoying the terrain and the fact that I was passing people made the whole thing even more enjoyable.

However, after a couple of hours of uphill running the novelty was beginning to wear off. The climb was relentless with absolutely no respite, though my legs felt okay I was knackered and beginning to struggle.

More than once I had to walk and as we climbed higher my energy levels got lower. Eventually I was reduced to counting 40 steps then stop, then 40 steps stop - this plan didn't last long as I had hopelessly overestimated my ability to walk the 40 steps. It was time for a rethink, 20 steps, stop, 20 steps stop.

It was during my 20 steps that the final indignity occurred:- whilst coughing, wheezing and farting my way up a particularly steep bit, I was passed not by a fellow athlete, no, that I could live with, but a local. Bad enough, but he was walking and carrying a load on his back that I doubted I could lift, whilst smoking and wearing wellies and he looked old enough to be my grandad. I'm sure I heard him giggling as he went by.

Pride, vanity, ego or my competitive instinct kicked in. I gave chase, determined to catch and pass him and I would have if he hadn't been plodding so bloody fast.

By now, other runners were catching and passing me. I was moving slowly, very, very slowly, so slow that I was beginning to get cold. This wasn't helped by the fact that it was now getting misty and damp (I later found out it wasn't mist - we had in fact run, well, passed through the clouds) and because I hadn't been listening to the briefing properly I didn't have the right kit.

Eventually and much to my relief I saw the 5km to go marker, 5km, thats 3 miles or 40 minutes to an hour till the finish.

It was nearly 2 hours before I reached the finish line. I was knackered and I just hoped that all the days weren't going to be like that, because if they were, I was, to put it bluntly, in the shit!

It had taken me 6 hours and 55 minutes and I had come in at 25th place.

The finish line on day one was at a place called Sandakphu - at a little over 11900ft it was to be the highest point that we would reach during the race.

There were a collection of trekker's huts that were to be our lodgings for the night - basic but very welcome.

I grabbed my kit bag - the one with my running kit in and made my way over to one of the huts, changed into warm clothing and took a short tour. It was a stunningly beautiful area and apparently the only place on Earth where you can see 4 of the 5 highest mountains in the world at the same time. With the mountains looking down at us and us looking down at the clouds, it was a fantastic photo opportunity.

The meal was an impressive affair considering where we were:- a vegetable soup, chicken and spaghetti with sauce, chapati and mixed vegetables and boiled potatoes. Pudding was a choice of fruit salad or apple pie! It was at moments like this that I really hated my loss of appetite but I tried.

All the runners were now in and a couple had decided that enough was enough and withdrew - altitude problems being the deciding factor.

Though I had struggled I actually felt good, the legs felt good and I was not suffering from headaches or nausea. I was just knackered and slow.

Over dinner we compared 'war stories' and exaggerated the day's events. I was sure that by the time we got home the stories would be very colourful indeed.

The room I was in was full, with 8 of us and it was freezing but once inside my borrowed 'arctic' sleeping bag I was toastie warm.

The downside of being toastie warm was a reluctance to get out of the bag - Mother Nature however dictated otherwise:- I needed the loo. I tried very hard to put off the inevitable but desperation forced my hand - with toilet roll in hand I made my way over to one of the small wooden outhouses, opened the door and gagged. The stench caught me by surprise and just like I had done during the run I was given no choice but to 'tough it out' and besides I was running out of time. I held my breath and entered. Unlike at home I hadn't the luxury of time. I was not able to savour the moment:- it was in, do the deed and get out.

And out it was like a drowning man breaking surface. I exited the 'thunderbox' at a great rate of knots and gasping for air.

11/11/98
Day 6

The second day's running was to be a 20 mile out and back route - remaining at the same altitude we would follow a rough but flatter (flatter being a relative term when referring to a route in the Himalayas,) track. The reality was that it was just not as steep as the day before, or as the official version described it, 'undulating'. I have done enough runs in the past to be able to translate the language that race organisers use and the word 'undulating' actually translates into normal language as lots of hills. However, the fact that we were still at an altitude of very nearly 12000ft made it a bit of a challenge.

We were to follow the trail for 10 miles reaching a place called Molle and then turn round and head back to Sandakphu where we would spend a second night.

It was a beautiful place to run and for most of the day we had 4 out of the 5 highest mountains in the world in view.

The day didn't get off to the best of starts:- there was some confusion as to when the actual start time was. It had been amended from 07:00 to 06:30 and not everybody knew. Unusually for me, I was actually listening for once.

The first mile or so was fine - however, it wasn't long before the 'undulating' bits made an appearance.

The ascents were steep enough to warrant walking while the descents were steep enough to require concentration, something I momentarily forgot and again went arse over apex. I actually slipped on a piece of ice. There wasn't that much of it about but because I was trying to admire the view and move forward I found one of the few bits that were there. As is usual in this situation the first thing I did was look around to see if anyone had noticed. They hadn't so my pride remained in tact.

The fact that we were running around one of the most beautiful places on the planet was not lost on me and consequently I stopped more than once to take photographs. It might have been a 'Race' but I realised that it was also an experience to be savoured.

With Everest, Kanchenjunga, Lhotse and Makalu, 4 out of the 5 highest mountains on earth as a backdrop even my photographs looked good.

I eventually reached the turnaround checkpoint in a little over 2 hours - I felt pretty good.

On the return journey I could see one or two runners really struggling and more than once I was asked "how much further?" that's never a good sign. Once again that nasty selfish thought of rather them than me crept up. However, this time it was tempered by the thought that my time will surely come.

The return journey was just as spectacular with clear blue cloudless skies, sunshine and snowcapped mountains - a more perfect running route would be hard to find.

I was lucky indeed to be here in the Himalayas and the fact that I was in a running race was almost forgotten.

I plodded on eventually finishing in a time of 4hrs and 39 minutes and in 20th position. I was pleased, my legs were tired but at least I had no blisters, chafing or headaches. Tired legs and a loss of appetite were a small price to pay.

A couple more runners dropped out today. Tomorrow is the longest day and at 26.2 was billed as 'The Everest Challenge Marathon'. Some runners will be arriving just to compete in this Marathon. I'm looking forward to it as we actually start descending and hopefully my speed and energy levels will improve.

12/11/98
Day 7

My marathon-running experience is somewhat limited with just two London Marathons under my belt. They had both hurt like hell. Even though I had followed a training schedule they had still hurt and I seem to remember the week to ten days prior to a marathon you are advised to 'taper' (slowly reduce the miles you run, giving your body a chance to rest) and here we were having just run forty four tough miles at altitude - not what I would call the best tapering in the world.

According to the race briefing we would now start descending. I think each of us was pleased. With the two days altitude training we had just done I was hoping that my overall speed would improve, ever the optimist me!

Now you would think with the acclimatisation of the previous two days and the fact that we were descending ie. indulging in a gravity-assisted run, we would fly down. Unfortunately, the severity of the descent required absolute concentration, something that for me has always been in short supply. The constant descending was costing:- my poor old toes were taking a real bashing constantly smacking the front of my trainers.

The lower down we got the more lush and green the area became with bamboos and rhododendrons offering some much welcome shade.

Passing through small populated areas and negotiating small narrow paths again required a bit of concentration and at one point I reached a bottleneck and had to give way to a small herd of oxen and their handler. So narrow was this section that they brushed my legs as I frantically clung on to some overhanging vegetation!

Once they were clear I carried on, the descent finally levelled out and I could hear the distinct sound of fast-flowing water. My imagination ran riot with thoughts of wading across fast-flowing deep rivers or, worse, swimming across. Hopefully there would be one of those rickety old rope bridges that swing when used and if we did have to cross over on an old rope bridge would I bottle it?

As I turned right, there in front of me was a pretty modern solid-looking steel bridge. Once across I tried to pick up the pace but all this achieved was that I stubbed my toes more often - my poor old toes were by this time really tender and each time I stubbed them I could have cried.

I plodded on and rounding a corner spotted the finishing line. I crossed the line in 11th place. I was pleased, pleased that it seemed to be the altitude that was slowing me down and not my incompetence.

The finish line/race HQ was at a tea house. I collected my kit bag and was shown to my room which was actually someone's bedroom.

I settled in and examined my feet. Though blister-free, all the toes were red raw and angry looking, battered and bashed. They would no doubt be bruised by the morning, even the nails hurt.

Once all the runners were in we were again treated to a fantastic meal, with a large communal bonfire blazing away. We all sat around while some of the staff sang and danced. There were some trekkers there who were astounded to hear that we had run from Mannybayang to Sandakphu in a single day:- it had taken them three days to do the same route.

13/11/98

Day 8

Today's section was a relatively short half-marathon and we were consequently treated to a bit of a late start:- 11:00.

However, the habit of getting up at 'daft o'clock' in the morning proved too difficult a habit to break so I was still up bright and early.

I had a walk around the small but very busy little village and found a postbox so posted some postcards. As I write this in 2013 the postcards have still not arrived.

At 11:00 we all stood on the start line, my toes were sore and just like I had done at the Marathon des Sables start lines I was trying to protect them from being trodden on.

Other than my toes I felt pretty good, legs were a bit stiff and felt well used but after running 70 miles in the Himalayas that was to be expected. Unlike some of the others I had no blisters, headaches or nausea, so let battle commence!

Once we were underway it was immediately time to switch on:- the descents were tricky, technical, cruel and unforgiving especially to tender toes.

The whole area was extremely hilly, so hilly in fact the buildings were built half on terra firma and half on stilts. There was literally not enough flat ground to build a whole building on.

Running along the road I had to move over as spread out over the road was some tarpaulins with various produce drying in the sun. Also, any passing traffic would do the crushing that was needed by running over the stuff.

The first 8-9 miles was composed of mainly tricky steep switchbacks but then the terrain slowly changed very gently and almost without noticing we started to climb and climb with the last couple of miles as steep as anything we had thus far encountered - in other words fucking steep, knee-grabbing, lung-busting, heart racing self-inflicted masochism.

I eventually crossed the finishing line in a time of 2:05hrs.

The evening was again a fantastic meal and great entertainment but the runners were becoming a little jaded - too jaded to join in.

14/11/98
Day 9

The last day's running was some 17 miles long. The finish line was at the start in Manybayang.

The atmosphere on the start line for this last day's running was a lot more relaxed with a lot more jovial chatter. The pressure was off:- the completion of the Himalayan 100 mile race was now just a formality, people could afford to relax a bit.

Three, two, one and we were off, the ground on which we were running was the best so far:- a well-maintained 'road', nice and hard, smooth underfoot. However, my tender feet didn't really appreciate the constant pounding and again complained.

To override the pain I employed the same tactic as I had during the 'Marathon des Sables':- keep the runner in front in sight - this gave me something to concentrate on other than my painful feet - it seemed to work as the miles slipped by.

It was another gorgeous crisp day with clear blue skies. Eventually I rounded a corner and could hear in the distance clapping and cheering. A few moments later the finish line came into view - I finally crossed the finish line.

I had come 16th overall, thoroughly enjoyed the Race and would recommend it to anyone considering having a go.

It was tough, yes, but survive the first couple of days and you should, with a little bit of luck, finish.

As I said earlier the 'Himalayan 100' is so much more than a running race - it really is a fantastic experience.

And, more importantly, I still had my complimentary bottle of Champagne.

What next?

*The
finish
line*

Caught walking through the clouds

Another day at the office

THE JORDAN DESERT CUP 2001

What is it: A single stage Desert Footrace

When: November 2001

Where: Jordan, Wadi Rum-Petra

Distance: 106 miles (170km)

It is: A great race, 60 miles of sand, the remainder in the mountains - either way it hurts!

See: darbaroud.com

---

222 starters   41 DNFs

Arriving at the airport at Amman I found myself going through my now familiar routine of trying to spot likely Jordan Desert Cup competitors.

This race was organised by Patrick Bauers - the same bloke who organises the Marathon Des Sables. This race was different in that, unlike the MDS, it was just one stage:- start and don't stop until you reach the finish line some 168 kms away.

Whilst looking around for the other like-minded lunatics I spotted Indiana Jones, aka Lloyd Scott. I had met Lloyd during our participation in the MDS. Lloyd was a phenomenal athlete, a former fireman, who had survived cancer and now raised funds for charity by taking part in extreme endurance events all over the world - a very tough if not slightly eccentric bloke.

Since I had last seen him he had had a bone marrow transplant and a hip replacement. He was, he told me, going to run the Jordan Desert Cup dressed as Indiana Jones including leather jacket, shirt, tie, trilby and the entire Elton John CD collection! These were after all, the days before the iPod!!

The British contingent arrived at Wadi Rum at 03:30. The whole camp was asleep and all available space seemed to have been taken so a bit of sneaking about was required:- a rearranging of peoples' kit bags, squeezing into any space that was wider than 8 inches, a diplomatic cough or two and I was in - sort of.

After what appeared to be a two minute sleep we were up and getting organised. First, over to the kit-check tent making sure we had all the compulsory food and safety equipment, ie torch, compass, whistle, emergency supplies etc.

That done it was off to the medical tent, ECG and Doctors note handed in, a few questions regarding medical history and I was good to go. Lloyd, however, was a different kettle of fish. First the French crew had tried to explain to him that he was supposed to be wearing his race kit not a trilby, shirt, tie, leather jacket and chino trousers (they accepted the training shoes he had on).

It took a lot of explaining and much head-scratching before they realised that "the crazy English bloke" was actually going to try and run the Jordan Desert Cup in fancy dress!

On to the medical tent. Lloyd, standing in front of the Doctors dressed as Indiana Jones proceeded to give them a medical history:- fire-damaged lungs (from his time in the fire service) hip replacement, bone marrow recipient and cancer survivor. I think all diplomatic relations were now severely strained and the Entente Cordiale that our two countries had thus far enjoyed was beginning to look decidedly shaky!

I think they let him proceed fully expecting the "Lunatic Brit" to last the first day before admitting defeat.

Thursday 7/11/01

After a long sleepless night we were up early. I attempted to eat breakfast and failed miserably. Got dressed, packed the rucksack and prepared the feet. With memories of the MDS still fresh in my memory, I knew that it was absolutely imperative to look after my feet. I had bought some small ankle gaiters and a large pot of Vaseline. I applied the Vaseline to anywhere I was likely to get friction and when I say anywhere, I really do mean anywhere. I put the ankle gaiters on and duct taped them into place: no sand, grit or gravel was getting in to my shoes this time.

All sorted out and ready to go, a short walk to the start line and I was already knackered - the super soft sand and racing heart rate I'm sure didn't help matters. Looking around at the others I couldn't help but ask myself - why does everyone else manage to have smaller, lighter packs than mine?

Once again here I was standing at the start line, hopelessly out of my depth, thinking to myself what the hell am I doing here? I'm a wannabe, I don't belong, square pegs and round holes, this race is for only proper athletes only and I'll get found out soon enough. Realising that it was now too late to do anything about it, I put those thoughts to one side and was busy listening to the excited and nervous chatter. Final instructions were given in multi languages - French, English and Japanese to name but three.

At bang on 08:30 we were off. CP1 was some 13km away and I managed to run the whole way. A 13km run easy? Wrong, running on super fine sand is anything but easy:- your feet go into the sand not onto the sand - real energy sapping stuff.

Leaving the first CP shortly after arriving, it was straight onto the next. Once again it was real knackering sand running. I still managed to run most of it but my poor old legs were letting me know that they weren't happy! At CP2 I decided to get rid of any items I thought I wouldn't need ie cooking fuel and foodstuffs. I wasn't the only one judging by the already overflowing bins. I was being fairly cautious in the amount I jettisoned, keeping just enough to get me to the finish line.

Onto CP3, a mixture of running and walking, about 60-40 in favour of walking. Finally I arrived. It was at this CP that the enormity of the race began to sink in. I was filled with negative thoughts about how I felt, the weight of my pack, the distance left, the difficulty of the terrain. Negative thoughts are without doubt the worst thing any Ultra-distance racer can have:- they start to erode away at your confidence, try to convince you to stop, suggest any reason to stop, from sore feet, too far to go, the heat, the cold, the pack is too heavy, you haven't got enough food, you're going too slow. The list is endless and your imagination adds to the list until you agree with something or other, anything that tells you to stop, because stopping is really the only sensible thing to do, the easy thing to do, the right thing to do.

I left CP3 and I left the negative thoughts there. I already had enough to carry. I wasn't doing too badly, some people looked bloody awful (with hindsight I probably looked bloody awful too).

From CP3 to CP4 I switched off, had tunnel vision and became very focused. I followed the path and I followed the runners ahead. I didn't sightsee or daydream like I normally do. I was struggling and tired and sightseeing was a luxury I could ill afford. I really remember nothing of note except footprints in the sand and the rucksack belonging to the runner ahead. I now just focused on getting to CP4 - nothing else mattered except the next CP.

I eventually arrived, collected some water and left. Plodding along, feeling sorry for myself, I decided that at CP5 I would have a rest. Unfortunately when I arrived I found very little space in the tent, it seems everyone else felt as knackered as me. I got my sleeping bag out and climbed in. An hour and a half after arriving I left. It was too bloody cold to sleep, I just laid there shivering, listening to somebody coughing and farting and someone else tossing and turning while wearing a tin foil space blanket. The noises were enough to get me up - I also reasoned that the energy I was using to shiver would be better spent on getting me to the finish line! I left CP5 feeling tired and a little anxious:- would I make it and where's my "bum bag?" The little bag worn around my waist containing some food, glucose tablets, small pencil torch and various bits and pieces needed whilst on the move, bollocks, must have left it at CP5. Too late now, pillock, I gave myself a verbal kick up the arse, get on with it and told myself in no uncertain terms to stop moaning!

I was now left with my emergency rations which, if opened, would disqualify me from the race so all I had to eat were two-thirds of a packet of jelly babies, half a packet of fruit pastilles and a packet of glucose sweets.

My already shattered confidence took another knock when I spoke to a fellow British runner who was extremely concerned that he might not have enough food despite having bags of the stuff.

I plodded on to CP6. I arrived at this CP safe in the knowledge that I would not have to make the decision to 'pull out', that decision was already made by the fact that I had so little food it would be virtually impossible to complete such an extreme race.

It was only this fact that got me out of CP6 - too much of a 'chicken' to make the decision myself, I would wait until lack of nutrition and energy forced me out!

I plodded on to CP7, another quick stop and I was off to CP8. It was now taking between 2:5 and 3 hours to reach each CP.

CP8 in and out. The difficulty I had in getting to CP9 was worrying, this must surely be as hard as it gets, it must get easier from here on in - wrong!

The difficulty I experienced between CP9 and 10 was one of frustration and exasperation. The terrain seemed to be full of 'switchbacks' zigzagging all over the place. To move forward a mile (as the crow flies) you seemed to be doing two or three. You look ahead and see someone apparently quite close and within catching distance only to realise that they were actually 3 or 4 miles away, absolutely soul-destroying.

My ability to judge time, distance and terrain were now non-existent. Ah well, head down, one foot in front of the other and get on with it.

Time for a treat: a couple of jelly babies, a glucose sweet and a sip of Lucozade sports drink and all was once again well in David's world.

When I finally reached CP10 it was with relief and this relief was helped by the fact that a few of the competitors not only looked bloody awful but were very vocal in their description of that last section. Expressions like "well that was BOLLOCKS" and the "fuckers are trying to break us, bastards".

I had a giggle, a drink and a 20 minute break and I was off. I left this CP and for the first time actually believed I could finish! Then bugger me if the terrain didn't get harder. We had now just about finished with the sand but were into the mountains. On leaving the CP we were immediately greeted with a climb, well, a climb and a half. It was relentless, constant and bloody hot.

But with 10 CPs done, just 3 remained. I reasoned that it would be cooler the higher we climbed and the worry of not enough food was for now not an issue. I wasn't hungry and felt reasonably strong. If I was suddenly attacked by pangs of hunger I would be more or less at CP 11, I'd have a rest and hopefully survive the last 2 CPs (ever the optimist!).

However, in the meantime I had to get CP 11. This was proving somewhat challenging, with some impressive and saucy climbs. The moment you left the CP you were climbing and a 1500 meter climb is always a challenge - even more so after a 135 or so kilometers of running through sandy desert, little sleep and very little to eat!

But onward and upward - keep going put one foot in front of the other. The climbing continued and then sort of levelled out. It was now late afternoon and I started to look hard for where the next CP was, with more optimism than realism, and besides, it gave me something to do and took my mind off the monotony of the terrain. Beautiful it may be but it was, at this point in time, just an obstacle to overcome!

Scanning the horizon ahead I saw nothing, then turning my head slightly to the right and down in a shallow depression there it was CP 11, 11 down 2 to go!

It was now 6 o' clock in the evening. I collected some water, ate 3 fruit pastilles, a jelly baby and a dextorol glucose sweet, put some warm clothes on, head torch and hat and I was then good to go. I left at 6:25.

So far, apart from one 20 minute stint, I had been on my own - only ever seeing the person ahead and that's if I was lucky. I refuse to look behind me during these races:- it serves no practical purpose. If I am going to get caught then so be it. I'm doing the best I can and it takes all my concentration to move myself forward. Worrying about things I have no control over is a pretty pointless exercise.

As the evening wore on it got windier and colder, tiredness was making me trip over my own feet and had anyone been watching me they may well have thought they were watching a drunk staggering home.

After a while I realised that I had not seen a single runner since leaving the previous CP. Then, scanning the terrain ahead I spotted a small white light. Without realising it my speed increased, why, I don't know. I can only assume that we humans must have some inbuilt "chasing" gene.

A little while later and after my 'increased speed' had decreased I realised that the 'runner' in front was not a runner but the CP.

Arriving at CP12 I was immediately asked if I would be sleeping, and am I okay? (I must have looked rough). When I politely said I wouldn't be staying they said that this was the last chance to sleep as the last CP had no facilities for sleeping. I think they were a little bored and just glad that someone had turned up.

After about 15 minutes I was off - now I was wondering if I should have stayed and slept - but too late and not having the balls to turn back, I kept plodding along. After a while the track became more defined and seemed to be littered with used bits of rubbish, old tyres and tins. Then the sound of dogs barking, the smell of smoke and finally lights, climbing a rather steep, twisting incline and suddenly I was in the village of Taiyiba. It was dark but there were a lot of people about.

Walking through the village I was joined be a small group of people, mainly children. They were intrigued and asked if I had run from Wadi Rum. They stayed with me for about a kilometre. Leaving the village the route took me onto the tarmaced road - this road was steep, cold and windy. Moving along the right hand side of the road, with thoughts of finishing, food, showers and bed I could see what appeared to be headlights approaching. They were moving fast and were very bright, then I realised we were on a collision course. Self-preservation took over (I'm glad I had not eaten or I may well have had an accident in my shorts) and I jumped down into a drainage ditch. The car stopped and I heard the car door open. I thought "Oh fuck, I've just covered God knows how far, I've nearly reached the end of this fantastic race and I'm about to be mugged!" Too bloody knackered to fight and too knackered to run I was working out what to do when I realised the car was a police car. The very helpful officer helped me up, asked if I was alright and was I one of the runners from Wadi Rum? He told me there was a CP up ahead and that it would be better if I was on the other side of the road. Phew!!

Within 30 minutes I was at CP13, the last CP. It was extremely cold and windy and I had decided to have a short break before the final few kilometres. However on arriving I saw that I was not the only one with that idea:- half a dozen runners were doing exactly that: huddled down beside the landcruiser that was the CP, it was too cold to hang around so I decided to plod on.

On leaving the CP I was given very clear and very precise instructions on how to proceed. The first km or so were apparently 'treacherous underfoot'. They weren't wrong:- it was very difficult, steep and slippery (I later found out that some of the runners huddling down at the CP had attempted to get down and discretion being the better part of valour had turned back and were waiting for daylight!). I slowly, very slowly, made my way down. The loose scree petered out, and finally the steepness started to level out. Just as I was getting the hang of moving along, the whole canyon lit up, bright light everywhere! I could momentarily see the whole steep canyon, sheer drops and narrow paths. Then as quickly as the light appeared it disappeared along with my 'night vision'. What the hell had just happened or was it the dreaded 'sleepmonsters' coming out to play?

I then heard a voice shouting and looking around I spotted a small light on the other side of the canyon. I shouted back and waved my head torch in the direction that I had seen the torch. It turned out that the runner was Spanish-he was okay but stuck. He had either taken a wrong turn or attempted a shortcut, whichever it was it was a mistake. The moment he used his flare he was out the race. What made it more galling was that he was so close to the finish - maybe 4 miles as the crow flies. I told him I would inform the race crew.

A little further on I started to notice the little green fluorescent glowsticks marking the way. Then turning a corner I was presented with the wonderful sight of the steps that led down to Petra, each step had on it a candle lighting the way (I still managed to trip over!).

Reaching the bottom and the familiar smell of camel wee and poo. Up past the famous Treasury and the final couple of km to the finish line, I crossed the finish line at 01:05 in 82nd place.

A very attractive French lady placed a medal around my neck, embraced me and kissed me on either cheek. Unfortunately for her I smelled like a rotting carcass and I knew it. I'm sure she was aware of it but was far too polite to mention it.

I sat down with my medal. Another finisher was there and a few moments later we were both taken to a hotel. I was lucky that I had a room to myself.

I unwrapped my feet and was pleasantly surprised to see just one small blister -I had got away with it virtually unscathed. I was chuffed. A quick shower and bed. As I stood in the shower washing away the accumulated grime I suddenly jumped and clenched. What the %^&* hell was that? It was like a bee sting, a sharp stabbing pain right between my buttocks. It continued and was very sore, sore enough to warrant further investigation so making good use of the full-length mirror I bent over and like a somewhat nervous amateur proctologist I set about checking the damage. What the *&^%$? The damage was severe, red-raw and angry, it looked and felt as if someone had sandpapered my arse.

Even though I thought I had been clever in applying Vaseline, I was wrong. The Vaseline/sand combination mixed together made a very effective abrasive!

Forty-one years old and suffering from nappy rash - did I get any sympathy from my wife? No, she laughed.

The Jordan Desert Cup was an odd race, though I thought it tougher than the Marathon des Sables, I had enjoyed it more. The one stage factor suited me more. I didn't like the stop start aspect of the stage races.

Lloyd Scott, aka Indiana Jones, annoyed the hell out of the French by finishing - still listening to his Elton John CD collection!

The following April, Lloyd completed the London marathon in his deep sea divers suit, a suit that weighed some 140 pounds. He managed to finish in a little over 5 days!!

What next?

A rather dapper looking Lloyd Scott AKA Indiana Jones

The calm before the storm!

Checkpoint 9 I felt worse than I look!

Getting organised

RAID AMAZONIE 2003

What is it:	An Ultra-distance jungle footrace
When:	March
Where:	French Guyana
Distance:	160 km (100miles)
It is:	Tough, hot, humid and unforgiving and was supported by the French Foreign Legion

What a nightmare start! I have travelled quite a lot in my life, from places as diverse as India and Sri Lanka, Jordan and Syria and even the Great Sahara Desert but nothing compares to the nightmare journey from Paris, Charles de Gaul airport to my hotel, the Hotel Escale.

For a start, the simple trip from Charles de Gaul to Orly (my connecting flight) was fraught with problems. I finally arrived at Orly, with the instructions to phone the hotel and a courtesy vehicle would come and pick me up.

However, my money was not good enough for the card only telephone so I decided to get a taxi to the hotel. Spotting a couple of taxis pulling away, I decided to wait for the next one - after waiting for sometime I decided to ask a member of staff about the taxis and was told that this was a drop off point only!

Taking the hint I gave up and went to buy a phone card. On my way I spotted the information kiosk and asked directions for the taxi rank - I then joined the world's longest taxi queue. After forty minutes I finally got into a taxi, though my French is limited and the taxi driver's English even more so. Luckily for me I had the address for the hotel written down. I passed the address to the driver, he nodded his head in acknowledgement and we were off. Paris and Rue Pierre-Marie Curie were found but the Hotel Escale was not - up and down we went checking each number one by one. We found the right number, 15, but the building was in complete darkness and most certainly was not a hotel - this was confirmed by the rather large lettering above the front door that said 'The Institute Geographic'.

Fortunately, I had tipped the driver well and he returned the favour by getting on his mobile and making a couple of enquiries. He seemed pleased and relieved so off we went. After some time and some miles he pulled up outside a taxi rank and asked fellow drivers for directions - this seemed to work and we were off, eventually finding the elusive Hotel Escale.

I ended up paying 90 euros for the taxi ride - I had only brought 100. It was now 23:15 and I was knackered and stressed before I had even got into the jungle!

At breakfast I met a few of the other runners, 3 of which I recognised from the Jordan Desert Cup, 2 years ago.

The flight was uneventful but long. We landed at Cayenne, the capital city of French Guiana and were met by the wild looking, bandana wearing and slightly eccentric race organiser Alain Gestain.

Alain met each one of us, shook our hands and herded us on to the waiting minibuses for the 4 and half hour drive to the town St. Laurent.

The hotel was run by a family that had settled here from

Vietnam - lovely hotel, very friendly and hospitable but the one drawback with this was the beds:- they were a little on the short side. I, however, am a little on the long side and not very good at Maths, but I could work out that a 6ft 4inch body would have a trouble with a 5ft 4inch bed. It would have been okay had the bed been one of those that would at least allow me to hang my feet over the end - not one of those that had a bed end so effectively not allowing my long legs to straighten out.

2/3/03

Up early - breakfast and a walk around the town Saint-Laurent-du- Maron.

This town was once a famous penal colony and a huge prison still stands on the banks of the river. Though no longer used as a prison it is open to the public and as I work for the prison service it seemed only right to take a tour.

Walking around was a bit of an eye opener. It was a tough place to do your time:- the humidity and the eerie atmosphere just added to the harshness of the place.

A little later I went for a wander around the town and even walking slowly I was sweating!

The colours and smells of the market place were fascinating. I only wish we had more time but it was lunch time. Lunch was (or would have been) lovely - a beautifully cooked and wonderfully aromatic Vietnamese meal. Unfortunately soon after lunch we were to run 20km - it sort of took the edge off most peoples' appetites. After lunch there was a race briefing, after which we were to be transported to the start line.

An afternoon start was somewhat unusual and after arriving at the start which was on a nondescript track, we were again given another quick talk.

This first section was a relatively short introductory course of 20km. This section was mainly on forest track and was therefore pretty straightforward.

Hard work, yes, hilly and bloody hot, but the chance of getting lost whilst running along a well-defined track were practically nil - I hoped!

After a few km I found myself running alongside another British runner. Jeremy had taken part in last year's race - we ran the remainder of the section together, our paces were perfectly matched.

The campsite was a collection of huts, there was no electricity. It was a question of finding a place for your hammock - we had all been issued with hammocks. I for one had never been in one let alone put one up so it was with some trepidation that I got into it. Would I roll out or would my knots come undone?

After a successful (I didn't fall out of the hammock) if not sweaty night, we got up and had breakfast - coffee, pain au chocolat, croissant, very typically French and very impressive but with the French Foreign Legion as our helpers we knew we would be well looked after.

3/3/03

07:30 start - incredibly tough run today. The terrain and distance were not the problem - challenging yes, but do-able. However, the heat and humidity were something else. I have run across deserts in hotter temperatures but this heat coupled with the humidity saps your strength and to add to my woes I am constipated - a new and rather unpleasant experience for me and a real pain in the arse, so to speak!

This night's camp is an amazing place:- Volpair - stunningly beautiful, tranquil and very peaceful, set beside a river.

After a little swim, I sat on the riverbank watching huge butterflies the size of pigeons apparently drinking from the river and resting on the shore. I was aware of an intense fluttering by my right ear causing me to swat whatever it was away - only to realise it was a hummingbird, no bigger than my little finger!

Butterflies the size of birds and birds the size of butterflies: very strange!

The intermittent downpours are impressive and heavy but refreshing. Some of the runners are off to see some waterfalls which are supposed to be a fantastic sight. However, the 5 mile round trip is more than I have to spare.

Lunch was once again fantastic. Apparently, the few people that did get to the waterfalls were less than impressed:- they were good but not that good!

That evening meal was delicious, but during the course of the meal we were given a big lecture on what to expect on tomorrow's section. The translation from French to English was done by an Irishman. The whole thing frightened everyone - it was to be 45km of hell on Earth, apparently!

4/4/03

Today's stage was incredible, the first 20km were undulating and challenging, but at the 18km mark I came across a box of Danish pastries - very surreal but very welcome.

Once we got to the halfway mark we had to swim across a river, watched by some Legionnaires.

I'm not a great swimmer and am prone to getting a touch of cramp in my feet when swimming, so I was now in a bit of a dilemma: Do I wear a life jacket or not? (Now I know how my wife must feel, "I just don't know what to wear") A difficult decision, the French Foreign Legion were there watching and acting as safety crew and they are not the sort I wanted to look wimpy in front of. I'll either look stupid putting one on or look stupid getting cramp floundering and need rescuing, bollocks. I decided to put one on and pretend that I thought they were compulsory. I put a life jacket on while trying to look macho, got into the water and sort of doggy-paddled over to the other side. A quick scramble up the bank and then into the jungle proper, thick and very dense. After a couple of kms, we came across a steel and wooden bridge, the steel was rusted and the wood was rotten. It required some nerves and a lot of concentration to cross. I managed to put my foot through one of the planks and then listened and watched as bits of rotten timber crashed to the river below! (It very nearly cured my constipation).

During this stage I once again teamed up with Jeremy, the English guy that had done the race the previous year. Trying to run in such difficult terrain was just about impossible so we speed-marched our way through and caught a couple of runners, we were certainly shifting because not once were we passed!

Stepping over a log that was lying across the path, I managed to catch sight of a grey snake right where I was about to place my foot. The thing never moved, I slowly pulled my leg back and decided to kick the log to frighten the snake into moving off, but no, this snake had balls. It just looked at me as if to say is that it, "Is that your best shot?" I'm no Dr Dolittle but I fully understood what the snake was telling me "Naf off, Sunshine" and, with discretion being the better part of valour I decided on this occasion to make a detour!

We finally emerged from the jungle after 7 hours.

The finish line was again on a river bank, in a small town called Apatou, not a lot seems to happen in this small town but the place is being modernised.

Tonight's accommodation is in what appears to be an old warehouse. The locals find us fascinating to the point of staring/studying us, picking up anything that gets discarded and watching our every move.

The evening meal was again preceded by another French

waffling session, officially called a briefing. The English and Irish contingent sat outside, the French managed to do enough clapping, cheering and self-appreciating for all of us!

5/3/03

Today's 20km section was along the river, running along forest tracks - these tracks were open and exposed and gave a short respite from the claustrophobic density of the jungle. However, being exposed to the sun's rays so close to the equator meant an increased risk of sunburn. Consequently I just wanted to get back into the jungle shade.

Running through the small villages we were always greeted with smiles and a friendly wave. The river and jungle made for a great run and I felt good all day. However, my running partner for the last 2 days, Jeremy, really seemed to struggle and came in a long way behind me. Not to worry, he seemed okay and I'm sure my bad day is just around the corner!

The jungle section was once again fantastic with more reported snake sightings.

At the finish line, which was a small clearing on the riverbank, we were collected by canoe and ferried over to the campsite, which was stunning.

Had a really good day:- felt good and ran well, the whole day was capped off by having a beautiful campsite!

Again the local children made an appearance and looked at us as if we had just landed from another planet!

6/3/03

Up early again, the mornings on the river are always beautiful. Breakfast was a cup of coffee or two, bread and chocolate spread sandwiches.

Whilst getting myself sorted out, by faffing and farting around as per usual, one of the runners asked about my shoes. They were Salomons and had no laces but had a unique 'quick-lacing system' - basically a thin Kevlar cord with a 'pull toggle'. Just slide toggle to fit and then tuck away into a small pocket on the tongue.

I took the shoe off to show how the thing works, explaining the benefits like a professional salesman:- speed, no laces to break, come undone or get clogged up with mud and crap etc. I wish I had been on a commission because he seemed impressed - with either the shoe or my salesman pitch I'm not sure.

Today's run was jungle and through more villages. We had a lot of support from the locals who were all very supportive. The rivers were fantastic - we crossed, swam, waded and canoed across half a dozen or so:- a great day.

Unfortunately, one little mistake occurred:- after my salesman's talk just prior the start, I didn't put my shoes on properly and consequently one got sucked off in a particularly boggy bit. It just so happened it was one of the bits that required a leap, thus I landed heavily or should I say deeply and the thing got sucked off! It disappeared into a rather deep hole and required a bit of digging around to retrieve it. Unfortunately, it was a narrow track and my faffing about was causing a bit of a traffic jam.

I continued on, my red embarrassed face disguised thanks to the extreme humidity. I finally finished a little over 2 hours later, feeling fresh and feeling good.

The village we stayed in was really just a small collection of huts and it had a bar that had apparently been hastily put together last night because the locals had heard that some runners were on their way and they like a drink!

We saw two dead armadillos that were apparently destined for the pot, not ours (I think) and a couple of the villagers had caught piranhas right outside our camp right where most of us had taken a dip!

Last night's sleep was slightly ruined by cockerels that decided to wake everyone up at 02:00. A great place though, Pinpin.

7/3/03
The last day!

Today's run was very difficult:- hard and long with a long jungle section that was extremely tough - bogs and the occasional swim.

Jungle swimming is fraught with potential problems - not only are there all sorts of unseen nasties waiting to eat, bite chew or sting you, the nastiest of them all being the 'toothpick fish' or to give it its correct name the Candiru:- a parasitic fish that has a very nasty way of attacking, so nasty in fact that given a choice I'd sooner have my legs chewed by piranhas. The numerous obstacles and rivers were all a bit tricky and very time-consuming.

On eventually emerging from the jungle we encountered a track that was open and exposed and consequently bloody hot!

This track was just 5km long but felt much longer, but maybe my tiredness and desperation to finish made it seem that much longer.

The finish was a complete shithole. There was nothing there except huts. Well, not exactly huts but roofs on stilts, and we had to spend the night.

I had a good run, coming in the top twenty - very pleased, especially as I was at one point in front of the Belgian marathon champion (female).

In the jungle my 6ft 4 inch height was a very distinct advantage:- bloody long legs, good for clambering over things. However, once on a track the champion was in her element and came storming past me.

The campsite was in the middle of nowhere with no facilities, unusual for a race: - normally you get shipped off somewhere nice, have a shower and plenty of food, but not here - it was up with the hammocks and wait until tomorrow.

The meal was again brilliant, the drinkers were drinking and we were all singing. What we were singing God only knows, a great evening, a great atmosphere - even the Legionnaires seemed to relax a bit!

8/3/03

This morning we could have had a lie-in, but force of habit kicked in and by six thirty the whole camp was up and faffing about - some feeling a touch delicate after downing too much celebration rum!

After breakfast and packing it was just hanging around until the transport arrived at ten, to take us back to St. Laurent.

After arriving we helped marshal a local children's running race. It was good fun and the kids loved having the 'international runners' helping.

At 12 o clock we had a presentation in the Mayor's office. All the runners received t-shirts, bottles of rum and a certificate. I also received a 'parang', a jungle knife which was given to the top twenty runners, my 19th place just qualifying me.

This race was fantastic:- the place, the people the looking around the prison and cell that the famous convict "papillon" was held, the flora, fauna and noises of the jungle all went to make it a fantastic experience.

WHAT NEXT?

The look of relief at having survived a few days in the jungle

The final campsite that flag goes with me on every race

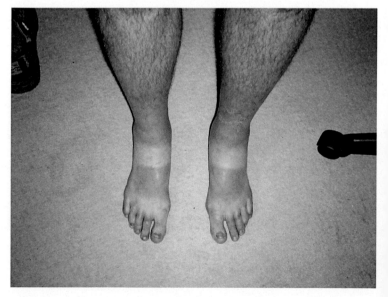

Back at home, it was a day or two before I could wear proper shoes

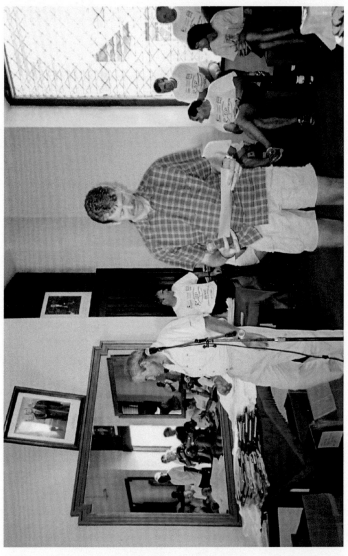

*Collecting my
Certificate
and - more
importantly -
my Machete,
awarded to the
top twenty -
I was
nineteenth*

*After a hard
day's work*

THE 3 PEAKS CHALLENGE 2003

What is it: A challenge to see if we could climb the 3 highest peaks in England, Scotland and Wales in 24 hours

When: Whenever - we did it in July

Where: Ben Nevis, Scotland, Scafell Pike, England and Snowdon, Wales

Distance: To the top of each of them!

See: thethreepeakschallenge.co.uk

The idea for this Challenge was first mooted by Mark, a friend and colleague from work.

The Challenge:- to scale the 3 highest peaks in England Wales and Scotland in under 24 hours. The 24 hours were to include the travelling time between each of the mountains.

Never being one to shy away from a challenge (or just plain stupid) I instantly said yes and as per usual I said yes without having a clue to what I had let myself in for.

We signed up two others to have a bash, Nigel and Jason, plus two support crew/drivers, Andy and Dave.

We spent the next few months training and getting organised - routes up to the summit of each mountain and the order they would be done.

Ben Nevis, Scotland, followed by Scafell Pyke, England and finally Snowdon in Wales.

With training and logistics all complete, it was time get on with it. The 4th of July 2003 saw the six of us, plus kit, packed into our rental vehicle.

The drive to Fort William was a long uneventful 9.5 hours.

We found the Glen Nevis Youth Hostel and realised that it was in the very best location possible:- right at the foot of Ben Nevis at 4,409ft our first and Britain's highest mountain. Looking up at it, it looked bloody impressive. We had 24 hours to kill so a decent meal and an early night was the order of the day.

The next day was spent trying to relax - plenty of food and a game of golf, well, pitch and putt. At 17:00 we made our way back to the foot of Ben Nevis, got ourselves organised, had our photos taken and then at exactly 18:00 we were off.

I needed a wee, I had been busting and told the others to carry on and did what needed to be done. Once finished I ran to catch up, I caught Mark and was surprised to see that he was already sweating and so soon! I looked at my watch and it was 12 minutes past 6, we had been going for 12 minutes and Mark was sweating and red in the face. I must admit at that point I wondered if he would be able to finish, but then I remembered that Mark was the most experienced one of us having done a shed load of Munros (climbed peaks of over 3000ft) and he had climbed each of the 3 mountains we were now attempting.

We carried on and the pace was pretty good, with Nigel leading the way, Jason not far behind him, myself and Mark bringing up the rear. We started to pass a few of the slower walkers. This part of the route was relatively straightforward as it was a well-defined path, though we were slightly spaced out (not the chemically-induced kind) we were always within sight of each other. This was something that we had discussed during our training sessions - it was agreed that whoever was leading was responsible for keeping us all within sight and shouting distance, purely as a safety precaution.

It was good to see Nigel was regularly checking behind. Eventually the terrain got steeper and suddenly we seemed to be clambering over huge boulders, tricky and steep enough to require both hands and feet!

The rocks and stones occasionally moved and I think we were all aware of the potential for loose stones and possible injury to whoever was below.

Eventually we reached the end of the tricky scrambling bit and when we were all together we walked on toward the summit, which we reached at 19:58. It had taken 1 hour 58 minutes to reach the top, we took a quick photo of us all on the summit and then started our descent.

I think we all understood that to descend the same way as we had just come up would, at best, be silly and worst just plain dangerous so we took the longer but safer so-called tourist route:- a well defined path that would take us right down to outside the Glen Nevis Youth Hostel. We were moving well and I was pretty impressed with how well everyone was doing, we were in good spirits and pleased with the time. I just hoped we could maintain it and had not gone too fast, too soon! As always pace would be the key, it was pointless to do one mountain fast and the other two at a snail's pace. When we were approximately halfway down, we used our Walkie Talkie radio to contact the support crew. The little radios only had a range of about 2 miles but were perfect for what we needed, instantly the support crew came back and informed us that they would be at the bottom ready for us.

Though the route down was a lot easier, it still required a degree of caution and the fact that we were working against the clock meant that we were now attempting little runs and consequently we had to switch on:- one trip could spell disaster.

We reached the bottom at 21:18. Our total time for Ben Nevis was 3 hours 18 minutes.

Once we were back on the little footbridge we again took a photo. The reason for the photos were twofold, one - an accurate and official record of our times, start, summit, and return to the start. We were very aware that yes, we could break the speed limits and race from mountain to mountain but that was not the point. We had an official AA confirmed drive time for the three mountains and if we had broken the speed limit our time would not count - we needed to do the thing properly. The second reason for the photos was so that we had a memento of this great adventure.

Once the photos were taken, we quickly got into the vehicle and headed for the next mountain, Scafell Pyke, in the Lake District.

With the 2 drivers in the front seat and the 4 of us trying to sort ourselves out in the rather cramped back seats. Six sweaty, flatulent blokes in a confined space had the potential to be rather unpleasant, we were fortunate in that it wasn't too bad. The drivers had the responsibility to get us to the next mountain on time - all we had to do was rest, refuel and recharge the batteries.

Whilst I was listening to music and pondering the challenge ahead I suddenly became very aware of a desperate Nigel pushing my seat and shouting that he was going to be sick. Now he was sitting directly behind me I was therefore and unfortunately in his direct line of fire and with this in mind I told the driver in no uncertain terms to pull over and QUICK. He did, I slid the door open, got out and was followed immediately by a rocket-like Nigel, just in time to see Nige produce a magnificent display of multi-coloured projectile vomiting. I watched in wonder and then for some unknown reason I joined in. There we both were, puking whilst hanging on to the 'people carrier'. I looked up only to realise that our driver had pulled into a car park belonging to a Little Chef restaurant and people that had only a minute ago been enjoying their meal were now watching the two of us honking up - whilst at the same time pushing their half-full plates to one side. We did the only thing we could:- we smiled, waved and got back in the vehicle and *&^%$ off.

We arrived at Wasdale at 02:35, a little quicker than we should have owing to the lack of traffic and our 'very efficient' drivers!

We had worked out that if we were to keep to the spirit of the challenge and not start prior to the official AA timings we could not start for another 13 minutes. We all agreed to keep to our agreed official timings - after all, 13 minutes is not that long, and besides, it gave us time for a wee and a quick cup of tea.

At exactly 02:48 a photo was taken and then we were off. Apparently, Scafell is the trickiest mountain, not the biggest, but the trickiest to navigate. This is where Mark would come into his own, having been up to the summit on more than one occasion, he would now be our unofficial guide.

Moving along a footpath we crossed a small river via a footbridge. We went along the path, eventually reaching a junction at a place called Lingmell Gill. We took the left turn that took us through another gate and then another small river and then onto some steeper climbing. I was glad Mark knew his way, it was dark and confusing and had I been on my own I would have at least got wet feet, or lost, or both!

Looking up ahead I noticed a procession of torches, obviously we weren't the only ones doing the Three Peaks this weekend. It was reassuring, if only to know we were going in the right direction, not that I didn't have faith in Mark's ability!

We plodded on and it was now that I realised our planning had been spot on, the reason for our 18:00 start was worked out so that we would be on Scafell for the absolute minimum time in the dark. I had just turned off my head torch, it had only been on for 45 minutes. We had climbed in the dark for only 45 minutes - it wasn't quite daylight but it was light enough.

As the old saying goes, perfect planning prevents piss poor performance or something like that.

We continued climbing and were catching and overtaking quite a few people. We eventually reached the summit at 04:29, another quick photo and then the descent.

I was still impressed with the way everyone was moving:- no signs of tiredness and we all remained together and always within talking distance.

I have always raced and trained on my own and I must admit I was expecting ego, tiredness or testosterone to somehow creep into the team dynamics. I was wrong - everyone seemed to gel into a single efficient happy working unit.

We finally reached our support crew at 05:46 - they were ready with the vehicle doors open and ready to go.

So far we had been at it for less than 12 hours and in that time we had climbed two out of the three and were all still in good shape.

We drove off toward Snowdon, well aware that barring some unforeseen accident we would complete the challenge in under the 24 hours.

We arrived at the Pen-Y-Pass car park at 10:16. This was to be the start for our ascent of Snowdon, going up the Miners track and descending the longer but easier Llanberis Path.

Again a quick photo and we were off, the path was well-defined and busy. I had never been on the miners track before, but had been to the summit of Snowdon twice - once via the Watkins path and once by the Llanberis Path. Passing by a small lake we carried on and on turning a corner came across an even larger lake which was divided by a causeway. Moving along we saw some old mine buildings and yet another small lake and then suddenly the leisurely stroll we had until now been enjoying came to a rather abrupt end. The route now started to climb sharply, the path seemed to get very busy and converge with another path. We carried on trying to stick together but the congestion was making that a bit difficult plus it was getting a little misty. Then suddenly we spotted a large finger of rock indicating that we were very close to the summit. Again we waited until we were all together and then walked the last little bit together, finally arriving on the Summit at 11:56. A quick photo and down - in less than 18 hours we had reached the summit of all three mountains. It now depended on how long it would take us to get to the bottom at Llanberis.

We descended as fast as we could but sore and tired legs really dictated our pace. We were now spread out a little and on reaching the halfway house, a tiny little place that sells refreshments, we regrouped for the final spurt to the finish line.

Once we were passing through a gate with a cattlegrid we radioed our support crew and told them where we were, so they could meet us. We then stepped on to a road that was a little steep, its steepness reminding our quads to take it easy and then we spotted our crew waiting by the Llanberis path start sign. We reached the bottom at 13:13.

We had completed the Three Peaks 24 hour Challenge in a time of 19 hours 13 minutes and with 4 hours and 47 minutes to spare.

We had also raised £1007.50 for our local Earl Mountbatten Hospice.

*From left to right. The Author, Mark, Nigel and Jason
On the Summit of Ben Nevis - one down two to go*

Scafell Pike, The Lake District

And - finally - Snowdon

The Team - From left to right.
Jason, The Author, Mark, Nigel and the two drivers - Andy and Dave

GUADARUN 2004

What is it:	A multi-staged Ultra-distance running race
When:	June (2004)
Where:	French Guadaloupe, Caribbean
Distance:	156km (98 miles)
It is:	Unusual, beautiful and a deceptively tough race - a hill climbers dream!

3rd June 2004

Up early to catch a flight from Southampton to Charles De Gaul Airport Paris and then shuttle bus to Orly airport. It sounds so simple when you say it quickly, it turned out to be a right nightmare. It all started with a flight delay caused by air traffic control staff having problems - at Southampton, that delay, though it was only an hour, very nearly gave me heart failure. With connections to be made, that hour delay may as well have been a fortnight.

With the time ticking by I sat working the logistics out:- the flight time to Paris plus the travel time to Orly equals catastrophe. If the flight doesn't leave in the next forty-five minutes, I'm in the shit. With this in mind I phoned my wife to let her know that I might, just might, be on my way home and then suddenly the tannoy system sprung to life, with the announcer announcing that the flight was now boarding.

Landing at Charles de Gaul I was very aware that time was now against me so instead of the shuttle bus I had no choice but to get a taxi (bloody expensive).

The taxi driver asked what time my flight was and when I told him, there was a very loud silence, broken only by a shake of the head and a sharp intake of breath, it did not look good. No matter how hard I tried, I could not stop looking at the clock, it seemed to be racing. The driver had done a brilliant job and got me there with about 20 minutes to spare. However, the gate for my flight was closed and I was told in no uncertain terms that was it, it was well and truly "FERME."

Thoroughly dejected, angry and annoyed I made my way back to the taxi rank. However, I was lucky indeed (I think the sight of a grown man crying helped):- when the staff on the Air France desk saw me and told me I might be able to get on my flight if I went and explained what had happened to the main Air France transfer desk one floor below.

I was very conscious of the time but got down to the desk asap. They couldn't help but they knew a man that could and after a phone call or two was made my ticket was stamped and I was allowed through. I met Nic, an old friend who had just about given up on me. He thought I had 'chickened out'.

Long old flight. But well worth it:- the place was beautiful, the hotel was lovely but slightly spoiled by the French love affair with all things ceremonial. Each of the 33 runners had to one by one go up and receive our race numbers and t-shirt. This was followed by a short interview!

Day 2

Up at 05:30, breakfast at 06:00 and then onto a bus for the 2 hour journey to the ferry terminal.

Great 45 minute trip, busy - bustling ferry plenty of rolling around and getting wet, one sea sick casualty. Arriving at the campsite my friend Nic and I claimed our tent and spent the rest of the day just hanging around. Slept on the beach and ate fantastic food. However, I am now actually looking forward to the running tomorrow.

Day 3

Up at 04:45 for a wee and noticed people already swimming in the sea. It looked very nice but not as nice as my sleeping bag!

Up again at 06:00 for breakfast, coffee, bread rolls and jam. At 08:00 everyone was on the start line and ready to go. Within 50 steps we were climbing and boy were we climbing. It was steep and hot. The climb continued for about 4 km before levelling out. Then a sharp descent back down to sea level and through a small village and then another seriously steep climb. This first day's run was only 17 km long but 10 of these kilometres were very serious climbs and a bit of an eye opener.

My eventual finish time was 2 hours 5 minutes and 17th place.

After lunch we had to pack up the tents and walk down to catch the ferry to the next island.

After arriving we went to what could best be described as a large shed/outhouse in someone's back garden - this conveniently doubled up as a restaurant. The meal was a typical local affair:- lots of savoury filled triangular pastries - lovely.

After the meal we were told that we would be driven to the next campsite and we would have to put up the tents. As it was already raining it would be an unpleasant job but on arrival we were greeted by the sight of two rows of erected tents.

My lack of French can sometimes work to my advantage and on this occasion the briefing was full of tales of woe about the horrors that would greet us tomorrow. This was confirmed when a local expert came in to tell us what to be wary of.

Apparently, if the expert, who would be out on the course, considered us unable to cope with the horrendous conditions he would pull us off the mountain 'for our own good'. The list of dos and don'ts were as long as your arm. I shall do what I normally do: give it my best shot!

Day 4

Today's run was bloody tough.

An 08:00 start. The first 3 km were relatively straightforward along a fairly decent trail, then a left turn that took you into the jungle and then, bang, you were climbing. It was so steep you had no choice but to use your hands and they went into mud, up to the wrist. It climbed, I climbed and cursed and lost my sense of humour. Then I came across a broken rotten old bridge, it took me a minute or two to work out how to cross the bleeding thing, then slowly I inched my way across. I slipped, tried to put on the brakes and pulled my quadricep muscle. I managed to get to the other side, moaned like a bloody moaning thing, applied some vigorous massage and hobbled off. Luckily, the damage was not severe (it turns out that part of last night's briefing referred to this bridge and we were told NOT to cross it but to go around!)

My race in the Amazon last year was now beginning to pay dividends. I knew how to move through this kind of terrain and was not too intimidated by it.

At 10:00 the race leader passed me on his way down, it would be another 45 minutes before I reached the summit and started the return journey.

The return journey proved to be worse than the climb up, with gravity conspiring against me and taking full advantage of my already tired legs. I slipped and tripped the whole way down. I eventually caught one runner who was fairing worse than me, he had injured himself and was struggling and suffering in equal measure. I stayed with him for a while and as we neared the track he was happy to be left. As I neared the track a film crew were filming. Vanity took over and I tried to look the part of an Ultra-distance runner in full flow, but ended up looking a right dick! They had obviously chosen their spot for a reason and that reason soon became apparent:- there was a huge and very deep puddle and yes, in I went - right up to my thigh. The look of surprise on my face must have been priceless. I'm 6ft 4 inches tall and any short arses must have made great footage.

Once I was back on to the road I just ran until I reached the campsite at 13:15 in a total time of 5hrs 15 minutes.

Day 5

Today we were told was a day off, however, that was not strictly true it was a day of travelling, travelling to the next island then hanging around. My friend Nic and I sat on a beautiful Caribbean beach eating ice creams. We looked at each other and agreed to never mention this part of Ultra-distance racing to anyone. We would, of course, mention the severe climbs, the oppressive heat, the nerve-jangling descents and the jungle-like terrain, but eating ice creams on white sandy beaches, swimming in turquoise waters on days off? No, some things it was decided, were best left unsaid!

Back at the hotel the official Race photographer asked us if we would be interested in buying some race photographs, a big yes on that one.

Day 6

Up early again, I say up early, but the thing with these races is that you usually finish the day's running mid to late afternoon then hang around for a bit, grab something to eat and then, well then, bed. On this race I have been getting to sleep at about 20:00 so even if the "up early again" is 06:00 you have had about 10 hours sleep.

Anyway, up and on - to board the coach that would take us to the start line, a lot was made of last night's briefing. It became apparent that navigation could be an issue during today's run. I was a little anxious in that my lack of French would prevent me from asking directions!

But the good news was that today's run would be a four-lap run, running around the island, so as long as I could keep a runner in sight on the first lap, I should remember the way. See: ever the optimist!

Such a simple plan on paper but the reality was that the runner I was trying to keep in sight was, I'm sure, trying to shake me off and I had to run my lungs out to keep him in sight. The one saving grace was that because I had run hundreds of kilometres across deserts my speed or technique across sandy beaches was better than his, so he never quite shook me off. But I was still glad when that first lap was done and I could afford to let him go.

Four laps sound okay but the repetition starts to play on your mind - you know what's ahead. I have to say I didn't enjoy the going round in circles.

I managed to finish without getting lost. However, it transpired that because we had a ferry to catch, some of the slower runners were prevented from completing the full four laps.

Day 7

Two more days running to go.

We arrived on the island of Grande Terre for today's 36 km. The run started off okay, but ended up a navigational nightmare. The first half went smoothly and according to plan - a nice steady comfortable pace. I was happy and felt good. I caught up with Nic, the only other British runner, we had a quick chat and I was off. Up ahead I could see another runner but I hadn't seen a route marker: too busy bloody talking. Just to make sure I turned around to see if I was being followed, I was. Nic and a French runner came into view. I was happy I was on the right track so to speak.

Eventually the French runner caught me up and appeared to be a little confused. He got his road book out (a small book explaining the route for the day). Unfortunately, it was written in French and consequently was of no use to me. However, he realised that we had somehow gone wrong, we were on the wrong road but heading in the right direction. We ploughed on but the French runner was getting a little concerned about his lack of water. I hadn't got a lot myself but gave him some glucose tablets and plodded on. It was bloody hot and very demoralising. Eventually, after an hour and a half one of the race vehicles came along the road, pulled up and gave us water and Coke, and, more importantly, told us we were now on the right road.

We carried on at a relatively slow pace because Lulu, as I found out his name was, was struggling. We looked back and another French runner was fast approaching. When he caught us up and I was happy Lulu was okay, I increased my speed before finally reaching the finish line.

It turned out to be one of my better days position wise, only because so many runners went off course.

The fact that we missed two water stations was potentially quite serious. My past experience has taught me to never drink all my water. To assume you will be at a water station soon is plain foolish. I only ever finish my water when I can see the next water station (I made that mistake once, and only once) - missing two water stations confirmed that.

Once all the runners were in it was back on the coach and on to the next Island Le Desirade.

Day 8

Le Desirade is a small, long beautiful island as are all the islands we have been on.

As usual the slower runners set off first followed by the mediocre runners (me) - then the racing snakes.

The first part of today's run took us through a small town, then on to a path that took us to the end of the island and the island's lighthouse. Here we turned around, headed back to town, then took a sharp right turn on to what I guessed was a service road. This road was steep and full of switchbacks. When eventually you reached the top you were met by a sea of wind turbines. It was here that I caught a couple of the slower runners including Nic. We had a quick chat and I was off.

Got to the end of the plateau, and then started the descent which was a damn site more painful than the ascent:- the toes were moaning, the knees were hurting.

The path eventually took us back down into town through the streets and finally to the finish line, which was on the beach.

This race has been fantastic and novel, island-hopping in the Caribbean for each day's run, challenging terrain and fantastic people. It was a fast-paced race and I'm not a fast runner. I'm a plodder, more suited to long slow plods.

I would recommend it - its stunning scenery alone makes it a race worth doing.

I was a little apprehensive - the competition looked pretty awesome

Giving it my best shot - it didn't last long

The first day - trying to look good for the photographer

THE YUKON ARCTIC ULTRA 2006

What is it: A multi-discipline (you chose one discipline) single stage cold weather race

When: February

Where: The Yukon region of Canada

Distance: Either 160, 480, or 690 (100, 300, or 430 miles)

It is: An extreme cold weather/mental challenge

See: arcticultra.de

This race is advertised as being 'The World's Coldest and Toughest Ultra' and as usual as long as it's the world's something est, ie: toughest, highest, coldest, hottest, wettest, it meets the criteria. I am officially interested and so it was that I again managed to talk myself into entering a race I knew nothing about.

The race, held annually in the Yukon area of Canada was undoubtedly tough. I bought the video of the previous year's race and once again studied the race gleaning as much information as I could.

It looked spectacular and challenging. I couldn't wait - I signed up and started training. I had entered the 100 mile race. There were 2 other distances, the marathon 26 miles or the monster 320 miler. I would love to have had the balls to have entered the 320 miler but being a bit of a chicken I'm afraid to say I bottled it!

Once again, time just seemed to fly past;- one minute I had months to train then weeks and before you know it just a few days. After a long 10 hour flight to Vancouver and a 4 hour wait for a connecting flight to the Yukon capital, Whitehorse, I had been awake for a little over 25 hours and I was amazed that even though I was one bag missing (I only had 2) and the missing bag happened to be my sledge with the bulk of my Arctic clothing in, I was pretty calm - helped in no small matter was that most people here seemed to have a bag or two missing.

It transpires that the small aircraft used as the link between Vancouver and Whitehorse just has not got the space for a large amount of luggage and the Yukon Arctic Ultra with all its visiting athletes and accompanying luggage highlights this every year. The good news is that the race organiser was here to calm frayed nerves and explain that "the left behind luggage always arrives in time, and not once has some piece of kit or other failed to turn up in time".

Luckily for me my kit eventually turned up at 15:15 the next day. I say luckily because the race training programme started at 15:00. I had managed to waffle and bluff my way out of having to do the training course, a course that would undoubtedly expose my very limited or should I say non-existent cold weather skills, by telling the race organiser that I had raced in the Himalayas, which was true, and that I had done a bit of climbing including Kilimanjaro (the others being, when I climbed the 3 highest summits in the UK during the Three Peaks Challenge).

I was really worried about being found out that this was my first time in these conditions and my cold weather experience was woeful to say the least!

Day 2

Spent the day looking around Whitehorse and faffing about with kit, buying last minute bits of things I really didn't need.

Had a good sleep, great breakfast, then attended the training course debrief. A lot was made of the fact that there would be a lot of overflow on the trail this year, certainly for the first few miles.

Overflow is when water appears on the surface of the ice you could be walking along and suddenly an inch, a foot, a meter of water will suddenly appear. In other words, be prepared to get wet feet or take evasive action. When asked what evasive action we could take, the first and most obvious one was to put on your Neos! Of course (what the hell were Neos? It transpires that Neos are a large waterproof overboot, that literally go over the footwear that you are already wearing).

Decision made, back into town to buy a pair Neos, the talk continued and the paper work was completed. A good night's sleep and a good meal and then Race day.

Race Day

Up early, shower and a hearty breakfast - the breakfast of a condemned man:- porridge, orange juice and a gallon of coffee. Back to the room, get dressed, final pack, ablutions complete and a gentle walk to the start.

62 competitors for the 3 distances, the marathon, 100 mile (me) and the monster 320 mile.

It was a great atmosphere with plenty of the locals there to cheer us on. I was trying to soak it up and appreciate the support. Film crews were filming and various athletes were being interviewed. It was a fantastic almost carnival like atmosphere.

And then the countdown, 3 2 1 and we were off - racers on bikes, skis and on foot and even one bloke skijoring (a skier being pulled by huskies). We dropped down onto the river and were in single file for the first few miles, then at approximately 13 miles we turned left on to the Takhini river and under a road bridge where people were standing and watching!

I noticed that quite a few people were stopping early on to adjust this or that, remove or add clothing or just have a bit of a breather. It didn't bode well that they were disorganised or knackered before the race had really started. Preparation and organisation was, I had decided, the key to this race.

The whole area was stunningly beautiful, I felt good and comfortable, overtaking more people than were overtaking me.

Hours into the race I came across the halfway marker, this was a bit of a downer because I thought I was nearly there!

Walking along a frozen river was a strange experience and would have been rather unnerving had I not been able to see other racers and see tracks left by snowmobiles. It didn't sound right, didn't feel right and didn't look right:- walking on a frozen river was just not natural. Most of the time you walked on snow-covered ice but occasionally the snow had been blown off and you were left with just bare ice clear enough to look through. Other times the gentle rhythmic tap of your poles would be interrupted be a dull thud, then the occasional crack. It took a while to realise that you were safe enough and you could uncross your fingers and unclench your buttocks.

Eventually we took a right hand turn that led off the river and up on to the bank and then inland to the first CP at North Sir Ranch.

In the meantime I had the little problem of trying to get up the bank:- it was extremely steep and traction was limited. I somehow grunted, pulled, and swore my way up on to terra firma. The hard work could now begin, unlike the smooth gliding ice down on the river, this was uneven soft snow with tussocks of grass peeping through. The sledge was not running as smoothly as before and required much more effort to pull, the difficulty of the terrain was unrelenting and no rhythm could be found: in a word or three, it was bloody hard work!

It was at this point, desperately looking for any signs saying North Sir Ranch that I remembered that a ranch out here could be the size of a small county.

Plodding along I eventually found a signpost saying North Sir Ranch and 20 minutes later I arrived. I checked in, had a cup of soup and a cup of tea. I was offered a beef roll but couldn't stomach it - usual thing for me - loss of appetite.

Before we could settle down we had to show the crew that we could light our stove and show them our sleeping system. This CP was a compulsory 4 hour stop and I wanted to spend as much of that 4 hours sleeping as I could so when the formalities were out of the way it was bed. Three and a half hours after arriving I was up. I had managed to find a sleeping space next to the guy who arrived just minutes before me so I knew he would be leaving just minutes before me and hopefully make enough noise to wake me! Fortunately my plan worked.

As I went to check out I was told that I still had 30 minutes to wait. I told them that I had checked in at 17:00 hours and it was now 21:00 (even with limited mathematical ability I could work out that was 4 hours) she rechecked, apologised and said I was free to go.

This next section to CP 2 the ominously named "Dog Grave Lake" was 38 miles long.

The one thing I have learned with these long races is not to race, the secret for me is to keep moving forward as comfortably as I can - the key word is keep! Consistency of pace, and my one saving grace I have is that I am a really good plodder, I can plod for ever, if plodding were an Olympic sport I would be a medallist.

I've noticed people passing me 3 or 4 times:- they race ahead, have a rest or a sleep, maybe have something to eat, then I plod pass them, then they get going and pass me and the whole thing starts again.

This section was huge and challenging, hilly and long:- very tiring. Eventually I came across the halfway marker and like before I thought I was way past halfway. But there you are: no ability to judge distance. Continuing on I spotted the 5km to go marker, however, that 5km was more like 5 miles: it never seemed to end. The final kick in the teeth was the fact that the CP was on the top of a very nasty short steep climb.

Entering the tent, I saw 4 other runners and, annoyingly, only 3 seats. I managed to find a little space to sit on one of the storage boxes and it was bliss just to be sitting. I was asked if I wanted something to eat. I wasn't really hungry but inquired as to what there was and whatever it was was still frozen. I asked if there was a hot drink available and was told that, yep, as soon as the water boiled I could have one - they were getting the water now. I filled up my water bottles using an old ladle, it was a tricky operation trying to fill a 'camelbak' up using a ladle. I had to take my gloves off and be quick! I had a hot drink and then decided to be on my way, so 50 minutes after arriving I left.

It was now ten to one in the afternoon, I had 36 miles to go. Three miles an hour would get me to the finish at about 01:00.

Plodding along this part of the route was the most enjoyable so far:- the terrain wasn't too challenging and the whole area was beautiful. Some places were rock hard, compact snow making forward motion relatively easy, other places the snow was soft and uneven, making it a little less enjoyable. A little after 7 hours I came across the *&^%$ing half way marker! Yet again I overestimated my speed and underestimated the distance I had covered. Ah well, that blows my 01:00 finish theory out of the window.

I now started to wonder if I had enough water - always difficult to judge when using a camelbak:- to check the thing I would have to stop, unhitch the sledge, get undressed, well remove my top layer, check and repeat the process in reverse and to be honest I couldn't be arsed. If I ran out I would just have to stop, get the stove out and melt snow. Anyway, the water situation was the least of my worries. I had started to develop a very unpleasant, sore and smelly sweat rash and without going into too much detail, I now wish I had some wet wipes or Sudocreme (nappy rash cream).

As time wore on I wore out. I was now bloody knackered and was having to stop little and often, a 30 second stop every 30/40 steps. Then to add to my woes I came across a huge section of overflow - the biggest yet. I tried in every direction to get around but there was, I discovered, no way round. I had no choice but to go through! Neos on, I unhitched the sledge deciding to pull it by hand - the reason being that my sledge could float, and I had no idea how deep the water was. I also didn't know how strong the ice was beneath the water, so if I went through I could at least let go of the sledge instead of going through the ice still attached to the thing. I carried both poles in one hand and the sledge in the other, gently using the poles to test the ice ahead and then approximately halfway across, the sheet of ice I was standing on dropped. The water rose - I clenched my teeth, I clenched the poles, the sledge and my very sore raw buttocks all in perfect unison. I had a split second to decide what to do and before that split second was up I was across and on the other side.

I put my sledge harness back on and moved off. I'm not at all religious but I have to confess I said a little "thank you". Moving along the trail I noticed that I was entering a wooded area. The trail was enclosed and claustrophobic, very sheltered and very eerie. My ears found the absolute silence a challenge:- straining to hear any sound and failing, the only noise was the tap tap tap of my walking poles and the sliding of my sledge.

I had long since given up trying to estimate my finish time but when I saw the 5km to go marker I looked at my watch: a little after 03:30. I now knew for the first time that I would finish some time today and that I was on the right track. See, I'm an optimist:- a glass half full kind of guy!

A little further on, perhaps 2km, the trail ahead was taped off and numerous spray-painted arrows pointed to the right and to the right was one mighty steep drop that went straight down on to a lake.

The severity of the drop required the utmost caution using my poles and the power of prayer. I went for it. It was a titanic struggle between my poles and my sledge, my poles acting as brakes to slow me down and my sledge pushing me on to speed me up. Somehow, a compromise was reached and I managed to stop just before going arse over apex.

Now, standing on what would normally be the shoreline and with memories of the earlier overflow still fresh in my mind, I tested the ice and continued to do so until I was across the lake.

It was with some relief that I stepped off the lake, however, that relief was short-lived. I figured I probably had 2km to go but the last little bit was created by a sadist with a sense of humour. There were roots, stumps and hills, branches, twists and turns - it was to all intense and purposes an obstacle course. At no time during that last couple of km was my sledge in full contact with the ground, either the front was in the air or the back was. It was up and down, or what race organisers euphemistically call 'undulating'.

Eventually the trees cleared and I came out into the open and then onto what appeared to be track. Up ahead I saw orange lights and realised that it could only be Braeburn and consequently the finish, but this race has a nasty way of kicking you in the nuts, so I didn't get my hopes up!

And then suddenly I saw a huge banner proclaiming 'Yukon Arctic Ultra 100 mile finish'. I saw the banner but didn't see anyone but I did see movement in a caravan - I knocked on the door and Stuart, a fellow British athlete opened it and pointed me in the right direction. I entered the building housing the official finish line at 05:50. It had taken me 17 hours to cover 36 miles.

I was in 4th position. The first British athlete and I was told that 9 people had dropped out. I was happy and relieved. It was the toughest race I had ever taken part in and I knew then and there that I would not be back:- it was just too damn tough. I had been lucky to have reached the finish and when Stuart left to continue his 300 miles race I had nothing but respect and admiration. 300 miles was just too *&^%$ much.

The Yukon Arctic Ultra is a fantastic race, extremely well organised, friendly, helpful and happy staff and as a bonus one of the most beautiful places I have ever raced in.

What Next!

The author now realises what the hell he has let himself in for

The accommodation was not the best I've stayed at.

West Wight
SPORTS CENTRE

TRIATHLON 2006

What is it:	Swim, Bike, Run
When:	September
Where:	On the Isle of Wight (West Wight)
Distance:	600 meter swim (24 lengths)
	35km bike (22 miles) 7.5 run (4.6 miles)
It is:	A beautiful triathlon, with a tough bike section
See:	westwight.co.uk

In 2005 I took part in a race called 7x7x7:- seven marathons, in seven days, in seven different ways - a challenging multi discipline race. I loved it.

Though I had taken part in numerous Ultra-distance races over the years, I had never taken part in a triathlon. The multi-discipline aspect of the 7x7x7 interested me enough to think of giving a triathlon a bash. The seven different sports that made up the 7x7x7 were mountain biking, road running, off-road running, kayaking, rowing machine, time trial cycling and the last day was a mixture of running, kayaking and cycling.

All those sports were ones I could 'bluff' my way through, the triathlon would be a little different!

No swimming:- I could run, I could just about cycle, but

swimming, yes I could get from one end of the pool to the other but to say I could swim from one end to the other might be stretching it a bit.

My arms did whatever was needed to move me forward, my legs did the same. A lot of faffing and flapping about using a lot of unnecessary effort - when I finally did reach the other end I would hold on for dear life whilst trying to get my breath back and when I did get my breath back it would be time for the return journey. It wasn't pleasant or pretty. I can't even say it was effective.

Even as I write this, I have no idea why I wanted to give triathlon a go - was it because I had been asked so often if I had done a triathlon? Or was it because in 2001 I had watched with utter fascination, the UK half Ironman, in Llanberis, Wales and I thought even then, that those guys were crazy, who the hell can swim 1.2 miles, let alone do the other stuff, cycling and running, immediately afterwards?

Whatever the reason, I was determined to do one, and luckily for me the West Wight Triathlon is right on my door step - a 600 metre pool swim, a 35 km bike ride and a 7.5 km run.

Held every September at the local sports centre, it was a popular triathlon but having never seen one other than on the television, I couldn't work out how the pool swimming was done.

It was, I decided, time for a bit of homework. I went and watched the next event and was pleasantly surprised - not just at the organisation and the turnout, but the fact that the swimmers were not all the super swimmers that I had seen on the television. Some were doing breaststroke and some were actually struggling and needing to hold on to the end of the pool to get their breath back!

My confidence soared, not in my ability to do well, but in my not looking so silly when I was splashing about in the pool. I would sign up for the next one, a year from now I would be in the pool, on the bike and out for a run.

As usual, I hadn't got a clue how to train. The one advantage I did posses was that I could run, not very fast but I could run. I cycle regularly to work, a round trip of about 20 miles. The cycling section was about 21.75 miles but swimming: that was a different kettle of fish. As mentioned earlier I can just about haul my carcass from one end of the pool to the other - with the triathlon 12 months away and my need to keep things simple, being the genius mathematician that I am, I quickly worked out that if I could increase my swimming by 2 lengths a month for the next 12 months, that would give me the required 24 lengths. Easy!

I had a few running races already booked for 2007, one being a 300 miler in Canada, so I didn't worry too much about training for the run. I upped my cycling and decided to go for a run immediately after getting off my bike. I have since found out that this bit of training is known as a 'brick'. Likewise with the swimming, I cycled to the pool, thereby necessitating my need to cycle home straight after a swim.

As the months crept by, I hoped my swim would improve: it didn't. Though the distance I could haul my carcass through the water did increase, it wasn't anything that could remotely be called improved technique. It was with a degree of fitness and with a bucketload of stubbornness that saw me complete each and every length.

Though I was attending the pool on a regular basis (notice I say attending, not swimming) I didn't really enjoy a single session. As far as I was concerned, it was on a par with going to a job interview or the dentist:- something that had to be done- a means to an end. In time I hoped the enjoyment would come, but it never did, the dread slightly decreased but that was all.

As the months and weeks ticked by, I read as much as I could about the sport of triathlon. Though the name triathlon suggests that there are three components to the sport, I realised that there are actually four, including transition. A lot of time can be wasted or gained from an efficient transition, so I decided to incorporate transitions into my training.

As usual Race day approached all too quickly - training had gone as well as I could have hoped. I had cycled the route three or four times, swam the distance three or four times, practised transition. Running the distance was not a problem, but running fast, that might be a problem.

Race day arrived and living only 4 miles from the start I decided to cycle, using it as a gentle warm up. Getting to the starting area and trying to look as if I knew what I was doing. I registered and was issued with my race number and had the number written on my arm and leg. Now I felt like a real triathlete.

Setting up my transition area would however show the world I was a fraud. I hadn't got a clue. I covertly watched the others and laid out my kit accordingly.

I nibbled on a banana, admired my handiwork, looked at my watch and realised it was time. Time to get changed and wander over like the condemned man I now was, to the gallows - sorry, I meant swimming pool. After finding out which lane I was in, and filled with absolute terror, I grabbed a seat, and for some reason held on tightly! I have in the past done some pretty daft things:- running across the Sahara desert, the Himalayan mountain range and through the Amazon jungle to name but three, but nothing (and I really do mean nothing) had me shaking and quaking as much as the impending 24 lengths at my local swimming pool that I was about to attempt!

I was in lane 3 and, in no time at all, three of us were called over. There were three swimmers to a lane. The first one got in - when he reached the far end, I got in (no diving was allowed) and finally swimmer number three got in, losing his goggles and making a splash in the process. I had to make a conscious effort to swim slowly, not that I was worried about catching anyone but I knew that if I did my usual splash and dash I'd be knackered and end up clinging on to one end of the pool or the other. It was hard work and I seemed to be in the pool for hours. I had no idea how many lengths I had done, the task of counting lengths and swimming was just too much. I could do one or the other. Then, thank the Lord, one of the Race marshals held out a '2 lengths to go' sign. I smiled and carried on. A few moments later I was trying to haul my carcass out of the water.

I got out of the pool and for some reason felt very self-conscious. Goggles off, swim cap off, stomach in and chest out.

Into the transition area and time to put into practice what, until now, had only been a mental exercise.

Stand on towel, a quick drink, then top on, socks on, shoes on, helmet and glasses on and go. A couple of minutes after arriving in transition I was pedalling away.

I had cycled the route three or four times and was well aware how hilly it was. Though only 35km long, there were a couple of steep climbs that needed to be respected - failure to do so could result in my failure to finish.

Having never done a triathlon before I decided to err on the side of caution and not push too hard, saving my legs for the run, the only discipline that I was confident with.

I managed to catch a couple of cyclists but started to regret not getting out of wet shorts! Whilst on the bike I managed to eat a Mars Bar and so was fuelled up in preparation for the run.

As I approached the transition area I again ran through a checklist of how to do a swift exit.

This transition was a lot easier: rack the bike, helmet glasses off and run - it literally took seconds. Once I got rid of my wobbly, jelly legs (legs that felt as if they had once belonged to Bambi), I pushed hard. The run route was nice and flat and again, having run the same route countless times, I could afford to go all out.

I eventually finished in a time of 02:03:02 the splits for each event were as follows Swim 14:13 Bike 1:11:06 Run 33:37.

I was as happy finishing a triathlon as I was any Ultra-distance race I had done.

What Next!

THE YUKON ARCTIC ULTRA 2007

What is it: A multi-discipline, single-stage cold weather race

When: February

Where: The Yukon region of Canada

Distance: Either 160, 480 or 690 kms (100, 300, or 430 miles)

It is: An extreme cold weather race

See: arcticultra.de

Once again here I am standing on the start line of the Yukon Arctic Ultra.

I say again because this time last year I was here in this exact same spot, waiting to race the 100 miles to Braeburn.

I thought then that I was mad, but no, like the addict I had now become, I was here waiting for my fix, as if last years 100 miles were not enough. I needed more and so it was that I signed up for the 320 miler!

24 hours ago the world famous Yukon Quest Dog sled race used this exact same starting line. The atmosphere then was electric. Yellow pee-stained snow, patches of straw and dog poo were scattered all around, spectators pushing and shoving for a better view, cameras clicking away, the overhead tannoy system blaring out information regarding the race, the teams and the handlers.

As each of the teams lined up, the countdown began, hardly audible against the muffled claps of gloved hands and enthusiastic cheers, the dogs sensing the time was rapidly approaching, time to race. As the countdown got nearer the dogs got louder, a mixture of barking and screaming. They each pulled and strained in a desperate attempt to get going, straining so hard that the sledges, anchors (a small spiked piece of metal that is stamped into the snow to either slow the team or hold the team) were not enough to hold them in place. Mushers and race crew had to hold onto the teams, the effort required was enormous. These dogs train by pulling 4x4 vehicles around and now that adrenalin raced through their bodies, the power that they produced was frightening. They pulled and barked, the cold, frigid air catching the breath of spectators, mushers and dogs alike. Plumes of what appeared to be smoke hung lazily for a few seconds before slowly evaporating.

As the countdown got to the 3 2 1, the anchor was pulled from the snow, the mushers gave instructions to the race crew to release the dogs and then, as if fired from a cannon, the whole team shot off at warp factor whatever, with the poor old musher hanging on for dear life whilst - I'm sure - praying and hoping that the dogs were going in the right direction, because if they weren't, there was precious little he could do about it.

Our start line antics were - not surprisingly - a little more subdued.

For me I was attempting to complete the 320 miles to Pelly Crossing. I was anxious: during last year's 100 miler I made mistakes and had suffered as a consequence. This year would be different:- I had trained harder, not got so much kit and learned valuable lessons about food, kit and pace.

It didn't help that because I was seen as experienced (only because I had been here the year before and not because of any impressive racing CV), people were asking me questions.

It might have stroked my ego a little but I was still very much a learner, keen to pick up any tips myself.

Standing at the start line with a few minutes to spare, trying to remember details of the route ahead, making a mental checklist of things that I should have with me and things that I should have done, put bodyglide on my feet, Sudocrem where Sudocrem needs to go etc.

And then it was our countdown. The spectators were not as numerous as they had been for the Yukon Quest but they were every bit as enthusiastic - clapping and cheering and, just like the dogs had done yesterday, we all set off much too quickly. Cameras seem to do that to racers and, as usual, as soon as the cameras were out of sight we all settled down into a far more sensible and somewhat sedate pace.

The pace was really dictated to us by the fact that we were on such a narrow little path that ran alongside the mighty Yukon river. The path was well defined and there was really only enough room for one person at a time and no possibility for overtaking: if you strayed off the path you risked going knee deep into soft snow.

After about a kilometre we dropped down onto the river itself.

I was about halfway down the field at this point, moving along quite nicely, when I noticed my sled started to have a mind of its own, trying to move to one side. I did what I usually do at a time like this and carried on, pretending it wasn't happening. Then bugger me if one of the poles decided to detach itself! I turned to see what had happened and realised that the left hand pole and sledge had parted company. I pulled over into the soft snow to investigate further. A few racers passed by. I unharnessed myself and took a quick look. The connecting piece of hose that joins the sledge to the pole by two jubilee clips had come apart because the clips had not been tightened.

It was a stupid mistake and my own fault for not checking.

I couldn't believe it - last year this same sledge had got me through 100 miles without a single problem and now, 2 miles into a 300 mile race I was having to make repairs.

I set to work and retrieved my repair kit from the sledge, tightening the offending jubilee clips with my leatherman multi tool, a simple job unfortunately made difficult by the fact that at -22 I was wearing gloves. The dexterity now required left me with little choice but to take them off - I did and I worked quickly, tightening all the clips (just in case).

To prevent the clips working loose I decided to put duct tape over them to hold them in place. It was whilst cutting the tape that I sliced the top of my finger. Now I had a broken sledge and a cut finger, racers were still passing and asking if every thing was okay. Of course I lied and said "yes, no problem" while at the same time trying to hide my now bleeding digit.

It was a deep cut - deep enough to warrant me getting out the first aid kit. I fished around in my sledge, getting blood over my sleeping bag and jacket.

After about twenty minutes I had repaired my sledge and patched up my finger and I was now in last place.

I put a bit of a spurt on. I did this for two reasons:- 1, to catch up and 2, to warm up. It worked on both counts and after about forty minutes I had joined the back of the queue.

After a while we turned left onto a part of the river I remembered from last year - this turning was roughly halfway to the first checkpoint and took us onto the Tahini river and under a road bridge.

The repair to the sledge was holding up but the repair to the finger was not:- it wouldn't stop bleeding so I wrapped it up in my buff.

Walking along the river it was getting noticeably colder, so rather than stop and put on another layer, I decided to speed up. Eventually the route markers pointed to the right and a small track that would take us off the river and onto the first checkpoint - Tahini Hotsprings.

However, first was the rather tricky task of getting off the river. The bank was steep and required an enormous amount of effort. It was while clambering up the bank that I noticed, just ahead, another British runner, Mark. He seemed to be struggling. I caught him up and he looked knackered.

Back at the Hotel in Whitehorse Mark had explained to me that this was his first Ultra-distance race, he had run numerous marathons but never an Ultra.

Now here he was in the Yukon racing the 320 miles to Pelly Crossing. I really hoped for his sake he had not got his ambition mixed up with his capability - this was, as I found out last year, a tough race.

Fortunately back at Whitehorse he was asking all the right questions, unfortunately he was ignoring all the answers. He looked totally disorganised, even to the point of having no compression straps. These straps, not only compress your sled load but, more importantly, they hold the bag in place. Now, every time he negotiated an incline his bag slipped off the back of his sledge, annoying for him but bloody funny for the rest of us.

We chatted and plodded along together before finally reaching the first checkpoint and the compulsory 4 hour stop.

My first job was to go and see Diane, the Race medic, to get my finger sorted - she took a quick look cleaned it and glued it together.

After a quick bite to eat I found a little spot and got into my sleeping bag - the spot I had chosen was fairly close to another runner who was already sleeping. The thinking was that when they started packing up I would hear them. I set my alarm and promptly fell asleep. 6 hours later I woke up. Bollocks - I never heard my alarm or the other runner.

I quickly packed up, all the time cursing my stupidity but looking on the bright side that I had had two hours more sleep more than anyone else. I went off to inform the organisers that I was now leaving and they thought I had already left!

I lied, as I explained that I had decided to have a good long sleep as there was still a very long way to go.

I left the checkpoint at the same time as Sean and we walked along together. Sean had tried this distance twice before and had failed on both occasions - he was now hoping that it was third time lucky. I admired his tenacious spirit and I did wonder if I would try again should I fail to finish, I honestly didn't know.

We walked along together for a while and after a couple of hours came across a runner sleeping in his bivi bag and then another and another. There must have been 15 to 20 runners all sleeping within a short 2 mile distance. I couldn't work out why they were sleeping here:- the first checkpoint was a compulsory 4 hour stop, so why leave that checkpoint only to stop, unpack and sleep just a couple of hours later?

We moved quietly through the sleepers and then Sean said he was going to stop for a while, I told him I would carry on for a bit.

Walking alone through the night in the Yukon is an amazing experience. Beautiful and tranquil, not a sound except for your walking poles hitting the crunchy snow followed by the gentle reassuring sound of the sledge gliding across the crisp surface. On a clear night, glistening trees cast elongated shadows, tiredness and shadows conspire to trick the mind into seeing elaborate shapes and figures, non-existent images entertain you and keep you guessing!

As a new day starts to break and the sun makes a welcome appearance your depleted energy levels get a much needed boost.

Plodding along, I try to remember the route and I recognise

nothing. Nothing is familiar, I can't work out how much further it is to the next checkpoint and then suddenly there it is: the first thing I recognise - a steep, no, a bloody steep hill, not big but bloody steep. However, I know the checkpoint is right on the top and that makes the nasty little climb just a bit more bearable. It's taken me 12 hours to get here.

As I entered the tent I was met by a familiar face:- Jessica, a volunteer who was here at this same checkpoint last year. She came up to me and said "I've got a surprise for you" and promptly handed me a jug.

The story behind the jug was that last year we had all been asked by the Race organiser what could be done to improve the race, a race I considered to be bloody well organised. The only thing I could think of that had annoyed me was the fact that we had to use a ladle to fill our respective camelbaks, bottles etc. As this was done outside and required you to remove your gloves, I had suggested using a jug - a simple solution - you could keep your gloves on and fill your chosen receptacle at twice the speed. And now the jug had made its first appearance.

I stayed for a couple of hours, eating the supplied dehydrated meal of reconstituted sawdust, drinking hot chocolate, and checking my feet - which for now looked to be in pretty good shape.

I was, however, keen to get going. I wanted to get to Braeburn, where I had planned to have a good sleep.

Leaving the tent, I harnessed up and moved off slowly. I remembered this part of the route from last year and was busy trying to work out how long it would take me to reach Braeburn, when I suddenly came across a racer sitting at the side of the trail. Andy was one of the 'big boys', going all the way to Dawson, 430 miles. He had got his stove out and was melting snow to make water, a bit confusing because the checkpoint we had just left was only about 3 hours back.

However, he explained that he had had a lot of problems with his sledge and had been so busy fixing it that he had forgotten to fill up with water. Not only that, he had somehow managed to mix up his Sudocrem and suntan lotion bottles, applying Sudocrem to his face and suntan lotion to a place where the sun ain't going to shine.

As one of the UK's most experienced cold weather racers and with a quite impressive racing CV I had no concerns about leaving him.

I was tired and keen to get to next checkpoint for some much needed sleep, however, my plans were thwarted when my sledge disintegrated - this time both poles had come loose. I wasn't angry or pissed off, there was no point. The only thing I could do was fix them and so once again it was out with leatherman and duct tape and as the temperature was hovering around -30 I worked quickly and carefully.

After a few minutes I was good to go. I moved off and, again, looking around I didn't recognise anything, which was not in the least bit surprising because last year I had done most of this section in the dark.

The one thing I did remember was that the 5km to go marker was in an avenue of trees and as I was now in an avenue of trees and had been for some time, I switched on and scoured the trail, desperately looking for the 5 km marker.

I realised I must have missed it because suddenly there was lots of marker tape and spray painted arrows pointing to the right - the Lake!

I was now only about 3km away from some hot food and a bed. I dropped down on to the lake and moved quickly knowing full well that once off the lake I would be negotiating a challenging last couple of km, more of an obstacle course.

It was as I remembered: horrible, back-breaking, frustrating, gnarly terrain but once done it was out of the trees and then the wonderful sight of the bright orange lights that surrounded the Braeburn Lodge.

As I made my way over to the entrance some people came out and were just about to get into a vehicle. They were some of the 100 mile racers who had finished and were now being taken back to Whitehorse.

Last year I reached this place at 05:50 and now I had got here some 5 hours quicker and I felt a whole lot better.

I entered the warm building, checked in and made way to one of the tables for something to eat. I made my choice and a few minutes later was getting stuck into a huge bowl of moose stew and hot chocolate, perfect.

Once I'd eaten, one of the race crew took me to my room. It all sounds very grand but the reality was that it was a portacabin with a couple of old beds in. I didn't care - it was warm and it had a bed. I quickly sorted some kit out, hung some stuff up to dry and got into my sleeping bag. Then, bugger me if someone didn't come in and get into the other bed.

Richard was part of the race crew and his dad was attempting the 320 miler. After 4 hours I woke up and started to get myself sorted and packed things into the sled bag. I then had a quick wash using wet wipes (when using wet wipes in Arctic conditions always have a few in your pocket, they tend to freeze otherwise, and let me tell you there is nothing worse or more shocking than the application of a frozen wet wipe!!!). I was just in the rather delicate process of re-applying the Sudocrem when Richard woke up. All he saw was a grown man with underpants around his knees applying a cream to his nether regions - not a pretty sight at the best of times and even worse when you have literally just woken up next to a complete stranger.

He politely pretended not to notice and rather diplomatically said he was going to get a coffee and did I want anything? I said I'd have a hot chocolate. He disappeared and returned a few minutes later with a large cup of hot chocolate, I finished packing and finished the chocolate, made my way over to the

Race HQ and told them I was now leaving.

This time last year I reached Braeburn knackered, I was beyond tired. I remember sitting down and watching as Stuart left to continue on his journey to Pelly Crossing. I was full of admiration and respect. It was beyond me how anybody could do that distance, it had taken every bit of willpower and experience I possessed just to get to the 100 mile mark. I couldn't have done any more.

Now that I was the one leaving, my thought process was totally different. This time Braeburn was not the finish, it was one-third of the distance done. I didn't look forward to arriving as I had last year, I looked forward to leaving.

The next checkpoint was Ken Lake some 48 miles away.

On leaving Braeburn I was given instructions to cross the road and follow the markers. After about half an hour I started to climb a beast of a hill and again it was one of those that once started there was no stopping until you reached the top.

On the top I took a moment to admire the scenery: it was beautiful, a tricky drop down onto the first of the lakes. I was now getting a bit warm so stopped for a quick break and took off my jacket.

This lake was the first of a series, one led onto another and so it continued, off the lake into the woods. The only way to get into the woods was usually by way of a lung-bursting energy-sapping climb.

This continued for most of the day until finally I arrived at a huge lake, surrounded on all sides by rolling hills. I was just taking in the enormity of the thing, when I heard the sound of a snow machine - a few minutes later it pulled up. Diane and Thomas were on their way to get the Ken Lake checkpoint sorted out and ready.

Once they left I had the place to myself. Nothing moved, no wind, no clouds, no wildlife, nothing. Everything was static and everything was quiet, not a sound.

I could see for miles ahead - I got my head down and moved quickly. An hour or so later I would look up and still nothing: it was like a dream when you are running away from some hidden danger running as fast as you can but not actually going anywhere.

I carried on and then, to my right hand side, just off the lake and high up on the bank, I could see a small cabin. At last I had something to focus on.

It took me nearly 4 hours to draw level with that little cabin and once I had passed it, it was back to the never-ending vista.

It was now late afternoon and would soon be getting dark so I got myself ready:- warm jacket, head torch on, a bite to eat and off.

At around midnight I spotted what appeared to be an orange light some way ahead and slightly to my left. I kept an eye on it, hoping that 1 - it was real and 2 - it was the checkpoint. As I got close to it I spotted bits of tape that led me up onto the bank and then once on the top, a cabin, a badly-damaged cabin. The door looked as if it had been put together by a four year-old in the dark. I opened the door and there was Diane and Thomas and another racer called Frank. Diane and Thomas looked to be in worse shape than me and Frank. They welcomed me in and offered me a hot drink, I was grateful and needed a sit down. It had taken me 19 hours to reach this checkpoint - it was now 01:40.

As I had something to eat, the whole story had come out that the snowmobile had crashed leaving them both shaken. When they had arrived at the cabin it had been semi-demolished by a hungry bear looking for food, hence the damage and then to round things off Thomas had received a nasty gash on his arm after slipping while drilling for water. (A large hand-held corkscrew device is used to drill through the ice to get fresh water).

Frank had been here a for about an hour and was unsure what to do: stay here or move on. We had a quick chat. I was keen to keep moving, as this was one of the checkpoints that you were not allowed to stay in. If you wanted to sleep you slept outside! Thomas said the temperature was dropping and would probably hit -35, we decided to leave together. After 2 hours we said our thanks and left the warm if not slightly damaged cabin.

Dropping back down onto the lake we soon got into a comfortable steady rhythm. Frank was in the lead and I needed a wee. As I was weeing away and making patterns in the snow, I noticed that Frank who was maybe 500 meters ahead, stop. Thinking he was waiting for me in case I had a problem, I hurried up, however as I caught him up I noticed that he was getting his bivi out explaining that he needed to get some sleep.

I was a little reluctant, by reluctant, I mean chicken. Sleeping out on a lake at -35 would not be pleasant, so I explained that I would carry on and probably kip later. I really just wanted to get off the lakes.

After about 3 hours I followed the trail off the lakes and into the woods. It was now daylight.

It wasn't long before I wished I was back on the lakes. They say be careful what you wish for:- I wanted off the lakes, but the alternative was now bloody hard work and lots of small steep climbs, trail markers were few and far between and I was beginning to doubt my navigation.

It was now mid-afternoon and as I looked up I saw in front of me a monster hill, long and very steep. It was one of those that you actually stop and stare at. I stood at the bottom working out how exactly to tackle the thing.

Fortunately, I wasn't blessed with multiple choices. I had one, climb it slowly and without stopping. I managed it, just, and as I stood on the top looking down at the thing, I heard the unmistakable sound of a snowmobile. Just as I left the summit, the snowmobile appeared. It was Mike, he got off and explained that Carmacks was about 3 miles ahead and would I like some coffee? The thought of a hot cup of coffee was tempting, but for some reason I declined. Mike said he was going on ahead a little to see if he could see anyone else, then promptly disappeared.

I carried on, came out of the woods and skirted around the rivers edge before climbing a small bank right beside a bridge. Then suddenly I was in Carmacks. Following the road that ran beside the river, a 4x4 vehicle slowed down, 2 British guys who were attempting to xc ski (cross country ski) leaned out of the window and wished me luck. I was a little confused - they either finished in record time or had for whatever reason been pulled from the race.

They were both military and had high hopes of doing well, having spent the best part of the winter training in the Cairngorms. I found out later that they had both suffered injuries.

I plodded on looking for the checkpoint when I heard a snowmobile coming up behind me. It was Mike, he told me that the checkpoint was up ahead and in someone's house. This was followed by those famous last words, "you can't miss it" Normally it would have been in the community hall but that was being used this year.

I thanked him and he again disappeared. I tried to speed up, all the time looking for the checkpoint, then I again spotted Mike who was now on foot and had come to show me the way - what a gent!

I arrived at the checkpoint at 17:00 and was greeted by some huge dogs - four slobbering, hairy, happy, curious dogs wagging their tails and sniffing me and my sledge. One went to cock his leg and claim the sledge as his own. I moved it quickly and Mike said "Lets get it inside". The inside was a workshop that had now doubled up as a checkpoint. The log-burning stove had warmed the place up. It was spacious and cosy, well, as cosy as a workshop can be.

Inside was the owner and Helke, a German athlete, who had

finished the 100 mile race and was now helping out.

I sat down next to the stove, removed my shoes and was presented with a very welcome bowl of moose stew and bread. It was lovely, so lovely I had another bowl.

I decided to get some sleep. After 3 hours of solid sleep I woke up and lying on the other side of the workshop was Frank. I tried to get back to sleep but failed. It was now a little after 22:00. I decided to get going, ate some more, refilled bottles and flasks and was packed and ready to leave. It was now 23:00. I had been here long enough.

As I made my way out into the frozen night I saw coming towards me another athlete, Andy. We had a quick word, shook hands and parted company.

I found the way without too much trouble - it was a pretty good track and was at one time a well-used miners track. It was, however, a bloody steep climb and I was having to work hard. It didn't matter because I was being treated to the most spectacular display of Aurora Borealis, the Northern Lights. They danced and teased their way across the night sky. So close did they seem that I actually tried to touch them with my walking pole. (Please don't tell anyone, they will think I'm nuts!)

This fantastic display went on for ages. Unfortunately, my constant gazing up had given me neck-ache. I carried on trying not to look up - this was made a little easier by the fact that I was now entering a wooded area and it was starting to get light.

The area that I was in was beautiful, every step of the way had been the same, but now its beauty was becoming just more of the same:- dare I say it - monotonous.

The trail was exactly that, a trail, a means to an end. I had plodded uphill, downhill, along rivers and across lakes, each section between checkpoints was uniquely challenging and tough.

I was now annoyed with myself for thinking that such a beautifully tranquil place - a place that I was very fortunate to be in - was monotonous.

I switched off from trying to work out the distance to the McCabe Creek checkpoint and just got on with it, one foot in front of the other.

Dropping down onto the river, I followed the markers. There were huge chunks of ice that required quite a detour, sort of zigzagging my way through. Eventually as I neared the shoreline I caught a whiff of a log burner, then as I clambered up the bank I saw a group of wooden buildings and Mike standing in front of one smoking his pipe. He saw me and signalled me over.

As I entered the McCabe checkpoint Marianne was there. Marianne had just had a bash at the 100 mile distance and was now helping out. She kindly offered food and drinks and a place to have a sleep, as it was now a little after 14:00.

Tempting though it was to stay, I wanted to get a move on and take advantage of the daylight.

Leaving the checkpoint I had to follow the track leading down to a main road, cross it and run alongside the road for approximately 4 miles. It was now dark and I had to concentrate hard to locate the turning, which thankfully led onto some proper trail away from the road. Though I saw only one vehicle I wanted to be away from the road.

After an hour or so I noticed some horrendous overflow that had frozen. It was 'run off' from the side of a hill and was right across my path. Trying to get across was tricky - a bit like trying to climb a child's slide in socks and without touching the sides. I had no choice but to put on my crampons and with the crampons and poles managed to inch my way across only going arse over tit once and even then I turned around to see if anyone had noticed.

I carried on and eventually reached the lakes, the advantage of moving on the lakes was that it was nice and flat and thus I could move quicker. Well, that's the theory.

I plodded on but was very aware of the sleep monster now

creeping up on me. My eyes kept closing, I was knackered.

I looked at my watch and it was a little after midnight I had had 3 hours sleep since Braeburn.

I tried everything to keep the monster at bay:- shutting my eyes for a few steps, shutting one eye at a time, washing my face with snow, nodding for a few seconds at a time while resting on my poles. They all worked for a minute or two but the reality was they were just delaying the inevitable. I knew if I could just keep awake I would make it to the checkpoint.

This was helped by the fact that I was now coming off the lakes and into some woods. I was getting close, just a bit further, I'm nearly there.

Moving through the woods I saw some people huddled together, talking. Thinking they were either support crew or a group of trappers, I approached but they rather rudely stopped talking and moved off. However, rounding a corner I saw them again and again they moved off. Thinking they might not have seen me I hurried after them and again they moved off, Bastards. I only wanted to ask them how much further to Pelly Crossing.

As I was deciding wether I should chase them or not, I wandered slightly off the trail and my walking pole disappeared into the thigh high snow. The shock woke me up with a start and I suddenly realised that there was no group of people wandering around the Yukon at 03:00 talking in huddled group whilst playing 'catch' to some poor unfortunate soul trying to get to Pelly Crossing.

The bloody sleep monster had sneaked up. I was close to Pelly but I knew I had to stop and get some sleep. So, reluctantly, I pulled my sledge to one side of the trail, got my bivi bag out and got into my sleeping bag then promptly fell asleep for nearly 3 hours.

I woke up feeling much better. The first thing I did was to see if anyone had passed me during my sleep - there didn't appear any fresh footprints but I couldn't be sure. I don't know why I did that, I wasn't racing, I was just trying to finish.

Unfortunately my camelbak had frozen, it was now just a block of ice and now I couldn't decide whether I should get my stove out and make a drink or plod on. I reasoned that I was close to the next checkpoint so opted to plod on. I put the block of ice on my back and moved off. It was now a little after 08:00 and I hadn't seen any trail markers for some time but owing to the fact that there were a lot of disgarded booties (little overboots that mushers use to protect the dogs feet) along the trail I knew I was going in the right direction.

After an hour or so I decided that I needed a poo, a number two, and started looking for a suitable spot whilst at the same time working out the logistics involved:- ie unharness my sledge, find the toilet tissue, remove my jacket to release braces, do I use walking poles to hold onto or do I rely on my balance, my legs are tired and well-used, the squatting position might be too stressful, I'll use poles etc etc. Also I realised that I hadn't been since I had started. Eventually I found just such a place, I unharnessed, fished out some toilet paper, made my way over to one side, selected the spot and then started the laborious process of removing clothing. Then I heard a vehicle, not a snowmobile but a proper vehicle:- now it was a question of do I or don't I? I stopped what I was doing, replaced the clothing, made my way back to the sledge, replaced the now unused toilet roll, harnessed up and moved off. I then saw, to my right, a wooden house, not a cabin but a house. Then I came to a road, followed it for maybe a km through Pelly Crossing and then saw the checkpoint banner. I arrived at 11:08.

On entering the place I was met by one of the medics, Eric, he welcomed me in, offered me a drink and some food which I gratefully accepted but not before I made good use of a proper toilet and washing facilities.

It's amazing what a good poo, washing and cleaning teeth can do for ones morale. After I had eaten and sorted some kit out and repacked my sledge I was keen to get going again. I wanted to make use of the daylight. I left at 13:46.

I made my way out of Pelly and crossed a road bridge. As I did so, I looked down onto the river and only then did I spot the trail markers. As I reached the other side I followed the trail markers up and off the river and rejoined the proper route.

After about 2 hours I spotted coming toward me, at a great rate of knots, the 2 Italians that made up Team Terraz. They looked shattered: limping and hobbling. We shook hands and they asked "how much further?" I didn't know the distance, but I told them that I had left the checkpoint at 13:46. They seemed happy, shook hands again. We wished each other good luck and went our separate ways.

Moving along the road I heard a vehicle coming up behind me, I turned around and saw that it was Robert, the race organiser and Diane, the medic, they asked if I was okay, I said that I was.

I asked about the next checkpoint at Pelly Farms, realising that I would be there in the early hours. Diane said "Don't worry they will have the kettle on for when you arrive, someone will be up."

They drove off and I was left to look forward to a decent sleep, some hot food and hot drinks.

At about 19:30 I came across the halfway marker, that also indicated that it was time to get back onto the river. I had a quick wee, something to eat and stepped onto the river. I felt good and had worked out that if it had taken me approx 6 hours to reach halfway (and that's with a slight detour and a couple of stops to chat) I should, fingers crossed, be at the checkpoint between 01:30 and 02:00. With this in mind and the thought of some sleep and food I got my arse in gear and started to push hard and fast.

The river was tricky and seemed to my tired mind to be going up hill, but following the route markers and feeling good I moved quickly. Then I spotted something, a cabin, all the lights were off. After gingerly knocking on the door I went in, looked around: nothing. Though I was in someone's home there was no sign of life. I called out a couple of times but nothing, I found the light switch, turned on the light, had a walk round, again nothing. I checked my watch, it was 00:46, slightly confused I realised that I way ahead of my predicted time, this couldn't be the checkpoint, after all, both Diane and Robert had said they would be up waiting for me and they knew I'd be arriving. I went outside and checked a couple outbuildings, nothing.

Realising I had cocked up, I harnessed up and moved off, figuring that the checkpoint was not much further and knowing I couldn't miss it as it was on the riverbank and I was on the river - simple.

My heart was saying that this WAS the checkpoint, but my oh-so-logical head kept telling me that it wasn't, because I had been told that someone would be up to meet me, with the kettle on.

Moving along, desperately trying to scan the riverbanks for any signs of the elusive Pelly Farms checkpoint. I applied every available sense I had: sight, smell and hearing all went into overdrive, nothing. It was now gone 04:00 and still nothing.

I was bloody annoyed with myself, for again overestimating my ability. I walked on, moaning to myself, cursing my stupidity, questioning my reason for being here in the Yukon, freezing my balls off, alone, fed up and pissed off. I'm 47 years old, I should know better. I could be at home in my bed, I don't have to be here. Ultra-distance running its a bloody stupid sport. Golf, now there's a proper sport, why don't I take up golf. That's what I'll do when I get back, I can wear a Pringle jumper and one of those funny gloves instead of these oversized Arctic mittens and a sensible pair of shoes. I'm never, ever coming to the Yukon again, this race will be my last, in fact when I get to Pelly I'll knock it on the head. I don't care if I don't finish. I wonder where the checkpoint is. I hope they have something nice to eat, I could do with a cup of tea.

On and on it went, me feeling sorry for myself and the fact that I was even contemplating playing golf was a sign of how bad things had become.

A quick look at my watch, nearly 06:00. I should have found the bloody checkpoint by now. I must have missed it, I'll turn back in a minute, just a little further it must be here somewhere. I couldn't have passed it. Trying to work out where I might have missed it. I didn't, couldn't have, I was desperate, which in turn had made me extra vigilant.

Another look at my watch, nearly 06:30. I should have been there four and a half, five hours ago, BOLLOCKS. I'll have to turn round BOLLOCKS, BOLLOCKS and BLOODY BOLLOCKS!

I'll go back to the cabin - maybe they know where bloody Pelly Farms is.

I, for some reason decided to write my name in the snow, taking my trekking pole, I wrote 'BERRIDGE 06:30' with an arrow pointing in my direction of travel. It was only after the race that I discovered this simple message had caused much confusion:- my tracks were going in both directions and a cryptic message was a great talking point between Frank and Andy, the two guys immediately behind me. It did, however, confirm to the world my stupidity (and the fact that I had done an extra 40km!).

I reluctantly turned around. Now I was pissed off, my shoulders dropped, as did my head, my walking poles had now become redundant, useless extensions, just dragging along behind me.

I was having an almighty sulk. My race was over, I've lost so much time I'll probably be last anyway, nobody cares, nobody loves me, blah blah bloody blah.

I carried on still feeling sorry for myself, whilst at the same time making up various ailments and injuries that I could use as an excuse to bail out with a little dignity. Then, up ahead, I spotted what I thought was a plume of smoke. Moving towards it more out of hope than anything, I saw the plume again and then as I got closer I saw 2 people - a man and a child.

As much as we men don't like to ask for directions, on this occasion I really didn't give a toss. I was going to ask them how to get to Pelly Farms.

Fortunately they spotted me, waved and called me over, then another person appeared at the door of the cabin. I was now in a dilemma:- if they invited me in and offered me a drink do I accept or not? If I do, my race is over as the rules state no outside help.

I was still making my mind up, when I heard Diane say "Welcome to Pelly Farms, we were expecting you last night." It was now a little after 11:00. Then the penny dropped: this was Pelly Farms, the place I had been last night. I had just walked for 10 hours to get to where I was! I hadn't recognised the place in daylight.

I explained that I was here last night and, to confirm it, I described the interior of the cabin, including a pair of white mittens with the name Kimberly written on them and the six bottles of mineral water on the sideboard. "How, when, what time did you get here?" I said "my watch said 00:46". They went on to apologise and explained that they were expecting me at around 02:00 and had set the alarm clock for 01:30.

The one time I actually get my arse in gear and move fast, it backfires. I didn't care. I needed a sit down, I was shattered. They explained that no one else other than the Italians had been through yet.

I couldn't believe it:- I was still in the race and was the first individual to reach this checkpoint. Dale and Sue, the owners, asked me what I was going to do. I was extremely tired, having had less than 6 hours sleep since Braeburn. My intention had always been to sleep here for 3 or 4 hours before leaving.

But after I had something to eat and drink, a little rest and the fact that I was only 30 miles from the finish, I decided to carry on. I felt good and I felt refreshed - just thirty miles, that's all!

Two hours after arriving, I left. It was a little after 13:00 and I worked out that if I pushed hard I would be finished in the early morning.

Sue came out and showed me which way to go, I thanked them for their hospitality (to which she again apologised for the timing fiasco).

I followed the track and, once out of sight, sorted myself out. I wanted to move fast and take full advantage of the remaining daylight. I proceeded down the narrow road and was moving well and the route was pretty good:- undulating, but well defined and easy to follow.

It was now getting dark and I was getting tired and consequently had slowed down to a more sensible pace. Eventually I reached the halfway marker - just 15 miles to go. I smiled and looked at my watch - it was 20:07. If it had taken me seven hours to do the last 15 miles I reasoned that I would be finished by 03:00, 04:00. Time to get my arse in gear. I had a quick bite to eat, a drink and was good to go.

Then my walking pole slipped on a patch of ice and then my sledge developed a mind of its own, weaving from side to side. I tried in vain to make it go straight but it just pulled me from one side of the trail to other. It was bloody annoying and I was getting pretty pissed off with the thing. My legs started to do the same, they refused to work properly. I gave them simple instructions which they totally ignored. I was trying to go forward on 'bambi legs' whilst trying to control an uncontrollable sledge, I was wandering all over the place, my walking poles weren't much help, just touching the ground whenever they felt like it, uncontrollable sledge, uncontrollable legs and now uncontrollable poles.

I stopped for a second, lent on my poles, trying to gather my thoughts and to try and work out what was going on, when suddenly I saw two headtorches coming toward me. They spoke to me in German, I replied in English. I don't know what I said but they were both wearing very concerned expressions, then in a limited English they asked if I was okay. I replied that I was and they seemed even more concerned, so I gave them the thumbs up looked at my watch - 02:10. What the fuck, I had only looked at my watch 10 minutes ago at the halfway mark, where the hell had those SIX hours gone? I turned around and saw my sledge was covered in snow as was the trail behind.

I walked on trying to work out what had happened. My watch must be broken:- six hours couldn't just disappear. If it was really 02:10 I should be just about finished. Then another strange thing happened - I heard someone talking to me, I ignored it, then a headtorch and voice were saying "Hi Dave." I turned around to see an animated Sean Brown. Like the 2 Germans, he seemed concerned.

This is an extract from Sean's race report:

"The forest rd was hard work but I felt good, on the way out I bumped into another athlete who was two hours from finishing, but as I slowed down to say hi and see how he was, I had to stop him from going straight past without acknowledging me, as soon as he started talking he made no sense whatsoever, he thought the race was over and I had been sent out to look for him he also started talking about the hotel he was staying in and the flight home.

I was concerned at first that he might be suffering hypothermia but the more we talked the more he started to come round he looked strong still and had only 2 hours to go, I realized he was suffering from sleep deprivation, I urged him to have some coffee I had in a flask with me, it was difficult to hold him back and once he assured me for the second time that he was fine he shot off, I watched him go and he was moving straight on the road, not wobbling.

I felt guilty I had been unable to persuade him to have some coffee and thought that if I felt he had hypothermia I would have physically stopped him and made him take some coffee (however he was bigger than me so this would have been easier said than done), I would also probably have gone back to Pelly Crossing with him to make sure he was OK.

I felt confident that he would get to Pelly fine as he looked so strong; however I couldn't stop thinking about it for a long time and wondered if I had done the right thing!"

Of this I was totally oblivious and it wasn't until after the race that Sean told me what had happened. Sleep deprivation: it's horrid and it's sneaky, slowly creeping up on you and making you see things that aren't there. It makes you make stupid and potentially dangerous decisions, irrational thoughts and fears. In this type of racing, one of the prerequisites is the ability to push hard, push very hard. However, there is a limit, when suddenly and, without realising it, you have pushed just a little too hard.

On this occasion I had pushed too hard and had been very fortunate to get away with it. It was another lesson learned (I hope). I carried on as if nothing had happened, then spotted the lights of Pelly.

The trail took me back on to the river and then under the road bridge and then it was just a short hop to the Community Centre and finish line. I arrived at 08:14 and it had taken me 164:44 hours and I was beaten only by the Italian team Terraz. Second place was Frank Jansenn who finished in a time of 174:36

It was the toughest race I had ever taken part in and I had been lucky:- lack of sleep and an extra 40kms could have been disastrous.

The Yukon Arctic Ultra is one of the most beautiful races I have ever run, but it is also the hardest and most unforgiving. You can have all the gear and all the training behind you but if you are not organised or you make mistakes, you are, to put it mildly in the SHIT!

WHAT NEXT!

IRONMAN UK 70.3 2007

What is it: A half Ironman distance triathlon

When: June

Where: Exmoor

Distance: 1.2 mile swim, 56 mile bike, 13.1 mile run
(1.9km, 90km, 21km)

It is: One of the toughest half Ironman triathlons
out there - Chris McCormack

See: ironmanuk.com

Last year I attempted a triathlon for the first time. As I hauled
myself across the finishing line I was grinning from ear to ear
and just like the addicted gambler who doesn't know when
to quit, I needed to push my luck just a little further.

The hunt was on for the next triathlon and being, as my wife
would say, bloody stupid, I wanted a tough one and my
searching drew me toward the Daddy of all triathlons:
the Ironman.

Last year's West Wight Triathlon paled into insignificance.
The Ironman was huge, the 600 meter swim that had so
terrified me was replaced by a 3800 meter (2.4 mile) open
water swim, the 35km bike section would be a 180km (112
mile) monster and the 7km run would now become a full

marathon at 42.2 km (26.2 mile).

The more I looked into it, the more I wanted to do it. But even me, someone who is by all accounts bloody stupid, realised that the Ironman was just too big - one step to far.

I had to rethink, and consequently came up with the Ironman 70.3. It still had the word Ironman in the title and that made me feel just a little better. It was, however, only half the distance (listen to me - ONLY half the distance).

I 'You Tubed' it and decided that it was possible, tough, yes, but possible none the less. The race also proudly states that there are 52 hills in its 56 mile bike route. With that I signed up there and then. I could, at this point, moan about the price: it was a little expensive for a triathlon (I have since learned that triathlon is not the cheapest of sports) but I am a glass half full kind of guy. I reasoned as I did with the 'Marathon Des Sables' that it was a lot of money to waste and if I didn't finish I would have wasted a lot of money - in other words I HAD to finish!

I started training with my usual naivety. As I had done for the West Wight Triathlon I decided that my running would, as long as I maintained my weekly average, take care of itself, the cycling would have to increase and improve. Luckily for me the Isle of Wight is a perfect place for cycling: beautiful and hilly. It was just a question of increasing both my mileage and hill work. Then there was swimming.

Swimming was most definitely my Achilles heel and so I decided to swim at least three times a week. The swim for the Ironman 70.3 was to be held in a reservoir and consequently all swimmers were obliged to wear a wetsuit.

So it was back on to the internet to begin my search for a wetsuit. I eventually found what I was looking for: a Blue Seventy Stealth. I sent my measurements off, placed the order and waited. A few days later it arrived. I was now beginning to feel like a real triathlete and couldn't wait to try it out.

Trying to get the thing on was a workout in itself, it was like trying to put a condom on a jelly: fraught with problems. I sweated, squeezed, squashed and yanked myself into it. I needed to perform a contortionist act just to pull the zip up and then I looked in the mirror. It didn't look right and it certainly didn't feel right, the arms and legs were twisted and certain parts of my anatomy were being strangled. I took it off and started again - this time was slightly more successful.

I had 8 months to get the hang of it. After a while I got more comfortable in the water and the added buoyancy that the wetsuit gave me was very welcome. My ability to swim the required distance was eventually reached and maintained, but to say I enjoyed swimming would be stretching it a bit.

Training was going well: I could swim and cycle, run and cycle and on a couple of occasions I actually managed to do a mini-triathlon.

As usual time, just seemed to whizz past, and all too soon the car was being packed and the ferry booked.

The drive through Exmoor National Park gave me the first indication of what the hell I had signed up for - it was, as the race organisers had promised, HILLY, very *&^%@ HILLY.

I had looked for another slightly more challenging triathlon and I had not disappointed myself. However, there was nothing slightly about it, it was a lot more challenging.

Now I thought back to last year's event when the winner Chris McCormack had said, quite categorically, that the UK half Ironman was the toughest in the world.

Bloody typical of me - the only time I get things right is when I am going to have to suffer for it!

The following day was registration day: sign in and collect the coloured bags that would be needed for each of the transitions. Then the most important job - to collect my official Ironman 70.3 bracelet, the bracelet that would let everyone know that I am a triathlete. The reality was very different: I was a nervous wreck.

I walked around the 'Expo' looking at impressive bits of triathlon kit. I spent half my time trying to work out what most of it did and the other half trying to look as if I belonged there, when I quite obviously didn't. I felt a fraud and it would not have surprised me if security had come up and escorted me out of the area, explaining on the way that "This area was for triathletes only, sir."

I managed to get away with my charade and we went for a walk to recce the swim route, which was down in the reservoir. Standing high above the thing I could see the buoys marking the route - it looked a bloody long way to swim. There were 11 buoys set out in a triangle shape. I had just finished counting when my darling wife kicked me in the nuts, well not quite, but that's what it felt like when she asked "Is it one lap or two!!!" I didn't honestly know, but I went all religious for a moment and prayed that it was just one!

The following day we arrived at the start early, it was still dark. I'd had a good night's sleep and for some bizarre reason I felt relaxed, and that worried me. I should have at least felt a little anxious or scared. I couldn't swim for toffees, couldn't bike very well and had not got a clue about transitions. The only thing I could do was run and even that was not a guaranteed after having swum and cycled a combined distance of a little over 57 miles.

It was still dark, damp and chilly. I sorted out my transition bags and made my way over to the large changing tent, had another wrestling match with my wetsuit and then wondered over to my allocated pen. Now my apprehension started, standing waiting and surrounded by some very fit and serious-looking athletes!

We stood waiting, slowly inching our way forward. The unfortunate thing was that I was in the 3rd wave and being so bloody tall could see the horrors that lay ahead. There was a lot of splashing and bashing going on, some people were being pulled out by kayaks and a couple of others turned around and made their way back to the safety of the shore.

It did not bode well. All the while that this maelstrom was taking place we were creeping our way forward - then all of a sudden I was ankle deep in water, the combination of wet mud seeping between my toes and the cold water had an immediate effect on my bladder, I needed a wee. I stood there savouring the moment, the relief and warming effect was instantaneous and very welcome.

As I waded into the water my rapidly diminishing confidence nosedived. I was now hopelessly out of my depth, in more ways than one!

Within moments of starting, I found myself in the middle of the splashing and bashing that I had earlier witnessed. I coughed and spluttered, inching my way forward, my heart rate was through the roof, I couldn't see a thing. I was beginning to panic and I wasn't even halfway to the first marker buoy.

I gathered my thoughts, rolled over onto my back and calmed both myself and my heart rate down - a few seconds was all it took. I rolled back over and decided that no matter what happened I would get to the first buoy. And with that, I gently swam forward, using the breast stroke technique that I had seen the little old ladies use in my local pool. It worked, by the time I reached the 1st buoy I had plenty of space and felt a lot better so I reverted back to the crawl and then on to the next buoy and then the next, until finally I turned a corner and could see the huge inflatable finishing banner.

I smiled to myself and continued on. I was now being passed by the swimmers that had started in the wave after mine, I didn't care, I hadn't drowned and I was going to make it.

Swimming along, keeping one eye on the approaching finish line, when suddenly I ran out of water and my fingertips stroked the silty bottom, bliss.

I had done it, finished 1.2 miles. I couldn't believe it. As I stood up, I wobbled like a drunk trying to get my balance, and fumbled with my zip, and like I'd seen on the television attempted to run to the transition area. Two things prevented me 1 - I was so knackered that I could hardly breath and 2 - the 400 metre climb to the transition area was bloody steep! Too bloody steep to run.

Eventually I reached the transition area, grabbed my bag and proceeded to get changed, while trying to eat a banana and have a drink. Once changed into my cycling kit (and now that I now I had recovered slightly) I attempted to run, found my bike. Helmet on, glasses on and then a walk out of the transition area and on to the bike!

It felt good to be on the bike and the first of the 52 hills soon appeared. It was steep enough to warm me up.

The bike route was a two-lap route and I decided to take the first lap fairly cautiously, not wanting to blow up too early.

The hills were as tricky going down as they were hard going up. Then just to make things a little more challenging, I took a left turn and was confronted with a very steep hill. It was one of those hills that was so steep that I needed to weave from side to side just to maintain forward momentum. I wasn't the only one weaving my way up:- there were quite a few people walking and because they were wearing cycling shoes it made their progress very interesting and rather entertaining - not for them I'm sure!

Continuing on, we at last came to a descent - at least I could now rest a bit and let gravity help me out, Wrong: the first clue to what lay ahead was a sign or several stating 'NO OVERTAKING.' It was just too bloody steep, coupled with the fact that the narrow lane we were on was covered in trees and the sunshine trying to peep its way through appeared to be flickering. It made the whole thing a bit like cycling down a bendy tube whilst blinking very fast!

Cycling along planning my transition in my head, a motorcycle, with cameraman came past. I had watched this event last year on Channel 4 so with thoughts of my TV appearance looming large, I tried to look the part of a serious triathlete. Just as I thought I had succeeded, a cyclist came storming past, the race leader - it was him they were filming and, to make matters worse, I realised he was at least twenty-six miles ahead of me. I must admit he looked bloody impressive.

I managed to complete the first lap with mixed emotions, glad to have survived the swim and lap one, but well aware that I still had lap two and a half-marathon to go!

Would my old legs carry me the rest of the way? During lap two I fuelled up: ate and drank as much as I could in preparation for the half-marathon.

As I finished the second and final lap I felt surprisingly good (I think the euphoria I was experienced helped dull any tiredness). Unlike the athletes I had seen on the television, I had no chance of dismounting whilst on the run. I had to stop the bike and slowly peel myself off the thing. I handed my bike over and hobbled off to get ready for the run.

I quickly sorted myself out and tried to run out of transition but unfortunately it felt as if I had borrowed Bambi's legs. It took a few minutes for them to settle down. I found a nice steady pace and felt reasonably comfortable, however, there was a nasty steep descent that pounded the quads up a bit. The run route was three laps - great for the spectators but was a little confusing for runners who were all over the place. Like a figure of eight, runners were going back and forth and I'm sure that some lost count and entered the finish area with another lap or two to go. Looking at the amount of people that were DSQd (disqualified) afterwards I realised that may well have been the case.

Suddenly I was on the last lap. I tried to speed up but I

must have left my speeding-up legs back at the hotel. I just continued with my now slow, if not efficient, pace. Then I turned right on to the red carpet and under the finish banner the clock said 7:12.33. I had finished a Half Ironman Triathlon - only my second attempt at triathlon. I was as chuffed with this finish as I was with finishing the 'Marathon Des Sables'.

My actual chip times were 44 minutes for the swim, 3:31 for bike and 2:02 for the run.

WHAT NEXT!

ATACAMA CROSSING 2009

What is it: Multi-stage, self-sufficient desert race

When: March 2009

Where: Chile

Distance: 250km (155 miles)

It is: Tough, the altitude, heat and cold make it hard

See: racingtheplanet.com

I have been looking forward to this race for some time. It's a race that I'd had in mind to do for a few years - it was to be all the more enjoyable because my wife was to join me. Marilyn has run several marathons and enjoyed them. That's not strictly true, she's enjoyed finishing them. I think curiosity had got the better of her after seeing this race on the TV. She needed to see for herself what all the fuss was about: why I always wanted to go and have a go at some ridiculous race or other (it's a fair question and one for which I still had no answer). I was just pleased that she was coming and I secretly/selfishly hoped that, like me, she would get the bug and want to do more.

The Atacama Crossing is a 250km long race across the Atacama Desert in Chile. It is held annually and uses the same format as the Marathon Des Sables - several stages with one long stage taking you through the night.

We flew to Santiago, Chile's capital via Madrid. We then had a short internal flight finally arriving at our hotel very nearly 40 hours after we had left home.

The Hotel Altiplanco was stunning, very beautiful and very peaceful, surrounded as it was by snow-capped peaks. The small town of San Pedro de Atacama was only a short walk away. It seemed very busy and bustling full of little shops catering for tourists wanting to explore the surrounding area. We walked around doing our own exploring and made our way to the race headquarters, located in another hotel. On returning to our hotel we noticed that we had both got a touch of sunburn. We were at altitude and I should have realised, it was annoying but not serious.

The next day it was back to race HQ for all the administration, equipment checks, medicals and the obligatory rucksack-weighing. Mine was 11 kgs and I thought that was heavy but someone had a rucksack weighing l5kgs. Marilyn's was 9kgs. The following day, after a hearty breakfast, we made our way back to the race HQ to board the coaches that would take us to the start. The start line was apparently way up into the mountains and would be at an altitude of a little over 3000 meters. On arriving at the campsite in the Arcoiris Valley, it was freezing - gloves hats, fleeces and anything else was put on. We were then shown to our tent, unlike other races this tent was named and to be used by those allocated to it for the duration of the race.

One Italian, two Danes, one American and three English. There was supposed to be a Japanese guy but he never made it (but it did give us a little more room).

After settling in we were given a lovely meal which was eaten around one of the many fires that were dotted around the campsite. Then, just to round things off, we were treated to some local music played by the camp staff. During the night there were some very strange sounds, weird animal-like noises coming from all around the camp. In the morning the source of the previous nights' cacophony became all too apparent:- a lot of people had become ill and a few of them had, in desperation, been running around clutching wet wipes and toilet tissue.

Day I - 35.2km

WOW, that was a shock to the system. Normally on races like this the first day or two is a short introduction - not this one. The very first steps were tricky: a very technical 50 meter descent, loose, rocky and very steep. The route choice was somewhat limited because so many of us were trying to squeeze ourselves through a very narrow corridor. Eventually we reached the bottom and then it was a nasty lung-bursting, heart-racing climb it required use of hands and feet and some rather colourful language on my part. It was a little difficult to concentrate with my wife's bottom hovering just inches above my head. When eventually we managed to reach the summit, we realised what the race organisers objective had been: to split the race up. They had achieved their objective, the racing snakes were off and into the distance. Us slower ones were left wondering why we hadn't trained harder.

The course for today would be what race organisers euphemistically call undulating and what we runners call a lot of bloody hills. Getting to the checkpoints was taking much longer than I had expected. By the afternoon Marilyn was feeling it - it was a very tough first day, lots of challenging hills at altitude and in the blazing sun the combination was making her first days 'ultra' extremely difficult. Using a nice steady pace we plodded on eventually reaching the campsite in the late afternoon. Marilyn had had a tough first day, a real baptism of fire. She had had to dig deep and push hard. I was surprised at the severity of the first day and was chuffed to bits for her - she'd had a real humdinger of a day. I was sure that after a bit of food and rest she would be as right as rain. After a meal and a rest I asked how she felt, she said she was tired but would be fine and planned to carry on.

Day 2 - 42kms

Today we were told that we would be getting our feet wet, we did. Shortly after starting we arrived at a gorge. Most of the time you were able to avoid getting wet feet, but occasionally you had no choice but to step in. The water was freezing - snow melt from the Andes. The one good thing about it being so cold was that you were encouraged to be bloody quick: it was just too cold to be hanging about. After a while we came across a section that was enclosed by sheer walls and for about 500 meters you were in ankle-to-knee deep water. Trying to rush through without falling over required a degree of concentration. I guess I wasn't concentrating because I tripped and was just thankful that my rucksack didn't get wet, the thought of a wet sleeping bag was just too much.

Looking back as you do when you fall over and make a complete tit of yourself, we noticed a small group of runners heading off in the wrong direction. I whistled as loud as I could and fortunately the fact that we were in a deep gorge meant that my whistle was heard, with a lot of frantic arm-waving we managed to get them back on track. They were very grateful.

My long legs (I'm 6"4 inches) and faster pace would normally be a distinct advantage in these races but this time they were a distinct disadvantage. I was always just slightly ahead and was having to stop regularly - the stopping and waiting meant that I was getting cold and I started to shiver!

Eventually we came out of the gorge and into the sunshine. CP 1 was a welcome sight. The terrain was a little better and the wet feet had a chance to dry, and just as they got nice and dry there was another small river to cross. The dry, warm feet were now once again cold and wet feet!

The river crossings came to a sudden end, with a sharp right turn and a monster climb. This climb was long and winding and took us to the entrance of an old miners' tunnel. Entering the tunnel was like going through a foggy tube. The fine dust that was disturbed by numerous pairs of feet was floating around and gave the appearance of fog! On leaving the tunnel you turned immediately left and another very steep climb. The views were stunning but you paid a high price for them.

The constant climbing combined with the heat were beginning to take their toll on Marilyn - she was needing to sit down every so often. It's never a good idea to sit out in the direct sunlight and at this height it was very unwise indeed, but I think she was suffering more than she was expecting and just needed short rests. It was during one of these rests that we saw a runner approaching from behind. He looked very fast and very strong, so much so that I couldn't work out why we were ahead of him. It turned out that he had taken a wrong turn and it had cost him dearly, not only in time but the extra distance he had to cover. We continued on and were now walking on an exposed ridge that dropped sharply away to the left. The ridge was slightly climbing and eventually we came across the markers that would take us down a very large and very steep sand dune. This large sand dune was a real test for Marilyn. There is a real knack to descending these sand dunes, and Marilyn struggled. I could tell she was having to work hard for every step and now the fun or the enjoyment or both had gone.

At the bottom of the sand dune was CP 2. It was at this checkpoint that Marilyn made the decision to stop. It was a courageous thing to do and I admired the way she had struggled without once complaining - she had survived what I considered to be the 2 toughest desert days I've ever done and she had the bollocks to give a very tough 'Ultra' a go. The good thing was that she was not upset or terribly disappointed but she knew that this race was too much for her.

I left the checkpoint, hoping that she was alright and not too despondent. The trail now descended down a track and across a road. I now picked up the pace and after about 40 minutes I could see up ahead a small group of runners. There were 3 of them and now my competitive instinct kicked in and I decided to give chase. It took very nearly an hour to catch and pass them. When I arrived at CP 3 I could see another runner having medical help on his feet. Being the mercenary that I am I left immediately after collecting some water. The terrain was now fairly flat. However, this soon changed to rougher stuff. Looking up ahead I could see a couple of runners. Eventually, after a lot of effort I managed to catch them. The trail was now more of a dusty road and from behind I could hear a vehicle approaching. Discretion being the better part of valour, I moved over, the 4x4 Toyota slowed down and I saw my wife sitting in one of the passenger seats along with a couple of other runners. I asked how she was and fortunately she was fine and smiling. Seeing her and knowing that she was okay had cheered me up a bit and I decided to run a bit, walk a bit. I saw the campsite up ahead 2 maybe 3 km away. There was also another runner ahead and I decided to chase them down. It's the little games like this, that I sometimes need to motivate me - it takes my mind off the monotonous miles and the agony! I finally reached the CP and my wife was there to meet me!

The campsite was in a beautiful location. But my feet were now beginning to resent the fact that I was once again abusing them. Blisters were now forming, especially on the heels. I spent quite a bit of time cleaning, draining and dressing them. The good thing with this race and unlike other desert races I've done in the past was that you didn't have to boil water! It's a small thing I know, but boiling water is not only very time-consuming (when you're knackered time is precious), it means that you also have to carry a stove and when the water is rationed do you drink it, prepare food with it, wash or clean teeth with it? This race has at each campsite large communal fires that have hot water constantly on the go. You walk or hobble your way over, fill your dehydrated ration pack, cup or flask and hobble back! Speaking to Marilyn she told me that she wasn't disappointed, it was the right thing to do. She should have trained harder, it was a lot harder than she was expecting (I told her that it was harder than I was expecting). Anyway, rather than go back to the hotel and just wait and get bored she had decided to stay and help with the race.

Day 3 - 40km

Today started much the same way as day one did, with a couple of challenging descents, followed by about 2 km of tricky and uneven terrain - terrain that required absolute concentration lest you trip or twist something. Eventually we found our way on to a track of sorts which enabled me to pick up the pace. Arriving at CP 1, I collected water and was off. With the trail now pretty good I took advantage and decided to run as much as I could, eventually arriving at what was a pretty good road. Unfortunately, we were to cross the road and not run along it. Reaching the other side we were met by a challenging (what I really mean by challenging is a *&"%@ nightmare) route - a quick look ahead confirmed this. Not one runner was running, everyone was now walking and/or struggling, the ground was uneven, hard and soft. If you were lucky you could take two steps. However, the reality was one step, stop and work out where to place the next one. Eventually as I picked and pondered my way through the 4 kms that was absolute misery (it was without doubt the toughest 4 km I had ever covered), I spotted the next checkpoint - up the side of a steep bank and across another road. Again I collected my water and was very kindly given directions, well, someone pointed. I was now too traumatised to hear what they were saying, I just followed the direction of the finger attached to the arm belonging to the person giving me instructions. I nodded and grinned in agreement and sauntered off!

After leaving the checkpoint the terrain was a little kinder, mainly rock with some sand. However, it was bloody hot and somewhat exposed and unfortunately I realised too late that we were in fact climbing. It was a climb so gradual that I was unaware of it until it was too late and I was bloody knackered.

Once I reached the top it was a pleasant descent, well, it would have been pleasant had I not caught sight of a runner crawling up the side of a monster sand dune away in the distance. I made my way down thinking all the time about the monster climb awaiting me, and then once I reached the bottom I reluctantly made my way up. Once on top of the dune I strained to see any sign of the finish but no such luck. All I could see were little pink flags urging me, enticing me, to follow them, over the next dune and then the next. Cresting the summit of yet another dune I at last caught sight of the campsite. It was still a couple of km away but the end was literally within sight.

I dropped down and approached the final ascent and what an ascent it was. The steepest climb yet and very unforgiving especially on tired old legs. I relied on the same technique I had learned during the Himalayan 100: a couple of steps, rest, a couple of steps, rest. Halfway up was a small irrigation channel. Two runners were sitting there and it was bloody tempting to sit and savour the ice-cold water with them, but I just wanted to reach the finish. I did however take my hat off, scoop up some water and pour it over me. I can't put into words how invigorating that simple act was - absolute BLISS!

I carried on and, nearing the top, caught site of my wife waiting for me. I had made it - camp Volcan Licancabar. After I had something to eat, I examined my feet, yes they were blistered and sore but I'd had worse. These were manageable, annoying but manageable. All in all I felt good and pretty strong, I was eating well and moving along okay. No major problems - YET!

Day 4 - 42.8km

The one everyone was dreading, though not the longest. This day was the now famous or should I say infamous Salt

Flat day. The atmosphere on the start line was a little more subdued than normal, I think everyone realised the magnitude of today. Horror stories of shredded shoes, knackered knees and blister-popping terrain were banded about last night. I decided to go gaiter-free, knowing that they would be shredded and I would need them for another couple of days. The countdown began. After our final instructions and last minute tales of woe, we shuffled slowly forward and then gradually increased our speed - mine increased from very slow to just plain slow. I didn't care: it was a comfortable steady pace and one which I knew I could maintain. The first section wasn't too bad, a combination of rocks and sand, eventually reaching a descent that took us down a large sand dune and into a river valley. Once we reached the bottom it was into knee-deep water (wet feet again), the water was cool and shaded and a very welcome relief from the now baking sun. Following the river for a short distance took us into a small village and the first checkpoint.

Once we left the village it was a case of following a very narrow path and then a fence line for a couple of km, turn right and follow the fence down the other side, drop down onto a road, cross over and head toward the dreaded salt flats. It was at this point that I started to get confused, it doesn't take much. Once I got myself into a nice steady rhythm I locked onto the runner in front and was slowly, very slowly catching him up. I recognised the runner as the American that had come into the last checkpoint just as I was leaving. I couldn't work out how or where they had passed me, the route from the last checkpoint was so narrow that in order to have passed me I would have had to move over and out of the way, and as that did not happen, I was now confused. This played on my mind for a while and then the penny dropped. There was a section of the fence that was missing and if you stepped through it you could have saved yourself over a kilometre! I was annoyed that would anyone cheat, take a short cut or be such an arsehole! I just couldn't work it out, and rather stupidly it got to me. I was fuming and made the decision - a decision that I knew was wrong, but I made it anyway. I wanted to show that cheats never prosper. I decided that no matter what, no matter how much it hurt, no matter what the cost, the cheating American was not, repeat not, going to beat me today. And so I slowly cranked up my pace, caught him, exchanged pleasantries and passed him, thankfully that was how it remained.

Moving along, still angry at the American, I spotted two British runners ahead. They seem to be struggling or at least slowing down, then one of them disappeared behind a bush, the only bush for miles around and, unfortunately for them, it was only about 2ft high, but when you've got to go you've got to go. I of course did that very British thing and pretended I couldn't see or hear a bloke crapping his life away not 10ft away from me. He was close enough for me to notice he had tears in his eyes and was clenching his fists in pain! There wasn't much of a breeze, but what there was was blowing in the wrong direction, so I could hear, see and smell that he was somewhat poorly. Poor sod, but hey ho, it could have been worse: it could have been me!

Carrying on, through some trees and then turning left I spotted the checkpoint, it was this checkpoint that we were informed the fun and games would begin:- The Salt Flats.

The official course notes said they were extremely difficult and they weren't wrong: crystallised, razor sharp, hard baked and uneven. The going was fraught with difficulty. Every single step required concentration and pre-planning, tired legs and sore feet moaned every step of the way. The fact that I was using poles didn't help, as they just got stuck and clogged up with salty deposits. The effort required to extricate them had now left me with aching arm muscles. Moving along at a snail's pace I eventually got to the halfway mark at 7kms and there was Alastair, one of the race crew, standing there offering encouragement and a small amount of water to each of the runners. Water that he had heroically carried on his back to this point. Water is bloody heavy and coupled with the fact that the terrain was so awful and that this was an unofficial water station, made this kind act very impressive indeed.

Carrying on, I eventually spotted the next checkpoint and once inside I grabbed a seat, desperate for a sit down. One of the crew came up and asked "How did you find the Salt Flats?" and I said that it was, without doubt, the hardest 14 km I had ever done, and that "You couldn't pay me my registration fee to cross them again" (that interview appeared on YouTube).

Leaving the checkpoint and with just 6 km to go until the campsite, I tried to speed up and failed miserably. I eventually arrived at camp Tebiquincbe Lagoon - hungry, knackered and relieved.

Tomorrow would be the long day, so tonight rest, eat and hydrate. Get the blisters cleaned and re-dressed and get rid of anything that was no longer required. Like everyone else I knew that once tomorrow was out of the way the last day was really just a formality.

Day 5 The long day - 73.6km

As is usual at the start line of a stage race's longest day, the atmosphere was a little less jovial. Always a strange feeling, anxiety and nervousness about the enormity of what we were about to take on, whilst at the same time, thoughts of just get today out of the way and there's just one small day left - a simple formality to reach the finish line.

The countdown began and then we were off. Unfortunately we were still on salt flats, not quite as bad as yesterday and slightly helped by the fact that we were on what seemed to be a small narrow path, so narrow in fact that it was impossible to overtake - bloody annoying if you were one of the fast ones and wanted to push on, but excellent if, like me, you needed to hold back and pace yourself for what was going to be a bloody long day.

Eventually the terrain got a little easier and the first couple of checkpoints were reached. Then we entered an area where it is as close to the moons surface as you can get here on planet Earth and consequently where the NASA's moon buggy was tested and put through its paces. It was a strangely beautiful, alien landscape. I could see why NASA had chosen it. Plodding along and lost in thought about all things extra-terrestrial, I spotted the next checkpoint and as per usual I tried to speed up and look impressive and, as per usual, entered the checkpoint hobbling, waddling and looking like a sack of shit.

However, this checkpoint had a rather nice surprise: we were all handed a can of Coke, not just any old can of Coke but COCA COLA, it was the real thing! I know, I know, but let me assure you that Coca Cola during a desert race is a truly wonderful thing. It is, I am certain, how Ambrosia would taste to Zeus himself, truly food of the Gods, well, maybe not, but you get the idea. It was very welcome and very much appreciated by all of us.

Moving on from the checkpoint the terrain was now a little better and it was now that some of the faster runners were catching me. They had started about an hour after us, just to try and get the runners finishing closer together.

The elite runners in any Ultra I have done have always impressed the hell out of me - they seem to run so well without pain or clumsiness:- a lovely economical, consistent pace that often beggars belief, as good on the last day as they were on the first. I carried on still following the little pink flags, occasionally being overtaken. Every so often I would lift my head and scan the horizon, trying to work out what lay ahead. On this particular horizon-scanning session, I saw something up ahead that looked very out of place, rock climbers. I did a double take, had a slurp of water and checked again, but they were real and still climbing. I smiled to myself and thought that they were even more crazy than us. The wall they were climbing looked horrible. I was either mesmerised or just glad to have something to take my mind of the monotony. I couldn't take my eyes off them. The flags were leading us towards the climbers and then a horrid thought occurred: the flags were leading us TO, not toward, the wall and the fact was that they were not climbers, but runners, became blatantly obvious the nearer I got!

Oh my God, they actually want us to climb the steepest wall, of what appeared to be the most hard-packed sand I had ever seen. One of those moments when I didn't know what to do, should I slow down and conserve as much energy as I should or speed up and get the bloody thing over and done with? I chose the latter.

I eventually reached the bottom and it looked even worse than I thought close up: it wasn't far off being vertical. I plucked up some courage, shortened my walking poles and proceeded to climb, using poles and legs in unison. Taking very small steps I inched my way forward. It was a tough and unforgiving climb. My heart rate went through the roof, my already tired legs were in agony, but inch by slow painful inch climbed higher. When I reached what I guessed to be halfway I stopped and turned around and could see runners heading toward the wall of death! I smiled to myself and continued. Eventually the severity of the climbing got less, until finally it levelled off before descending. After a few minutes I spotted the next checkpoint about a kilometre away.

I arrived just as someone was leaving and I promptly grabbed the now vacant chair - my days of being a gentleman were over. Normally, I would have asked. Vacant - it was MINE ALL MINE. I refilled my water bottles, moaned to anyone who was listening about the climb and then 5 minutes after arriving I sauntered off just as the two Danes who were in the same tent as me arrived. They were moaning about the climb far more eloquently than I.

The terrain was now flat and consequently the going was a lot easier, it was now late afternoon. I tried to speed up, hoping to get to the next checkpoint before it got dark. I even managed to catch four runners though this was tempered by the fact that at least four runners passed me. We were now in what I guessed to be a valley and after a while we turned right and onto what seemed like a dried up river bed. I continued on, all the time looking out for the next checkpoint. It was now early evening and starting to get dark. I was just deciding should I stop and get my head torch and fleece out, when I spotted the checkpoint. With just one more checkpoint left before the finish I quickly got organised:- head torch on, lightweight fleece on and flashing red light attached to my rucksack on, a quick fill of my water bottle and I was gone.

Green glowing snapsticks had now replaced the little pink flags, marking the way. We followed a stony track that climbed and climbed. Though I had felt reasonably strong all day, after an hour or so I could feel myself slowing down. This was confirmed by the fact that people were now overtaking me. I still felt good but had just lost whatever small amount of speed I had possessed. The track continued right and seemed to be going in a huge circle that disappeared into a mountain range. Entering the range there was a small but steep climb and then the checkpoint. This was a fantastic one and had been kitted out for people who were going to stay the night. Plenty of room and plenty of staff, it was mighty tempting to stay longer than was necessary. It was now, according to the race handbook, only 9.4 difficult kms to the end. I pushed on and promptly spent the next half an hour telling myself I should have stayed longer.

Leaving the checkpoint there was an immediate and challenging climb, whatever small reserves of energy I possessed were now rapidly being used up. I plodded on and was very aware that I was being overtaken by lots of runners. There was nothing I could do about it but accept it and grind out the kms. The climbing was constant and I remembered what the race handbook had said about this last little bit, it was very difficult. And I had always thought that it was the British that had mastered the art of the understatement! After finally reaching the top, I was looking forward to the descent. However, the route down was challenging, twisting, turning, maze-like channels that led downward. Fortunately, the steep narrow channel walls were so narrow that you could place a hand on either side, and lower yourself gently down. The overhanging rocks were now becoming more numerous until eventually they blocked out the entire night sky.

Not only did they block out the sky, they were also getting lower and lower, until eventually I was forced onto my knees. The whole adventure had suddenly changed from a running race to a crash course in Speleology (the scientific study of caves). Crawling along on hands and knees, the way out was marked by green snapsticks. I obediently followed, occasionally scraping my back. I could feel my poor old quads tightening up. I needed to get out quick, then just add to my misery - a Dutch girl crawled past me, looking and sounding as if she was enjoying herself. We got out the other side and continued on then turning a tight corner, we came face to face with a severe drop, so severe that we were given instructions by the waiting race crew that we were to wait and climb down one at a time with the help of a crew member! I was now so desperate to finish, that even my macho pride gratefully accepted any help offered even by a girl! The Dutch girl went first, slowly and with clear concise instructions, she reached the bottom and then I started my descent, the crew member explaining where hand and footholds were. My tired muscles were now rebelling and each time I found a foothold and put my weight on my already overused muscles they started shaking and quivering. To the casual observer it must have looked as if I was shaking and quaking with fear. This whole descending route had by now turned into one huge adventure playground. Climbing, crawling and sliding down on my arse, it was certainly one of the more entertaining races that I had taken part in. Once I reached the bottom, I was told that there were just 2 km to go. Once I emerged from the rocky maze, it was just a short hop to the campsite Kari Gorge. Arriving at approx 01:30 I was surprised to see that my wife was up and waiting. The whole camp was very busy, with runners eating and telling war stories. After something to eat and drink and a few slightly exaggerated war stories of my own it was bedtime.

Day 6 The last day - 10km

The last day of the Atacama Crossing was, at 10km, the shortest last day of any Ultra I had done. Breakfast was a very unhurried and somewhat relaxed affair, owing to the late start, with just 6 miles to go. The race was scheduled to finish at lunchtime in the town square in San Pedro de Atacama.

The slowest runners would start at 09:00, the middle runners (me) went at 10:00 and the super fast racing snakes left at 10:45. I wanted to get the day's running over and done with as quickly as I could, so had set myself a little challenge:- not only would I attempt to run the whole 10km non stop, I also would try and do it without being overtaken by any of the group that would start 45 minutes after me. At breakfast the whole camp was a hive of activity, the race crew were sorting the camp out and packing, the racers were doing the same sorting themselves out and packing.

Both groups were excited and happy for a job well done. Once the first group started to make their way to the start line, it became very noticeable how different the runners were from the start line of the first day. Then, the runners had been dressed in clean, branded, colourful race kit. That kit had now been replaced by grimy, dusty, sweat-stained, salt-encrusted smelly, rag-like clothing!

The apprehension and slight fear that had been present on that first start line had now been replaced by big smiles and half-empty rucksacks. As the first group left, it was a somewhat bizarre spectacle. Some tried to run, some hobbled and some waddled, strange gaits and even stranger facial expressions, as blisters popped, chaffing rubbed and stiff muscles were all rudely activated! An hour later it was my turn and as the countdown began we all shuffled our way forward, 3, 2, 1 and we were off. Some sprinted off and some walked but whatever our chosen style of locomotion we all moved forward. I ran, well, sort of`ran - it was definitely meant to be a run. At home it might have been called a walk but here I could get away with calling it a run. It was slow going as the terrain was very technical: a narrow path and lots of up and downs, eventually giving way to flatter, firmer ground that led us onto a dusty track, which in turn took us toward a green belt of trees and bushes. The first part of my own private challenge was still going according to plan. I was still running, however, part two was over as a couple of the faster runners caught me.

The trees and bushes were hiding various small buildings. Moving along, people, buildings and livestock were becoming more numerous and then suddenly I could hear music, clapping and cheering. People going about their daily business clapped and cheered as we went past. I was still sort of running when I spotted, up ahead, the two Danish guys from my tent. I accelerated and tried to catch them and then suddenly I was on the last little bit of road before the square. The noise was terrific. I looked up to see if I could catch the Danish guys, just in time to see them reach the finishing banner. The road I was on was getting narrower and narrower. The supporters were fantastic and a couple of minutes after the Danes, I crossed the same finishing line.

The whole square was packed full of runners' supporters and race crew, noisy and colourful music and dancers: a fantastic party-like atmosphere. It felt like the whole town had come out to see us. I crossed the line with the same old familiar feeling - one minute I was desperate to finish and the next I was sad it was all over. A medal was presented, as was a race t-shirt, pizza and Coca Cola.

Then I had a hug from my wife and a sit down in a shaded area. My shoes, like my feet, were now shredded, torn and tatty. They went into the nearest rubbish bin. The last runner finally made it. Alastair had taken 4.5 hours to cover the 10km - what were once his feet had now been replaced by bloody raw wounds. But when he crossed the finish line he wore the biggest smile of us all!

The Atacama Crossing was a fantastic if not tough race. Incredibly well organised, the route was the best marked route I had ever seen. Crew were helpful and friendly. Not the cheapest desert run but I would recommend it - maybe not as a first one because, in my opinion, it is a toughie.

WHAT NEXT !

Approaching the finish line.

*Approaching
a check point.*

The author and his wife, Marilyn, 2nd and 3rd from right.

They're off.

THE NORSEMAN
EXTREME TRIATHLON 2010

What is it: Ironman distance Extreme triathlon

When: August

Where: Norway

Distance: 250km (155 miles)

It is: Simply the world's toughest Triathlon

See: nxtri.com

This Ironman distance Triathlon has a fearsome reputation, but having said that, I consider any triathlon to be fearsome.

As if swimming 2:4 miles, cycling 112 miles and then for good measure running the marathon distance of 26:2 miles are not enough, the Norseman for some unknown reason makes each of those three just a little bit more challenging.

Take the swim for example. It starts in the dark, it's in a Norwegian fjord and has jellyfish to keep you company, oh, and did I mention the fact that you have to jump off a car ferry, much like walking the plank of days gone by.

If you survive the jump, the jelly fish, the cold and the distance, you will be allowed to get on your bike and cycle the equivalent of a mountain stage in the Tour de France. Then and only then have you earned the privilege of running the marathon, only this marathon finishes on the summit of a mountain.

So when I started looking for a challenge that was a little different from my usual ultras, I decided to have a bash at an Ironman distance triathlon. Only me being me, I decided to have a go at the toughest. After doing a bit of research the general consensus was that the Norseman was it. Watching 'You Tube' clips of poor unfortunates leaping into the dark waters of a Norwegian fjord, cycling up things that I would have trouble walking up, before finally running up to the mountain summit of Gaustatopen convinced me that I should have a bash!

The triathlon as the name implies has three sports. I am reasonable at one: running, or should I say marathon-running.

Cycling, well, I cycle to work and back - a round trip of roughly 20 miles. Lastly, swimming, now this one could be problem, I can swim, well, when I say swim, I can get to one end of the pool without having to touch the sides!

Time to do a bit of homework: to swim 2:4 miles I would need to swim 154 lengths of my local pool. To cycle 112 miles I would need to cycle around the island (I live on the Isle of Wight) 2 and a bit times. The running, I reasoned, would take care of itself.

The more I studied the Norseman the more I realised what a beast it was. The two triathlons I had previously done were completed by huffing and bluffing my way round. The Norseman, however, was an entirely different proposition. I would still be huffing but there would be absolutely no chance of bluffing.

With this in mind I decided to splash out on a Triathlon Training Manual, written by an experienced former Ironman athlete, who was now a very well-respected Ironman coach.

The book arrived and like an enthusiastic student I set about studying it, applying a vigour that I had not used since my school days.

The book was comprehensive and detailed and it seemed to have been written by an academic:- flow charts, pie charts, graphs and spread sheets. I was introduced to new words such as macrocycle, mesocycle, lactate threshold and muscle capillary density. It was a very impressive peace of work.

Unfortunately, however, I'm a man whose eyes glaze over when trying to decipher the instructions for flat-pack furniture, a man who has yet to unravel the complexities of even the simplest instruction manuals.

I persevered, I tried and employed the same determination and focus that I had used during my previous Ultra-distance races. I slogged on and chipped away at it.

But then, alas, it happened, the submaximum heart rate, VO2 max, lactate threshold, base level this and anaerobic that, charts and graphs measuring velocity and critical power output was all too much: my head exploded!

I got up, put the book away and went for a run.

I gave up on the studying for two reasons:- 1 - I hadn't got a clue what they were talking about, and 2 - I wasn't enjoying it.

The Norseman is held in August, a year from now, so I should, if disciplined enough, be able to still train for it. I cherry-picked bits from the book and used it as a guide only. I was back on track.

Spend the next 12 months training, easy.

I was keenly aware that my previous two triathlons had been completed on a mixture of luck and bluff. Fitness and stubbornness were my two main assets - they had been enough, just, to get me to the finish line.

The Norseman was different - any flaws in my training would soon be exposed and the price for any such flaws would be high.

The Norseman, in a word, commanded respect. I would need to train properly, a real Ironman training schedule is what I needed to focus on. The kit would have to be spot on and according to the race rules I would need to provide a support crew.

First things first, a training schedule. With this in mind I cherry-picked what I thought to be the relevant bits, drew up a plan of action and started training.

The one fly in the ointment was the fact that nine weeks after The Norseman I would be racing across the Kalahari Desert in a race called Augrabies Extreme Ultra Marathon and fourteen weeks after that I would be in the Yukon to race in a 430 mile race called the Yukon Arctic Ultra.

So, unfortunately, my running would have to take priority.

Training for so many tough events was pushing my luck a bit. I couldn't afford to get injured and I couldn't afford to skip sessions. As is always the case, training, working and being a husband (those 3 things are not in any particular order, HONEST) is always going to be difficult and so it proved.

My wife works unsociable shifts and runs marathons and half-marathons with the occasional triathlon so was sort of understanding about the training. So I could either train when she was at work or train when she trains.

Time was still tight and required the skills of a master juggler. Fortunately the training was progressing nicely, with regular 60 mile bike rides and regular 100 length session in the pool, with an occasional open water swim.

As The Norseman crept ever closer so my training increased, maxing out with a 110 length swim session which was done a couple of times and a 104 mile bike ride which I did on 4 occasions.

I felt good, I felt confident, I was ready.

Arriving at Eidfiord, the small Norwegian town that was once again to host The Norseman, and meeting the other athletes I suddenly wondered if I hadn't once again, bitten off more than I could chew. There were some very fit-looking athletes here, all with stories of multi Ironman races, and previous Norsemans.

Too late now - we will see tomorrow.

The Race

Arriving at the ferry in the dark and wearing a wetsuit, I for some bizarre reason, was not in the least bit nervous. After a while people started making their way up onto the deck. It was still dark and the lights in the town of Eijdfjord were twinkling away like the stars in the sky - they certainly appeared to be the same distance away. I made my way to the ramp, that had now become an impromptu diving board. It was some 4 meters above the water, the intention being to recce the thing before getting my head round the fact that I was about to jump off a Norwegian ferry at daft o'clock in the morning. However, things conspired against me, the ramp was slippery and wet. The moment I stepped on to the thing I was committed to the jump. The swim booties I was wearing afforded no traction, in other words I couldn't get back up and so it was a very undignified start. As I left the ferry I seemed to be suspended in space - it took ages to hit the water and if I thought it took ages to hit the water it took bloody ages to hit the surface.

It was now that I realised the 2:4 mile swim was at least 400 meters longer, it was at least that distance to the start line. As I turned back to the lights on the ferry it reminded me of the scene in the film the Titanic, when passengers were jumping for their lives.

As the last of the athletes made their way over to the start, we were guided into position by kayakers and then bang on 05:00 the ship's horn sounded and the Norseman 2010 was officially under way.

I settled into a nice steady pace and by steady I mean slow. However, as I glanced back I could see many swimmers way behind. I swam along and some time later looked behind and saw half a dozen or so swimmers. One of them was actually doing backstroke. At about half way I realised that I was last.

I could now see the finish line which was right outside a large hotel, the Hotel Voss. However, as I tried to swim toward it, the kayakers had other ideas and kept guiding me to the right. Eventually I lost site of the finish. Then I saw the reason: a marker buoy that I had to go round. I made it round and was now just in front of the hotel. As I got to the finish I realised that I was the only swimmer in the water and had been for some time, all the kayakers were there just for me. As my feet touched the beach I needed a bit of assistance. I had been swimming for two and a half hours (my actual swim time was 2:13). As I was guided up to the first transition and helped out of my wetsuit, I could see just 2 bikes - mine and the bloke who was just leaving.

I got dressed tried to eat then left, hoping that the sooner I got going the sooner I would warm up.

It wasn't long before the climbing started. I felt good and was certain to catch the others. Last out of the swim was a first for me, so to speak. I have never been in last place (but by the same token I have never been in first place!). I knew swimming was my weakest discipline, just not that weak.

Ah well, should have trained harder. After about 60 km I realised that I had not seen a single cyclist and now that I was on a plateau and could see for miles ahead, and I still couldn't see a cyclist.

On reaching the halfway CP I saw one of the Austrian athletes who had withdrawn and I felt a bit sorry for him, but I am afraid to say, for some reason, it made me feel better.

Now we were at the halfway mark the real work could begin. Five climbs, one after the other, the longest of the climbs was some 10 km long. Bizarrely, it was whilst on the climbs that I not only saw my first cyclist but actually caught him - this cat and mouse continued. I caught him while climbing, only for him to pass me on the descent and the flat. Eventually the climbing ended and the long 30 km descent began, full of switchbacks and very technical: great care was needed.

My cycling is a lot like my running. I can climb pretty well but when it comes to descending I am a wuss, very slow and overly cautious. It annoys the hell out of me because I always lose so much time.

Ah well, I was now watching the distance markers counting down to the next transition. Then turning a corner, there it was - The Norseman banner and flags indicating the transition.

On arriving I was greeted by my support crew and told "You'll have to hurry, you've got 7 minutes." After spending a little over 9 hours cycling and knowing that most of those precious 7 minutes would be required to just get me off the bike, I made a decision that I had never made before in 14 years of racing some of the toughest races in the world:- I withdrew, scratched, pulled out, retired, whatever name you want to give it. I knew that with what the swimming had taken out of me and the 9 hour monster bike ride, a mountain marathon was one step too far. I knew with my hand on my heart that I hadn't trained enough and had grossly overestimated my ability.

Glad that swimming is over - wish I had trained harder!

Above - not only was I last out of the water, but I was having a bad hair day.

I was lulling the others into a false sense of security by giving them all a head start!

THE AUGRABIES EXTREME ULTRA MARATHON 2010

What is it: Ultra-distance Desert stage footrace

When: October

Where: South Africa, the Northern Cape Province

Distance: 155 miles (250km)

It is: Bloody hot and bloody tough

See: extrememarathons.com

This was another one of those races that I'd had my eye on for some time.

The race is held every October, in the Augrabies National Park. A stunningly beautiful area located in the Northern Cape Province of South Africa.

I flew out with Nic, a friend and fellow Ultra-race enthusiast. After a long 11 hour flight to Johannesburg, we were met at the airport by Ed, the British race representative and lover of the race - a race that he had entered and completed 4 times.

Me being me and thus able to apply a simpleton's logic, reasoned that the race couldn't be that bad if someone was prepared to return time and time again!

Whilst at the hotel, a few of the other racers started to arrive and as usual it was a complete mixed bag. The one thing we did have in common was the fact that we were all a little nervous.

The next day was a long drive to the Augrabies National

Park. Arriving late afternoon we were presented with our race number, chalet key and, most important of all, our 'goodie bag'. I don't know what it is about the goodie bag but they always seem to bring out the child in me. I played it cool and resisted the urge to look inside. Once inside the chalet however, I would be like a seven year-old at Christmas: desperate to look inside, to see what goodies I've got.

After a quick introduction and brief chat about the dos and don'ts, we were shown our chalet. On entering the chalet the first thing I noticed was the bed. Now I like Nic, I consider him a friend, but there are limits to our friendship and sharing a bed is most definitely not within those limits. I was rapidly forming a plan as to whether we should paper scissor rock, or toss a coin for it, when he pointed out that it was in fact two singles pushed together!

During the registration we got a good look at the other runners and there were some tough-looking South Africans and some very lean-looking racing snakes.

More than once we were told to be careful of the monkeys that roam around and live close to the chalets. They had been brought up living with tourists and consequently have little fear of humans and are opportunist thieves. They will nick anything that they can get their hands on, and more than once they have been seen running through the campsite with their ill-gotten gains which include absolutely anything from glasses, underwear, hats and bits of food - including energy gels and sweets.

During the registration we showed the race crew the bits of kit that we were obliged to have:- sleeping bag, compass, first aid etc, and then we had our rucksacks weighed. Mine weighed in at 7 kilos, a weight that I could only dream of achieving in my earlier desert races. It looked as if I was finally getting the hang of this desert racing malarkey.

The shoes I had decided to wear were made by the British company called UK Gear, I had first seen these specialist desert shoes with their shoe, gaiter combination, during last year's Atacama Crossing. A guy called Mark Cockbain was wearing them. Mark is a very experienced and well respected Ultra Runner. He is not only sponsored by UK Gear but also told me that they were without doubt the best desert racing shoe he had ever worn. If they were good enough for him they would, I reasoned, be good enough for me! Standing at the start line the following day, my shoe gaiter combination was attracting a lot of attention. I fully understood why - the knee-high gaiters were the same colour as the shoes and it looked as if I was wearing wellies.

Once we were all on the start line, the usual nervous waffle began and, as usual, as soon as the countdown began, the waffle died down. The cameramen and women jostled for position, 3, 2, 1, and we were off. Clapping and cheering, cameras clicking and runners doing their usual running whist trying to look good for that all important photograph, and, as usual, as soon as the photographers were out of sight a more sensible pace was adopted and for some that pace was walking.

It was already bloody hot and thankfully this first day was not too long at 28km, however, I decided that I would like to get the day over and done with as quickly as possible - the less time I spent in the baking heat the better.

My photographers' posing run felt good and reasonably comfortable and I decided to keep it going for as long as I could. I found myself running with a small group, the pace was comfortable so I decided to hang around with them for a while. That was until one of the group who was experiencing all sorts of problems slowed the group down for the third time to retrieve another dropped piece of kit. My very limited patience got dropped with it and I carried on, on my own.

The terrain was a mixture of jeep tracks, small, steep undulating hills one after the other (requiring constant climbing and descending) loose gravel and sharp tricky rocks. It was technical running at its best, every step needed concentration.

I continued running and all the time kept an eye out for the route markers. It was hot and slowly getting hotter, reaching

42 degrees at one of the checkpoints.

Everything felt good, the rucksack, shoes and clothing were performing well, no hot spots (areas that get hot prior to a blister developing). I was using a camelbak that contained an electrolyte drink and in my hand I carried a 750ml bottle of water - the theory being that I would be able to top up just my water bottle in seconds as opposed to the minutes it would take to refill a camelbak.

I was doing well and felt comfortable. No-one had overtaken me, however, about three km from the finish line I was overtaken by the group I had been running with earlier. They looked strong, too strong for me. I know my pace and I was running at a pace I knew I could maintain for a long time. Unfortunately, the problem with that pace is that there is no acceleration: I could only watch the group go.

I carried on trying to work out my overall position in the field and then about a kilometre from the end, the bite valve, a small rubber mouthpiece that fits on to the end of the drinking straw on the camelbak, came off and fell into the sand, I bent down to retrieve the thing only for the contents of the camelbak to come pouring out and onto my shoes and so it was that I finished my first days desert running with wet feet!

Arriving at the campsite I was pleasantly surprised:- it was not only in a beautiful location but the clincher was that it was on the banks of a river, a reward that I hoped would be repeated. (It wasn't!)

After a quick swim, which in turn had two important benefits: one was to cool me down and the other was to wash away the stench and grime, I made my way over to the gazebo which was to be our home throughout the race. On my way, however, I caught the faint smell of barbecued steak - the smell was wonderful and I instantly decided that the support crew were sadists, deliberately cooking steaks, so that the poor unfortunate racer with his sawdust-like concoction would cry and salivate and beg forgiveness. I was stronger than that and pretended I couldn't see or smell the wonderful aroma of freshly-cooked, juicy, barbecued steaks. I walked past the support crew area - the surprising thing was that the smell just got stronger. Then I realised that it wasn't the support crew at all, but some of our so-called fellow racers, the bastards had the foresight to bring with them, for a first night treat, some vacuum-packed steaks.

I reflected on the first day, and for me it had been textbook - everything had gone perfectly, I was in a good position, had no blisters, no hot spots or chaffing.

I lay there eating my rather unappetising rehydrated pack of sawdust, when I suddenly realised that so-called perfect day hadn't been as mishap-free as I had thought. My inflatable mattress had developed a slow puncture. I quickly realised that the puncture had occurred because I had strapped it to the top of my rucksack and brushed against a camelthorn. These nasty thorn-laden bushes wait for the unsuspecting innocent Ultra-distance runner to brush past and then attack, by shredding anything that touches it - clothes, skin or inflatable mattresses. This could be a disaster - the ground was rock hard, no mattress would mean no sleep. The whole thing left me feeling a little deflated, sorry, I couldn't help it!

I located the hole and set about repairing the thing with duct tape. It sort of worked, but, in reality, the slow puncture became just a little slower.

Unfortunately, not everyone had had such a good day: one of the girls had missed one of the route markers and ventured off the route. This consequently had added another 8 miles to her total distance. Not only that, she had frightened herself and knocked her self-confidence. The 42 degree heat and the fact she was low on water, combined with not knowing where the hell she was had really scared her. It was only when one of the race crew realised that she was not where she should have been that he worked out where she could have gone wrong. He then back tracked and luckily found the now distraught but relieved runner, he then guided her back onto the proper trail.

As the last runner came in, at a time of six and a half hours - as opposed to the first person who came in at two hours eleven minutes - we all cheered them in.

The first casualty of the race was a heatstroke victim, though he had made it across the finish line the race medics were a little concerned and checked him out, and to err on the side of caution were taken to the local hospital where the decision was made to not allow the runner to continue.

Day 2

Today the race organisers had decided to split the race start into two groups: the slower runners would be starting an hour before the faster ones. For some reason I had been classed as one of the faster runners and was in the second group. The theory was that all the runners would be finishing closer together, rather than being so spread out.

The first kilometre was beautiful and straightforward - a run along the riverbank, the calm before the storm. After a while we turned left, which I thought a little surprising because there wasn't a left or, should I say, that the left was actually a sheer wall of rock and looking at the group ahead I saw, to my horror, route markers attached to the rocks above.

I arrived at the foot of the wall we were now expected to scale. Within a few minutes I was using my arms and hands as much as my feet, and the fact that I was actually breathing out of my arse was a sure sign that I should have trained a bit harder for this climbing malarkey.

Some of the runners that had started an hour before us looked decidedly uncomfortable. It was hard laborious work. Finally I reached what I hoped was the top, and low and behold, checkpoint one. A few people were there taking a breather - I just left as quickly as I could. Today was a lot cooler than yesterday, and once I left the checkpoint and back onto the now easy to read trail I picked up the pace, not by much but enough.

It wasn't long before I was catching and passing a few of the slower runners.

The route markings were okay as long as you were vigilant, and being not only a coward who was frightened of getting lost, but also lazy enough to not want to do any more than was absolutely necessary, consequently I was very vigilant indeed.

Like yesterday, I was feeling good - no signs of blisters or chafing, the heat was okay and the terrain not too bad.

A nice steady, sensible pace and I finally reached the finish line. No riverside campsite today, so it was just a question of collecting my water and making myself a meal - well, pouring and stirring myself a meal. Whilst eating and waiting for the last few runners to arrive we sat around talking bollocks and catching up on the gossip. Apparently, the guy who came in first place yesterday missed one of the trail markers (reassuring that even the elite guys make mistakes) and had ended up doing an extra six km and he came in 27 minutes behind his arch rival.

Two more runners were out. One guy got to checkpoint one but could go no further, he had suffered with the heat yesterday and had not yet fully recovered. Arriving at the first checkpoint the medics immediately pulled him from the race and placed him on an intravenous drip, and then took him back to the lodges to recover. The second casualty was for blisters: blisters are the bane of a desert runners' life and I am sure that he will not be the only one to suffer with them.

Day 3

Today's stage was 30km. The terrain was now becoming more desert-like with a lot more sand. Running on sand is always hard work and energy-sapping. My shoe gaiter combination was holding up well and doing a great job of protecting my feet. I felt good and was making good progress. Plodding along and trying to take in the sheer beauty of the place I noticed some rather strange-looking objects in the trees. The trees weren't huge: maybe 20, 25 feet high but they had in them massive nests, these nests reaching about two metres in diameter are more like small towns to the hundreds of weaver birds that nest in them, community living at its best.

After taking a few photographs, I carried on. The temperature was slowly rising and I was glad to get to the campsite. This campsite was another beauty, sitting in a small clearing and in the shadow of a giant monolith, a huge clump of free-standing rock.

I chilled out eating and drinking whilst watching the youngsters who, with their surplus energy and bravado, were busy climbing the thing. I thought about joining them, but knowing my luck, would have fallen off, so I chose instead to have an extra helping of apple and custard pudding!

Day 4

Today was the day that every desert runner gets apprehensive about: the Long Day, at 76km, and with the forecast being for a hot one, there was a real sense of foreboding going around the campsite. Like the previous days there was to be a staggered start - only this time the groups were smaller and more numerous. The organisers were very aware of the tremendous difference in the runners' ability and they would in all probability be reaching the finish line as much as 10/12 hours apart. With this thought in mind the first group would be departing at 06:00 and the last group (the fast racing snakes) would leave at 13:00 - a full 7 hours later.

The group I was in was the 11:00 group. I was a little annoyed because I had wanted leave a little earlier knowing that I would be starting in just about the hottest part of the day.

I was in a bit of a dilemma:- my pride and ego wanted to push hard and fast, but I was very aware that in 14 weeks I would be racing some 430 miles in the Yukon Arctic Ultra. I needed to be in reasonable shape to complete that race, I didn't want to knacker myself completely.

As each of the small groups left, the temperature crept up. When my group left we were told that it was 48 degrees.

As we left I formulated a 'cunning plan':- I would run non-stop for the first three checkpoints. No matter how slow, and no matter how painful I would not stop running until I got to the checkpoint. Another part of my little self-motivational exercise would be that I would not get caught by the two guys who were leading the race until at least 18:00 and they would be starting at 13:00 - some two hours after me.

It was these little personal challenges that I needed to survive the long painful hours ahead. If I had nothing to focus on, except the monotonous miles, pain and misery, my day would automatically become just that bit harder. I really wanted to, needed to, not make the day ahead any harder than it already was.

As 11:00 approached, we took our positions on the start line, shook hands wished each other good luck, bon voyage, and sterkte. With the pleasantries over with, it was time to get going.

Immediately after starting, a couple of the guys shot off. I followed, albeit at a more sensible pace. I was very conscious of the difficult 76 km ahead.

We were running on a reasonably run-friendly jeep track and I quickly lost sight of the two lead guys. I wasn't too sure how far behind the other runners were because, as usual, I refused to look behind.

I plodded along, comfortable with the pace and before I knew it, the first checkpoint came into view. Quickly topping up my water bottle and pinching a sneaky look behind confirmed that there was no-one there. I was both surprised and pleased.

I still felt comfortable and the terrain, though initially sandy, started to become rocky and easier to run on. My legs felt fine and strong, my feet felt the same and still had no hotspots or blisters. The fly in the ointment was the heat. I have raced in hot places before but this was by far the hottest day's racing I had ever done. The sand had all but disappeared and now the rocky, gravelly track (though easier to run) became undulating. Small challenging little climbs broke the rhythm.

Checkpoint two arrived and not a moment too soon:- the heat

was so intense that I was drinking water at an alarming rate. It was a catch 22 situation. Do I run faster to get to each checkpoint quickly, a consequence of which is to drink faster to keep cool, or go slower and conserve my water and lessen my chance of overheating?

Mulling all this over, I decided to just stick to my original plan:- after all, it was working and I felt good. I carried on, finally reaching checkpoint three. I left quickly, trying to look fresh. However the moment I was out of sight I started walking, mixing walking with running. I plodded along and after a while I realised that my water bottle was nearly empty. It wasn't a problem because I still had my camelbak which contained an electrolyte drink. Unfortunately, it was warm, a somewhat sickly sweet, syrupy infusion. It was not pleasant but it would have to do. I carried on only taking the occasional sip, then I remembered that I had a couple of fruit pastilles. I popped one into my mouth and, wow, never has a single fruit pastille tasted so nice - it made me smile, lifted my morale and tasted wonderful. Fruit pastilles, like Peter Kay's garlic bread, are the future.

I was bloody relieved to get to checkpoint four. I topped up my camelbak with lovely cool water, topped up my water bottle and drank like there was no tomorrow. I think that my running out of water had given me a bit of a scare; running out of water in this heat was both stupid and frightening - I vowed to be more careful.

Moving along towards the next checkpoint I came across a race crew member taking pictures. He told me that it was 52 degrees - no bloody wonder I was suffering. For some rather bizarre reason I thanked him.

Arriving at checkpoint five was a blessed relief - it was now late in the afternoon and I decided that I would take a twenty minute break. I still had a long way to go. Unfortunately when I got there, I was met by a scene of absolute carnage - it was like arriving at a battlefield hospital triage unit: there were bodies lying about everywhere, strange, twisted contortions - some suffering from cramp, some pouring water over themselves, some puking. A couple were just sitting staring at nothing in particular. Every bit of shaded area had some poor soul desperately trying to avoid the sun, staff were wetting bits of cloth to place on the overheated runners. Shoes and socks lay scattered about, t-shirts, hats and bits of blister dressing were on the floor. Some were trying to patch themselves up, before leaving.

I just wanted to get the hell out of there. There were two reasons for my rapid exit, one, was purely mercenary: I could take advantage of the carnage that lay before me and improve my position in the race, and the second reason was fear, fear that if I stayed I would convince myself that I too really needed a slightly longer rest or should sort myself out and take a bit of time to recover and cool down, or it would be better to leave when it cooled down a bit.

I left and I thought about the distance ahead, (a little over 30km). It should, I reasoned, be an easier 30km than the last 30. With the sun gone it should be cooler.

The dusty track I was now on came to an abrupt end, it was time to stop daydreaming and switch on: which way do I go? I looked around and finally spotted up ahead some marker tape. I followed what had now become a small road.

The road was pretty good and seemed to be well used, consequently I decided to take full advantage and speed up. I made all the right moves, pumping my arms etc but the reality was that I may well have been walking in a running style.

Now that I was confident I was going in the right direction I could resume my daydreaming. Unfortunately this was short-lived. I heard a vehicle coming up behind me, instinctively I moved over not wanting to get run over, then bugger me if the thing didn't slow down right behind me. I could hear loud music coming from within, the car pulled up, rolled down the windows and just as I had in Jordan a few years earlier I thought I was going to get mugged. But no, they asked if I was okay and did I want a lift? I explained that I was in a race and that I was fine, I thanked them for their concern, they wished me well, wound up the windows and shot off as if it were the most natural thing in the world to see a fifty year old Englishman traipsing through the African desert at night.

I carried on with my daydreaming and again was interrupted, this time by one of the lead runners who came storming past looking very strong. We gave each other a thumbs up and I thought at least I had achieved both my little projects.

A few minutes after, another vehicle came up behind me, this time it was a race support vehicle - they slowed down, asked how I was and disappeared. I followed their little red back lights as they moved further and further ahead. After a while they turned left and then disappeared. I now knew the route ahead would be turning to the left. I carried on and tried to speed up but, as usual, failed miserably - then I spotted some lights and hoped against hope that they belonged to the next checkpoint.

As I got closer to the lights I realised that they were in fact part of a small farmhouse and then I spotted the markers that informed me that this was indeed the race checkpoint.

I sat on the veranda taking a five minute break, when suddenly another runner appeared. Owen was one of the faster runners but now he looked like a beaten man. He said that he had struggled all day and the intense heat had really taken it out of him and he had been slowly cooked throughout the day. He had a quick drink and was gone, eager to make up some time now that it was a little cooler.

I left a few minutes after, and even though it was now nighttime the heat was still there: even with the slight breeze that was now blowing it was still bloody hot.

Following what I guessed was a sandy jeep track, I felt good, navigating wasn't too bad. Every so often I could make out bits of marker tape, gently fluttering, making a noise and casting curious shadows. Every now and then a flashing red LED light would confirm that we were still going in the right direction.

Arriving at the next checkpoint I was asked how I was and how were the blisters? I said I felt fine and good (I would never admit to anyone that I felt like a bag of cack!) and then rather smugly I told them that I hadn't got any blisters.

Shortly after leaving the checkpoint I tried to pick up the pace. However, it was a rather short-lived affair and didn't last long. Not only had the running slowed down but I was now having to walk. Then I felt that old familiar feeling:- hotspots - I was now having to pay the price for being a smug git, and saying I hadn't got any blisters. They were now well and truly on their way.

On the plus side, the hotspots gave me something to think about, other than the monotony of the night time miles. At least during the day, there were distractions to be had: the beauty of the landscape, the wildlife and even the other runners. At night, just the darkness and the trail. I plodded on, one marker at a time, creeping ever closer to the end.

Suddenly the next checkpoint came into view, it seemed to be quite busy. A couple of the girls were there and they seemed to be somewhat fatigued and sounded even worse. I planned to stay just long enough to top up my water bottle, then leave asap. As I was screwing on the top of my water bottle one of the girls asked me how long I planned to stay. I told her that I wasn't staying, I was leaving now. She then said that her friend was struggling and was having a bit of a break, and that she wasn't confident in travelling alone at night - so could she run with me for a bit? I told her that it would be okay and she was welcome.

We moved off together and she immediately apologised for her rather strange gait. She went on to explain that everything hurt, she had blisters, backache, sunburn and God knows what else - she had also developed a touch of verbal diarrhoea: she just couldn't stop talking - she talked and talked. What she was talking about I had no idea and I am sure that if I'd had the balls to ask her she wouldn't have known either. I decided that her incessant chatter was her way of coping with the pain and misery that she was going through, so being the gentleman that I am I let her waffle away. Having been married for twenty-five years, I put into practice my best 'pretend to be listening' skills. It worked, she never suspected a thing - or she was too knackered to care.

The track we were on eventually led us down to some industrial-type buildings, slightly to our left and with cultivated foliage all around. We guessed we were now passing through a vineyard - as we were looking around trying to figure things out, we spotted, coming up behind us, a couple of runners. One was my companion's friend and she now looked a whole lot better than the corpse-like figure we had left behind at the checkpoint. The other was a member of the race crew, who had completed the race the previous year and was now helping out, and so it was that I found myself in the company of three women. It could have been a whole lot worse it could have been three blokes.

Now we moved along as a little group, following a fence line and safe in the knowledge that we had nearly finished. As we ambled along using the fence as our guide, we suddenly spotted a parked car - inside were three sleeping bodies. At least we all hoped they were sleeping bodies and not just bodies. As we peered inside the car, our headlights must have woken them up. When finally they were awake enough, they said that they were part of the race crew and were here to point us in the right direction and show us over the stile. I looked around and spotted a huge nine foot high stile - we were to climb over the thing.

The stile itself was not a problem, the problem was me: being the gentleman I elected to go last and help the now knackered, slightly un-coordinated ladies over it. It wasn't as easy as it may sound, as every time I looked up my head torch shone at places that ladies would prefer a bloke's head torch not to shine.

I felt awkward like some old pervert, but hey, we all got over the thing without incident. After about half an hour we finally reached the campsite and the finishing line, each of us glad to have survived the 76km long blast furnace.

Even though it was a little after midnight when we arrived, the camp was a hive of activity. Many of the runners were in but an equal amount were still out on the course. Some of the slower runners had already been out for over 18 hours - in many ways they were the real heroes. Yes, the fast runners were bloody impressive and great athletes, worthy of our respect but the slower runners are out on the course for twice as long and their recovery time was that much shorter owing to their earlier starts.

They are also great athletes, not as fast but none the less just as tough and equally impressive. After a quick bite to eat, I found myself a space and settled down for some much-needed sleep.

Day 5

Today was a rest day - a chance to recover and sort out and patch up the injured bits. My injured bits were just a couple annoying of blisters, I couldn't moan too much, because, compared to some of the runners, I had got off relatively lightly.

Looking around the campsite was interesting: it looked like a battle had just taken place and a few weary survivors were now aimlessly wandering around, limping and waddling in what appeared to be a state of utter confusion.

It wasn't the best campsite we'd had, but it was a day off and, as usual, on one of these days off, I would try to rest, but keep moving, eat and drink as much as I could and then indulge in the traditional tale-swapping, war and horror stories of yesterday's epic. Like the three main characters in the film Jaws, we each told each other of the horrors experienced and the superhuman effort required to overcome such an horrendous day.

I spent most of the day just lying around eating, going through my rucksack to try to get rid of the things I now knew I wouldn't be needing. With just two more days to go I only needed one more meal, but I still had loads, so I set about eating the two apple and custard puddings, the two shepherds pies and the rice pudding as well as two packets of fruit pastilles.

Another job that needed my attention was my feet - the two

annoying blisters needed popping, cleaning and dressing. By mid afternoon I was fed, watered, patched and ready for the next stage.

Day 6

At 46km - not exactly a short day, but at least it was a little cooler. As the various groups departed, the camp became quieter and more sombre. People were packing up and I'm sure that the lead runners were working out what needed to be done to either improve or maintain their present position. Today we were warned that there were some tricky navigational sections so we had to be switched on and concentrate at all times. I decided to use my tried and trusted old navigational trick and just keep close to some ne who knew what they were doing!

As my small group left, the four of us were pretty evenly-matched and, barring a catastrophe, whatever our present position was now, it was unlikely to change.

The good thing was that the furnace-like conditions of the last day's running were now gone. Another good thing was that because I had to concentrate and would have to work hard to be in the company of others (in case I got lost) the day should in theory not be monotonous or boring - thereby making the day go that much quicker. Well, that was the theory.

Today's route seemed to be a complete mixture of terrain: one minute we were running along nice jeep tracks, then a sudden off would find us running on what appeared to be a dried up river. Then, just as quickly we would be climbing out of the riverbed and onto to stony tracks and then just to make things a little more interesting, we would be running on some really difficult, tricky sections - sections that the race director had euphemistically called 'technical'.

Arriving at checkpoint two without any major mishaps ie getting lost, was a blessed relief. Unfortunately, one of the runners was pulled from the race - what had once been the soles of his feet were now just open, raw, infected sores. How the bloke had survived thus far was beyond the rest of us and a mighty impressive feat (sorry, no pun intended). What made his withdrawal all the more galling was the fact that tomorrow was the last day: so close and yet so far.

The terrain had so far been good enough to allow me to maintain a steady pace, and by way of a bonus there was abundant wildlife. Running along with giraffes staring at you was a little bit strange and, interestingly, pleasant.

The scorching heat kept away and with the trail now runner-friendly, I managed to get a good steady pace going.

Once I spotted the campsite I tried to speed up and look all macho but as usual failed miserably. My tired old legs had other ideas and kept me at a far more sedate pace.

When I did finally manage to haul my carcass across the finish line, I thought that I deserved a little treat, so went over to the massage table and had the most wonderful massage. It was pure bliss and worth running every kilometre for.

Tomorrow was thankfully the last day. Even though it was the last day it was still an impressive 26 km, roughly 16 miles.

Day 7

This morning was the last morning of this fantastic race and, as usual, everyone was more relaxed: laughing and chatty. We all knew, bar the shouting, we would make it.

As the small groups left it was noticeable how small the rucksacks were, compared to day one - normally each group seemed reluctant to leave and trundled off slowly. Now, however, even the slowest of the runners seemed to find a fresher pair of legs and couldn't wait to get going.

As my group left, we sort of understood that the final placings were already sorted - it was a sort of gentlemen's agreement that we would run together. Nothing was actually said but we all understood it. The terrain was straight forward and really easy to navigate: small, well-used roads - nothing complicated. We plodded along, occasionally chatting, inching ever closer to the finish line.

Then we came to a rather steep hill - any chatting was now suspended as we each hauled ourselves up and over the thing. Once on the top it was a quick top up of the water bottles and then off and back to talking. We carried on as a small group, eventually reaching an area that was a little more green and fertile. Then the terrain changed: no more sandy bits and no more gravelly bits. We were now running in what appeared to be a maze of rocks.

Running on the rock meant that we could run faster - however, the solid rock we were on also meant that we really had to switch on and look for markers. There were no tracks or footprints to follow. Again, working as a small team, we each managed to pick out the markers that led the way. Eventually we came to a part of the course that we had been told about - there was a small stream that if we waded through it it would be a shorter more direct line to the finish. However, if we took a left turn it would be slightly longer and over some rocks - we all decided to keep dry feet and went over the rocks.

Dropping off the rocks and back onto a small road we became aware of the noise: people clapping and cheering and rounding a corner was the beautiful sight of the finish line. Multi-national flags adorned the route, the cheering and clapping got louder the nearer we got.

Crossing the finish line was a fantastic relief. Coca Cola, beer, sandwiches smiles and hugs were handed out to each of us.

Ironically, the fastest time of the day was by a bloke called Tim. Tim had struggled every inch of the way - I personally didn't think he would survive day two, but hey, on the last day he found a real determination or was it a real desperation? Whatever it was it worked and got him across the finish line.

The Augrabies Extreme Ultra Marathon is tough, beautiful and fascinating - an incredibly, challenging adventure. If you get the chance, give it a go - go on you know you want to.

What Next?

*Trying to look
the part of an
Ultra-distance
athlete.*

At last - the end of a tough days running!

The rock that I was too chicken to climb.

Photography by James King

One slightly cooked and shell-shocked author.

THE YUKON ARCTIC ULTRA 2011

It is not strength of body but rather strength of will which carries a man farthest where mind and body are taxed at the same time to their utmost limit.

Apsley Cherry-Garrard

"The worst journey in the world"

What is it: A multi-discipline (you choose either xc ski, foot or bike) Ultra-distance race. Single stage, cold weather race.

When: February

Where: The Yukon region of Canada

Distance: 430 miles, 690 km

It is: An extreme cold weather/mental challenge

See: arcticultra.de

---

14 weeks ago I was in the Kalahari Desert taking part in a race called the 'Augrabies Extreme Ultra Marathon'. Temperatures had at one point hit +52 degrees celsius (126 fahrenheit), it was bloody hot, and now like a fool I'm in Canada and about to take part in a race called the 'Yukon Arctic Ultra'. It's bloody cold and furthermore the temperatures are quite likely to hit -52 degrees.

The few days prior to the start had been worryingly warm.

While I was out for a little three mile run and a quick recce of the new start line (which had recently been put in place owing to there being so little snow on the original start line) I saw a dog team that had just come off the river - the very river that we would be travelling along in a couple of days' time. The worrying thing was that they were soaking wet. I made my way over to them and introduced myself, explaining that I would shortly be travelling along the river, and asked what the conditions were like.

The two mushers explained that they had just come from Braeburn (which was a race checkpoint) and for the last twenty to thirty miles they had really struggled with 'overflow' and the dogs had suffered as a consequence. It was exactly what I did not want to hear: soft, wet, slushy overflow.

Now, standing on the start line, the temperatures had fortunately dropped to -17.

Seventy-eight athletes of all shapes, sizes, ability and age stood on the start line - twenty of us now no doubt regretting our decision to race the four hundred and thirty odd miles to Dawson.

The journey would mean that we would all be following the famous Yukon Quest dog sled race.

Standing shivering, whilst at the same time trying to give the appearance of confident Ultra-distance athlete was not easy. Mulling over the route, the kit, the distance and the sheer stupidity of the challenge that lay ahead - after all, there had only ever been nine finishers.

Then the countdown - 3, 2, 1, bought me back to reality. A mixture of inexperienced anxious racers, experienced super slow plodders (my group) and uber-competitive experienced racing snakes!

We made our way along the single track and down onto the mighty Yukon River. The nervous chatter petered out as the racers themselves started to spread out.

This first part of the route was familiar as I had raced here twice before. Still in single file, we plodded along. After reaching the 13 mile mark, we were to take a left turn and onto the Tahini river. Immediately after turning we followed the trail that took us under a road bridge - this bridge had on it a few waving and cheering well-wishers.

This bridge also marked the halfway point to the first check point at Rivendale Farm. The field was now pretty stretched out. I caught a couple of runners that were doing the 100 miles to Braeburn. The race numbers that we had been issued denoted what distance we were doing, ie numbers 101 plus were doing the 100 miles, 301 plus the 300 and the 400 plus were going all the way to Dawson.

I plodded along eating chocolates. Rolos were my weapon of choice: they are the perfect size and shape and they never froze when kept in my chest pocket. This was my fourth time racing in the Arctic and I was only just getting the hang of it. The first time, I had made the mistake of bringing bars of chocolate - these granite-hard, frozen blocks are impossible to eat. Small bite-size snacks that can be kept in the pocket is without doubt, the most efficient way to eat whilst moving along the snow and ice.

I finally managed to reach the Rivendale checkpoint at 15:42. I checked in, had a quick cup of soup and checked out - a full 7 minutes after arriving. I knew from experience that this first checkpoint would get busy and congested - I just wanted to take advantage of the fact that I felt good and had no real reason to stop.

One checkpoint down, seven to go. It was now late afternoon and getting noticeably colder. The next checkpoint at Dog Grave Lake (there really is a dog's grave there) was nearly 40 miles away.

After a few miles the trail turned off the river up, onto a steep bank and into the wooded trail.

At around midnight I decided that it was bedtime, so kept my eyes peeled for the next lot of straw. These occasional clumps of straw were left over from the Yukon Quest dog sled race - the straw had been used as the dog's beds and with recycling being the in thing, I decided that they were now the perfect insulation for a weary racer to sleep on.

I found the perfect straw bed and after a cursory glance to make sure that it was poo free, I set about making myself at home. Then, just as I was getting into my sleeping bag and about to zip up, a couple of friends came past. We had a quick chat and they explained that they would bivi down about an hour from now. In that short conversation my gloveless fingers got attacked by the -35/40 temperatures and were now in agony. I quickly shoved them onto the warmest part of my body - my, well, the warmest part of my body is enough information.

Two and a half hours later I was up and on the move. Finally reaching Dog Grave Lake at 06:25. After a quick bite to eat, a top up of water bottles and Camelbak I was good to go and left the warmth of the checkpoint exactly one hour after arriving 07:25.

One of the temptations of these sort of races is the temptation to stay in the relative luxury of a checkpoint - this temptation must be fought against, a bit like the alarm clock going off and you roll over and think "Just a few more minutes" - absolutely fatal. There is a piece of advise for Ultra-distance racers that states you should never give up, drop out, or scratch at a checkpoint! It's just too damned easy, and those that do usually realise they could have gone on and consequently regret the decision.

This next bit of the trail to Braeburn is beautiful and familiar. What's more: I was on my own. I always race on my own - I love the isolation, peace and quiet. Moving through the snow-covered trees, appreciating the absolute beauty, the peace and tranquillity, the deafening silence (save for the sound of my poles hitting the hard packed snow) I was in heaven!

Then suddenly, as I turned a corner, I spotted something that was out of place: a sleeping bag. As I approached I realised that it was a racer, Shelly Gallatly. She was just getting into her sleeping bag - this totally confused me. It was mid-afternoon, Shelly is one of the strongest most experienced racers and she lives here in the Yukon. I reckoned that the next checkpoint at Braeburn was maybe three hours away. If I knew that, Shelly certainly knew it, so why had she stopped? As I approached, I asked if everything was okay. She explained that she was suffering and in a lot of pain - she then went on to explain that she "would rest a while - see how she felt." I told her that I would explain the situation once I got to Braeburn. She wished me luck and I felt rather guilty about leaving her but I knew she was the most experienced cold weather racer in the race and every year she gives the Yukon Arctic Ultra racers a talk on how to race and survive in the Yukon.

Fortunately for me, any guilty feelings I had didn't last long, because within half an hour of leaving her, a snowmobile came toward me. I explained the situation and he went off to pick her up.

I plodded on, eventually arriving at the Braeburn 100 mile checkpoint at 18:12. It was here that I had decided to have my first good long rest. I was very aware that I wasn't even a quarter of the way to Dawson and the need to pace myself was paramount.

Braeburn was one of the better checkpoints, with a bed, hot food and hot drinks. I was going to take full advantage. After a good meal and a six hour good quality sleep I reluctantly left at 02:18. The next checkpoint at Ken Lake was some 43 miles away.

Braeburn to Ken Lake

Immediately after leaving the checkpoint we crossed the main road and shortly after that there was a severe, nasty climb and trying to pull a 35 kg sled up the hill turned the severe climb into a severe challenge - the knack was to go fast enough to keep the thing moving, because if you slowed down or stopped for a quick breather, gravity would do its very best to pull you and your sled back down. It required effort to have a breather, in other words, I had to pick a pace that I knew would get me to the top without the need to stop.

After this initial climb, it was a gradual descent on to a series of lakes. For some reason I just couldn't get myself organised - straps needed adjusting, clothing was too tight and constricting. Lots of little things - the harness didn't feel right, I needed a wee, I needed a drink, the headtorch kept slipping, my constant faffing and farting about was beginning to annoy me, the sensible thing would have been to stop and sort things out, but no, I plodded on adjusting things as I went.

Then the 'Coup de Grace': one of my poles broke, (the aluminium pole that connects my harness to my sled). Luckily for me it was a break I had seen happen to someone before - they had been using an identical sled to mine so I had worked out how to fix it should the same thing happen to me. That bit of pre-planning would now pay dividends:- a leatherman multi tool, jubilee clip and a short screw were already in my pocket and in less than five minutes the repair had been made. (The repair lasted until the finish of the race).

The lakes, though extremely beautiful, became monotonous: hour after hour of non-stop plodding took the edge off their beauty. The scenery never changed, flat and bloody long, nothing to focus on, nothing to take your mind off the sheer monotony of putting one foot in front of the other.

I carried on until eventually I spotted smoke rising from a small wooden lakeside cabin, then as I got nearer a large Yukon Arctic Ultra race banner declared that this was indeed the Ken Lake checkpoint. I arrived at 17:40, planned to have a short break and then get going. Whilst I was there another racer, Mark Hines, came in. Mark had completed the 430 mile race before and was the first person to ever attempt it twice.

As we were talking, a call came through to the crew. A racer was in trouble and needed evacuating from the course - the crew asked myself and Mark if we had seen anyone in trouble as the location had been given as being not far from this checkpoint. The only person that both Mark and I had seen was Sam, another British racer - when I had seen him he was making a brew. Mark had spoken to him and he had told Mark that he did not feel great - the good thing was that he was only about 3 km away. Kev, one of the crew, got on his snowmobile and went out to bring him in.

One hour after arriving, I left. The next checkpoint was Carmacks - some 35 miles away, I had planned to have a pretty good rest there, so was keen to get going.

After three hours more on the lakes, the trail led me into the woods. I was glad to be back on the trail proper. However, my joy was short-lived - the trail was challenging with one climb after another, lots of small awkward hills and the cumulative effect of so many hills was knackering.

Once I finally managed to find my way out of the woods, the trail dropped down onto the Yukon river for a mile or so before finally arriving in the small town of Carmacks. Following the well-marked route took me to the checkpoint which was housed in the leisure centre. I arrived at 07:30, I had now been on the go for about 28 hours, with just the one hour stop at Ken Lake.

I picked up my drop bag, had something to eat and a wash, cleaned my teeth and then decided to get some sleep.

This checkpoint had an area reserved for racers to have a sleep. My fear of over-sleeping was such that I grabbed a chair and dozed. When I woke a couple of hours later it was more food then time to go. I left the checkpoint at 12:30.

Carmacks to McCabe

The next checkpoint at McCabe was 38 miles away and some

211 miles from the start, even then I wouldn't be halfway to Dawson. I tried to grasp the enormity of the race, but right now I was having trouble finding my way out of Carmacks. It's funny how, when in the wilds, navigation and route-finding never seems to be a problem. As soon as I try to find my way through a town, I'm hopeless. However, this was not helped by the fact that some local kids had apparently thought it was great fun to nick the route markers. I personally couldn't see the funny side of it, but that's just me. Bah humbug and all that!

Eventually, I found my way back on to the trail, which was a well defined old miners' track. I remembered this part of the trail from when I did the 320 mile race, as it was here that I had been treated to the most spectacular display of the Northern lights. I was remembering that light show when I caught sight of something moving just ahead of me, and low and behold it was a moose - a huge clumsy-looking thing the size of a horse, but ironically it moved very gracefully. Mesmerized, I stopped and just watched it before it disappeared into some trees - how it did it I don't know, so densely-packed were the trees that I would have had trouble squeezing myself through.

It was now early evening and cold. I guessed it was about -30. I came off the well-defined track and into the woods, before dropping back down onto the river. Following the route markers that took me back into the woods and some serious climbing, then the trail got wider and became what appeared to be fire traps:- wide tree-free swathes cut through the forest to prevent fire spreading. The undulating trail continued as did the on, off sections of river.

Coming out of one section of the woods, I could see a couple of buildings and then the wonderful smell of a log-burning stove and the McCabe checkpoint. The time was 03:20.

Everyone was asleep when I got in, but then a couple of them got up asked if I needed anything and then they took a couple of photos. All I needed was a place to sleep, I was knackered and was fortunate to get a real bed. I slept for three hours. When I got up another racer was there. I faffed about, ate and drank as much as I could then left at 09:40.

McCabe to Pelly Crossing

Leaving McCabe I was to follow the half mile track to the main road, cross over and pick up the trail and follow the overhead power lines. After a while I came across what appeared to be a power substation, the trail then took a right turn and then it was back on the proper trail.

More undulating terrain was made a little more interesting by the fact that sections of overflow were scattered about - the fact that this overflow was not only "run off" from the adjacent hills and consequently on a slant, but had also been covered with a light dusting of powdered snow, now every single step had to be worked out and thought about. I toyed with the idea of putting my crampons (a small spiked device that fits over your shoes to prevent sliding) on, but as usual I couldn't decide whether to stop and faff about or carry on.

As I plodded along in a world of indecision an athlete came past - he was certainly moving fast. As he passed I realised that it was the athlete that had arrived at McCabe when I was asleep - he continued off down the trail and before long he was out of sight.

A short time after this minor humiliation, the trail led down onto some lakes. The flatness was a blessing after the overflow-laden trail. As I looked at the trail ahead, I spotted something that appeared to be out of place I strained my eyes trying to make out what it was, however, as I got nearer I realised that right slap bang in the middle of the lake, were a circle of chairs. One of the chairs had a china mug on it and two of the others had empty beer bottles on them. I then realised that someone had been ice fishing.

I carried on, before finally coming off the lakes late in the afternoon. Then I spotted some lights in the distance - coming down from the higher ground the lights became more numerous and then to my right was a cabin - a little further on was the road that I recognised from the last time I was here. A short time later I arrived at the Pelly Crossing checkpoint, the time was 18:20.

Pelly Crossing to Pelly Farms

Arriving in the small town of Pelly Crossing, my original plan had been to cut the stop here really short, if only because the next checkpoint at Pelly Farms was for the 430 mile racers: a compulsory 8 hour stop. However, the fact that it was now snowing confirmed that a short break was wise. If the snowing continued as was forecast the trail would not only disappear but would become bloody hard-going.

So the plan was a quick cup of coffee or two, something to eat and then leave. There were a few racers already at the checkpoint, predominately Spanish, all of them attempting the 320 miler, however, some were going no further. Either they had been pulled out (one in particular had a nasty touch of frost bite on each of his fingers, caused by the fact that he had spilt cooker fuel on them which had immediately frozen the skin) or had decided that enough was enough.

One of the guys spoke English and asked how long I was going to stay. I told him that I would be leaving shortly - he explained this to one of the guys, the one who I had seen at McCabe and the one that had passed me so impressively earlier on in the day. He then asked if Jorge could tag along and accompany me to Pelly Farms. I didn't mind and was glad of the company for what I expected to be a tough, long night and the clincher was that he spoke no English.

So fifty minutes after arriving we left, the fact that it was snowing and the very obvious fact that the trail was disappearing before our eyes, meant that we both understood the need to move quickly while the trail was still visible.

Leaving the checkpoint we immediately dropped down on to the Yukon River. I think we both understood the need for speed: we had to move fast while there was still some visible trail. I led the way and pushed hard, far harder than I would normally have pushed - this was helped by the fact that I was a chicken and did not really want to be stuck out in the wilderness, with no route markings.

Even though we were still on the river the going was far from easy; huge blocks of ice (I say huge, some were the size of small lorries) were scattered here and there and caused us to follow a zig-zaggy route. My headlight beam was reflecting off the falling snow, causing me to squint and concentrate, and, as my wife has pointed out on more than one occasion, I can't concentrate on anything for more than a few minutes, it was getting to be a little unpleasant. After several hours of straining to follow the now invisible route, Jorge came up beside me with his GPS in hand and showed me that we only had 9 km to go - a little over five miles, 3 hours later we were still plodding along, we had another look at the GPS and we were apparently still 4 km away. It doesn't take much to confuse my simple mind and even less when I'm tired and desperate, but the readings did not make sense. If it had taken 3 hours to do the last 5 km, we were moving at 1 mile an hour. I smiled, shook my head in a very positive manner, gave him the thumbs up and thought to myself "What the *&^%$?"

We moved off, Jorge then took over the lead, and we plodded on, me eating Rolos which had now become comfort food, whilst trying to work out what the &^%$ was going on, and with Jorge now slowly pulling away from me.

Then, just as I was begining to feel really sorry for myself, we spotted what we thought was a light and as we got nearer, we could see that it was Dale - the owner of Pelly Farms: he had come out to meet us.

He guided us to the checkpoint and explained that they had been watching our progress on the computer. It had taken us 11 hours to get here. Little did we know that we had been extremely lucky - other athletes would experience a real nightmare journey.

Pelly Farms is regarded as one of the best checkpoints because it is actually in someone's home: a beautiful log cabin, cosy, nice and warm, plenty of food and the owners love having us, helping in anyway they can. This checkpoint was for the 430 mile racers a compulsory 8 hour stop so I ate and drank, had a quick sleep of a couple of hours, picked up my drop bag and sorted out my kit, dried what I could, replenished my food supplies, topped up flasks and then at 14:10 and, with the greatest trepidation, left the comfort of Pelly Farms for the formidable 70 mile (roughly) section to Scroggie creek and the next checkpoint - a checkpoint that had only ever seen 9 previous racers.

Pelly Farms to Scroggie Creek

It was still snowing and bloody cold. I had achieved one of my goals and had left the Pelly Farms checkpoint before any other athlete had arrived. I now knew that my position was second place and with at least an 8 hour lead over the runner in third place.

However, this next section was the beginning of the real hard work, with soft snow underfoot, more difficult and challenging terrain and the biggest section of the race without a checkpoint, and the already accumulated 275 miles.

Within half an hour of leaving the checkpoint I had to stop, remove my down jacket and put on my snowshoes. The difference the snowshoes made was instant - I was walking on the snow instead of through the snow.

The trail was difficult to read but was fortunately through an avenue of trees, making navigating a little easier. It was now early evening and I was moving surprisingly well, when I spotted a "20 miles" sign that someone had written in the snow. I couldn't work out what the 20 miles meant:- 20

miles from where to where? I certainly hadn't done 20 miles
and, therefore, had more than 20 miles to go before scroggie.
I plodded on in my own little world of confusion when
suddenly I realised that I was climbing. This went on for ages
and was bloody hard work. As daylight made a welcome
appearance, I could begin to appreciate the harsh beauty of
the place, the absolute silence and stillness. I could have been
walking in a huge painting: nothing either moved or made a
noise, there was literally no sign of life. On and on I plodded,
then I noticed on the trail in front of me footprints, footprints
belonging to what I didn't know but whatever had made them
was, I reasoned, not that far ahead. It was still snowing and
the prints had virtually no snow on them. I followed them,
fascinated, and after a couple of hours heard the faint sound
of a snowmobile. Then suddenly coming toward me a beautiful
yellow snowmobile. It stopped beside me and the driver got
off and introduced himself, Pete. He said he was a trapper,
he then said "You guys are crazy." Whitehorse to Dawson on
foot, crazy. When he finished stating the obvious he offered
me a cup of hot coffee, I was very grateful and the coffee
was wonderful. We chatted for a few minutes as I drank his
coffee then I asked him what the footprints were. He replied
that they were WOLF prints, not one but two - they follow
the dogs on the Yukon Quest and scavenge any bits the race
leaves behind - he also said that I shouldn't worry, because I
would never see them and they will do everything to avoid
seeing me. I thanked him for the coffee and plodded on,
hoping and praying that I really didn't see any wolves.

With Pete gone the monotony returned - plodding along like
the proverbial beast of burden: one foot in front of the other,
hour after hour of slow, relentless grind. The boredom was
only slightly relieved by the fact that I was having to carefully
negotiate my way through several sections of overflow.
After a while of working my way through the overflow, I
noticed that I was either getting weaker or my pulk was
getting heavier, it felt like a fat bloke had decided to hitch a
lift on my pulk. I was struggling and stopping with alarming

regularity, and was getting a little concerned - concerned enough to stop, unharness and check what the hell was going on. On checking the underside of the pulk I could see that for some reason snow was sticking to it. I scraped off what I could, left it in the sun for 10/15 minutes while I had something to eat. It seemed to do the trick and then it was back to plodding.

It was now late afternoon and getting noticeably colder, so it was on with my jacket and headtorch, ready for the evening session.The trail was now closing in, with more trees on either side of the trail. Then, at about 18:30 I heard the wonderful sound of a snowmobile. A few minutes later, not one, but two snowmobiles came up from behind. Greg and Spence stopped and explained that they were part of the race crew and were now going to Scroggie. They also said that I was doing well because there was no one behind me. We had a quick chat, with me in all likelihood jibbering like an idiot, then it happened I tried not to but it just sort of came out, I asked how much further to Scroggie, Greg checked his GPS and, low and behold - there was only 28/29 kms left - ALL THAT WAS LEFT? I really had thought that there was maybe 5/6 miles, not the 17/18 that Greg had told me.

I smiled, put on my very British stiff upper lip and said thank you. I was determined not to cry or moan in front of the Canadians.

When they left, I tried to work out how long it would take me: even at 2 miles an hour it would take me 9 hours. I had been moving constantly for twenty-nine hours - could I hold out for just a bit longer? I reasoned that I could, just push hard for nine more hours and then I could have a bloody good sleep - easy.

It was now getting late, then at just gone 23:00 I was relieved to hear voices - the checkpoint. I was bloody close, if I could just keep going for a bit longer. The voices grew louder, laughing and joking, waiting for me. I pushed forward looking for the checkpoint, the voices got louder and were coming from the left, which surprised me as I thought the Scroggie Creek checkpoint would be on my right. I kept on moving forward, desperate to find the thing. The fresh snow had covered the route, I decided to use my initiative and take a short, more direct route toward the voices. Gingerly I stepped off the trail and down onto a small ice-covered pond, up the other side and through some densely packed trees. I pushed my way forward, breaking branches and making a lot of noise in the process. The trees got more and more densely-packed, leaving me with no choice but to retreat and return to the trail. Trying to reverse through the trees whilst wearing a pulk was not easy, so difficult in fact that I unharnessed myself, walked back to the pulk, grabbed the back of the pulk, and roughly man-handled it back onto to the trail proper. Tired and frustrated, I really was in no mood to treat the thing with caution lest I damage or break it.

Once back on the trail, I decided to have a quick break and gather my thoughts. I sat on my pulk, closed my eyes and only then did I realise that the sneaky bastard 'sleepmonster' had finally caught me - there were no people out drinking, laughing and cracking jokes at nearly midnight in temperatures of -40 plus.

I needed sleep - I was close, but not close enough. The fact that I'd had only two hours sleep since the McCabe checkpoint some three days ago had now caught up with me, so reluctantly I admitted defeat, pressed my SPOT tracking device to let them know that I was okay and withdrew to the comfort of my sleeping bag and bivi.

After what felt like a 10 minute catnap, I woke up, looked at my watch and realised I had in fact slept for a little over 6 hours.

Annoyed with myself, I got up - but not before checking the soft snow to see if anyone had passed by in the night. They hadn't: the snow ahead had no footprints. I don't know why I do that - there is precious little I can do about it, even if someone had passed by. I'm not racing, just plodding and trying to finish.

It was now a little after 08:30 - I moved off. After about an hour I heard the beautiful sound of snow mobiles. A few moments later, two machines appeared in front of me - Greg and Spence - they dismounted and approached with a flask of hot tea and a hot sandwich. I was grateful, hungry and thirsty and like a half-starved gannet was busy devouring the sandwich so enthusiastically that I was not really paying much attention to the route description Greg was so kindly describing.

Once I'd had my second cup of tea and finished eating, we bade farewell, Greg and Spence explaining that they were off up the trail to see if any other athlete was on the way.

I carried on down the trail towards the elusive Scroggie Creek checkpoint, fed and rested and safe in the knowledge that I was close.

I rather bizarrely started planning my next adventure. I had got a couple of races lined up in the UK including a half-marathon four weeks from now, but a race called the Namib Desert Challenge had caught my eye. I made the decision to do it. Whilst working things out, not least how, and more importantly, when to broach the subject to my wife. I spotted, nailed to a tree, a hand-painted sign saying "Scroggie Creek" - a few minutes later, and to my right, was the very wonderful sight of the two cabins that I had spent a very tough 46 hours to reach. I arrived at 12:05.

Ever the gentleman, I knocked on the door, Jessica and Mike welcomed me with hot drinks and hot food. Mike explained that I was to be held here until the weather improved - apparently there were horrendous blizzards ahead, with the temperature in the -40s and with two mountains to clamber over it was deemed to dangerous to continue. I had to wait until the weather improved.

I wasn't too concerned - I had planned to have a really good 6 or 7 hour rest anyway. I would use the time wisely: resting, eating and drinking, cleaning and sorting kit out. I was lucky I had no blisters - chafing, just a bit of frostnip on the tips of my fingers and thumbs, that was it. However, after about nine hours of inactivity I really wanted to get moving but the trail was covered in fresh snow - the blizzards were still raging. I was informed that I could be held for some time yet.

I went to bed feeling a little fed up, stopping for this length of time could only have a detrimental effect, ie: the muscles would start to get sore and stiff, my body would think that the race was over and start to shut down and then start the recovery process. Annoyingly, my feet were already starting to swell up - this only usually happens when I have finished a race.

The reality was that I still had over 100 miles to go and two mountains to climb.

I was lying in my sleeping bag, tossing and turning, and trying to sleep when suddenly the cabin door opened and in stepped an ice-covered athlete. Mark Hines had made it to Scroggie, the time was 03:00 and I now knew my position: 2nd overall and some 15 hours ahead of the third-placed athlete.

Mark annoyingly looked to be in pretty good shape and after a nine hour rest we were given the all clear to proceed - on condition we travelled to the next checkpoint together.

Scroggie Creek to Indian River

Shortly after leaving the Scroggie Creek checkpoint, we dropped down onto a river but after 24 hours of inactivity the body was a little stiff and would need a bit of time and distance to get the muscles warmed up and working.

I was plodding along, breaking trail in the fresh soft snow, when Mark called out and said that he was needed a comfort break. As I waited I could feel the cold trying to creep in. Luckily it was so cold that Mark had no choice but to be bloody quick - a few moments was all it took and then we were off.

Plodding along with someone was a new experience for me. I've raced consistently for 15 years and never once had a partner - I've always raced on my own, but I fully understood the reasons we were now together. It was different and interesting - two completely different styles. Mark with his faster pace but regular short breaks and me with my slow nonstop plod.

After about four miles, we got off the river, with me still in the front and then like a prat I took the wrong turn. Fortunately for me, Mark was switched on and quickly realised he was following a buffoon. He shouted out, ran up to me and got me back on track. It was only a short distance but I was annoyed with myself (and if I'm honest, a little embarrassed). We were now walking through some very soft and very fresh snow, consequently the going was slow and I was having to work hard.

Late on in the afternoon, we started to see old bits of derelict mining equipment. The temperature seemed to drop a few degrees. To our left were a couple of old cranes. We decided to have a quick teabreak and got into one them and had a hot drink and a bit of food. After about half an hour, we moved off.

For some reason I was really struggling - the pace wasn't particularly fast, just the opposite in fact. I was tired and didn't seem to have my usual oomph. I felt fine, good in fact, but just lacked my usual energy. I could only put it down to the enforced 24 hour stop - that much inactivity during a race would have only ever had a detrimental effect and so it proved.

During the early evening we started to look for somewhere to bivi down when we came across a disused, slightly dilapidated, wooden building. We got inside and in one of the rooms was an old calendar dated 2002 on the wall. We got our sleeping bags out, had a hot drink and some food (of which I was beginning to get pretty low) and then some much-needed sleep.

After several hours, it was time to bite the bullet and get

going - today we would be clambering the first of the two mountains: Eureka Dome, not the highest but the steepest.

It was whilst getting ready that I realised I had made a stupid, schoolboy error: I had left my shoes outside of my sleeping bag and now they had frozen solid. Forcing my nice warm feet into the now blocks of ice, was, I, decided not the best way to start the day.

Fortunately, it had finally stopped snowing, the going was still bloody hard work and by late morning we had reached the foot of the Dome. Normally I climb quite well - this mountain, I decided, would require slow nonstop plodding, my speciality.

It was steep and never-ending,. Slowly pushing my way forward with a metronome-like consistency, inch by inch I progressed, then suddenly I realised Mark had caught me up and was asking if I was okay. Unbeknownst to me my pace had been getting slower. I assured him that I was fine but I was struggling. Mark took the lead and I followed, glad of the rest: breaking trail had been bloody hard work.

Eventually we reached the summit. We didn't immediately start descending, the euphemistically named Dome actually levelled off for quite some time before starting its descent. The views were stunning, absolutely breathtaking (mind you, that might have been the arduous climbing, that had actually taken my breath away!) - so beautiful that Mark was busy taking photographs. When I eventually caught him up, we took advantage of the impromptu break and had a quick teabreak. Mark voiced his concerns about his running low on food, I hadn't the heart to tell him that he had loads more than me. I tried to allay his worries by telling him that it will be okay and "Whatever happens, don't dwell on the negative." I knew from bitter experience that once negative thoughts take hold they often spiral out of control. I also knew that no matter what, we would make it, we would get to Dawson.

We started our descent Mark seemed to be pulling away

from me and I had to work hard to keep him in sight. Then, late in the afternoon, I spotted the 5km to go marker. Mark had added an exclamation mark. I smiled to myself and moved on. Three miles to the checkpoint - an hour and a half max - however, the checkpoint proved elusive - it was not where it should have been. Owing to the severe weather conditions, the organisers had abandoned the idea of using a tent (as had been used previously) and instead had decided to use a small cabin a little further along, so the 3 miles became a several mile epic.

Mark was moving well and was ahead of me. I was still struggling, still trying to recover from such a long rest, still trying to convince my old body that we had not quite finished yet.

My feet were sore, the tips of my fingers were numb and my energy levels at an all-time low. We crossed a bridge and then I looked up and Mark was gone - envious of his speed I ploughed on. I continued for the best part of an hour before the penny dropped: I must have walked past the checkpoint - bollocks, bloody, bollocks. I turned around and backtracked to where I had last seen Mark - the bridge - scouring every inch of the trail, I couldn't find the checkpoint. When I reached the bridge, I turned around and walked along this part of the trail for the third time and then I heard the most beautiful sound in the world: a snow machine. Kevin, who I had last seen at the Ken Lake checkpoint taking Sam to Carmacks. He got off and explained that the checkpoint was about 2km away, all I had to do was keep going. After about half an hour I arrived and pinned to the cabin wall was a large sign post saying "The Last Checkpoint."

Once in the warmth of the small but cosy cabin, the 2 race crew went out of their way to make sure I had food and drink - like concerned parents, they made drinks and offered food. I sat next to the small log-burning stove, savouring both the seat and the warmth. As I thawed out and started to remove my shoes and socks, I realised that my socks were in fact frozen to my feet - try as I might gentle coaxing was not going to work, brute force was what was required. I literally ripped the socks off, bits of green sock remained firmly attached to my frozen feet. I threw the socks into the bin. Now, sitting in the corner like a naughty child, I tried to very discreetly look at what sort of damage had been done. I wish I hadn't: three toes on my right foot were aubergine in colour. I was shocked and now the stupidity of my neglecting to put the bloody shoes in my sleeping bag was confirmed. I'm no doctor but I guessed that aubergine-coloured toes meant only one thing:- frostbite. I did the only thing I could do, I held my frozen toes in my hand hoping against hope that I could thaw them out before anyone spotted them.

After several minutes of covert toe-thawing, Kev became suspicious and asked to have a quick look at my feet. I had no choice but to oblige - (part of the support crew's duties were to keep an eye out for exhaustion, frostbite etc) I moved my hand away and without missing a beat he said that my feet were frostbitten and that my race was over. I didn't, couldn't, argue - I knew that one stupid mistake had cost me.

There was nothing for it, except to get some sleep and eat. Sleep, however, was out of the question. The pain was excruciating, coming in waves, fist and buttock-clenching waves of pure agony. I was reduced to a simpering wimp, lying there waiting for the next jolt of absolute agony. I laid awake, comfort-eating the last of my chocolate, shortbread, crisps and sweets.

I had covered the best part of 400 miles, was in a good position but one lapse, (one silly, preventable mistake) had cost me the race. Those 400 miles were for nothing. I would have been better off bailing out at the first checkpoint. I lay there pondering and realised that I had been fortunate - fortunate to have seen and experienced so much of the Canadian wilderness: the place was beautiful. I couldn't regret the past few days, so few people would ever get to where I had been. I had given it my best but fucked it up, no one to blame but me. At least I had a go and would have been annoyed with myself and regretted forever, not having a go.

The morning eventually arrived and Mark was understandably keen to get going. The temperature outside was -46 degrees, which in turn meant that the crew were unable to get the snowmobiles started. Consequently, the crew were not happy about sending Mark off on his own. They would be unable to get to him should anything happen. He just had to wait a bit until the machines could be started.

Meanwhile, Kev wanted to have a quick look at my feet to see what damage had been done. I showed him the wretched things and much to his surprise and mine they were much better: the aubergine colour had been replaced with red, blotchy and blistered toes. I was asked how they felt and of course I lied, said they felt slightly tender but otherwise fine and promptly gave an impromptu demonstration of my walking ability. Confused by this sudden turn of events he said we'll leave it until midday and see how they are.

Mark finally got the all clear to go at 11:30. I got the all clear, well sort of, after much warning about not letting my now very susceptible feet getting frostbitten again:- the damage, I was warned, would be severe and permanent ie; I could lose bits!

I promised to be careful and check them periodically, uncrossed my fingers and left the Indian river checkpoint an hour after Mark.

As I hobbled off, I was mentally drained. One minute my race was over, now it was back on, I had frostbitten feet, frost-damaged finger-tips, no food and had had no sleep. I needed to finish within 14 hours of Mark to keep my second place and worked out that it would take me (if I was lucky) some 18/20 hours of nonstop plodding to finish - I love a challenge!

Indian River to Dawson

Leaving the checkpoint I put on an act of bravado - my raw and blistered feet were bloody painful. They hurt with every step, but there was no way, absolutely no way that I was going to let anyone see the seriousness of the injuries, in case they decided to err on the side of caution and pull me from the race a second time.

However, as soon as I was left alone and out of sight, I could hobble and limp away to my heart's content.

The trail was pretty good and the intense cold ensured that the snow was hard-packed enough for me to walk on as opposed to having to walk through. Walking along, appreciating the beauty and absolute tranquillity, I realised that I had been very lucky:- to be pulled from a race and then reinstated was something I had never heard of in any race. I also was lucky to be back on my own - as much as I like Mark, it was the solitude that these races offered that was one of the attractions.

Lost in my own little world of thought and counting my blessings, I rounded a corner and there in the distance King Solomons Dome at 4000ft - the highest mountain we had to climb, and approximately 20 miles from Dawson. Now, for the first time, I was beginning to think that I might actually reach the finish line.

If I could just keep plodding along, if I could just get to the top, if my feet could hold out, so many ifs. It was now late afternoon and the climbing started, Fortunately, it was not like Eureka where the climb was severe, this was more of a gentle incline. Following the trail was pretty straightforward and I finally reached the summit at 21:00 hours. It was too cold to hang about, so I continued on. A little while later I had a quick break, it was too cold to hang about so got going as soon as I had put on my down jacket.

The trail was changing: old bits of abandoned machinery and signposts were becoming more numerous, then after a few twists and turns the trail widened and became more defined. It was wider, well-ploughed and maintained. I continued on and then spotted some lights, then as I got a little closer I could see the lights belonged to mobile homes or caravans. It was about 03:00 in the morning and my presence had not gone unnoticed: every dog within a 5 mile radius seemed to be barking. Then, I noticed that I was not alone - a few of the more inquisitive among them came out to investigate. I carried on, too tired to be concerned about noisy, nosey dogs. Then a few moments later and with the dogs still in tow, a vehicle approached - I waved, hoping that the thing would stop so that I could ask for directions into Dawson and to my surprise it was Robert the race director - he had been following my progress on the computer (we all had SPOT tracking devices that relayed our position to race HQ) and had come out to give me directions into Dawson.

I removed my goggles and hat while he explained how to get to the finish line. I thanked him and continued off down the road with a spring in my step. Well, I would have if the weren't so bloody painful.

An hour and a half later I finally hauled my carcass over the finish line, only the 11th person to have completed this epic footrace. The Yukon Arctic Ultra 430 miler is so much more than a race, it is an incredible experience. I honestly - with my hand on my heart, did not enter to race. I entered to finish - yes, once I realised I was in a good position I wanted to remain there but if I had started out to race I don't think I would have been able to finish.

The final placings were:

Greg McHale in a time of	200:15 Hours
David Berridge	249:10 Hours
Mark Hines	251:55 Hours
Jerym Brunton	307:00 Hours

The Dog Grave checkpoint at about 64 miles.

Arriving at Braeburn - the 100 mile checkpoint.

Nearly finished - pretending my frostbitten feet don't hurt.

Spent hours sucking on my icicles.

Left exposed for just 3 hours - that'll teach me!

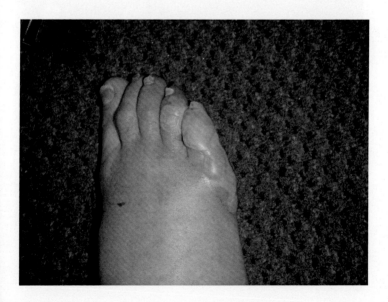

4 days after finishing - swollen and blistered, frostbitten tootsies.

Early on in the race -trying to look as though I know what I'm doing.

THE NAMIB DESERT CHALLENGE 2012

What is it: A multi-stage Desert Footrace

When: October and July

Where: Namibia

Distance: 220km (137 miles)

It is: An ideal introduction to Desert running - the fact that you don't carry your kit and are fed every night makes it ideal - it doesn't get any better!

See: namibdesertchallenge.com

Flying to Windhoek, the capital city of Namibia, to take part in a multi-day ultra-distance running race, consisting of 220km of desert running. The country of Namibia was a pleasant surprise: green, fertile country with friendly people.

After a long 5 hour drive to the Soussvlei race HQ, it rained - rain I ask you! Pay a bleeding fortune to race in some exotic hot desert environment and it rains and rains.

The usual - it has not rained in theses parts since anyone can remember.

To make matters worse, we were to be lodged in tents. Tents that were designed for hot environments meaning that they were anything but waterproof. We were wet before we started and trying to dry anything in a wet, leaking tent was a bit like poor old King Canute trying to stop the tide coming in!

Meeting the other competitors is always one of the fun bits. A few I recognised from previous races and a some even remembered me!

Our tent area had 5 tents. Richard, a lean looking racing snake type, Jo, a 25 year-old Australian female who was attempting a multi-day running race for the first time, my wife and an old friend called Nic.

My wife and I decided to have a tent each but this idea was soon changed after my tent sprung a leak and got everything wet including (and most annoyingly) my down sleeping bag. Even a decent nights sleep was taken away from me.

After the race briefing, kit checks etc, we made our way over to the tents and tried in vain to get some sleep and tried was (on this occasion) the operative word. The thunderclaps and lighting had other ideas and I am afraid to say that one particular thunderclap made me jump - just a little jump but a jump all the same.

Morning could not come soon enough. I just wanted to get out of the wet tent, the wet sleeping bag and get dressed into my wet trainers, wet clothes and wet kit, I decided that at least if I was moving I would get warm and if, by some miracle, it stopped raining I might even get dry.

It was not to be:- it rained for the next two days!

Day 1

Today's running was to be 42km ie a marathon.

The terrain was not too bad, the rain making it cool, slightly rocky underfoot. I ran alongside a South African - we chatted as we went, it was a nice steady pace and one I felt I could maintain. Patrick eased off slightly, I carried on, my hips started to complain but I put that down to the fact that I had been sat on my arse for so long, and had slept in a wet sleeping bag, and my very old age!

The terrain remained pretty constant - slightly rocky track, climbing occasionally and going through grass. After a while, another runner caught me up, Dave, a guy I had met a couple of years earlier during a race called the augrabies extreme marathon (a race through the Kalahari desert).

We ran together for a while, after approx 30km the terrain changed and started to climb. The grasses were thinning out and were gradually being replaced by rock.

Tricky and technical, we were reduced to walking for fear of injury - my long legs always come into their own when I have to walk over tricky terrain and so it was that Dave dropped behind. I continued on and after negotiating some tricky twisting and undulating sections, I came across a turning. Peering around the thing, I noticed a quite severe descent. Descending always causes problems tired legs: gravity, fear and an eagerness to get down unfortunately leaves me prone to mistakes so I knew I had to switch on and proceed with the utmost caution. Luckily for me one of the race organisers (who had obviously heard about my total ineptitude when it came to descending) had stationed themselves on the very top and was kindly issuing advice on how best to descend. I could see the way down - steep, loose, tricky and a little unnerving, I, like a fool, tried to speed up and very nearly came a cropper, with the loose stuff moving beneath me!

Once I managed to get halfway down, some thoughtful soul had gone to the trouble of laying concrete in an attempt to try and stabilise the loose stuff. It looked inviting, I now had the luxury of choice:- either loose and moving or stable but slippery - I chose the slippery, stable option and carefully inched my way down.

Once at the bottom, I was met by another of the race crew who informed me that the worst was over - it was now a flat ten km to the end.

I doubted what he said was true but the part of the route I

could see was flat and as long as it was flat I would run. I ran the whole lot and he was telling the truth - it was really 10 flat km. Annoyingly, about 500 meters from the finish line, a bloody big German came storming past like an express train and pipped me to the post.

I couldn't complain. I had had a good day and felt good and when I was informed that I was in eighth place I was chuffed to pieces. Finally, I was getting the hang of Desert running, or was it the fact that I wasn't having to carry a rucksack and it was wet and cloudy? More like English weather than the dry arid desert conditions that we had hoped for!

Namibia day 2

The overnight downpour had apparently caused a lot of damage to not only our campsite, but also to today's intended route. Localised flooding had meant that the race organisers had spent a sleepless night working out alternatives.

Happily, we runners were totally oblivious to all this, although we had also had a sleepless night!

As the briefing began we politely listened but we were, I'm sure, unanimous in our thoughts - just point us in the right direction and let us go.

Briefing over and on to the coach, a coach load of slightly damp, nervous runners soon had the windows steamed up.

As we drove along, we could see what we had been told was the longest sand dune. We all studied the monster only because we had been told that we would be running along it later.

As we disembarked from the coaches and made our way over to the start line, we were given last minute up-to-date instructions. The damp clothes and waiting around had made me shiver. The trouble with this type of desert race was that I had only bought two tops, one for running in and one for 'evening wear'.

Tent life, wet kit and constant rain were not exactly the ideal conditions for running. Then, at last, the countdown began and then we were off.

The route wasn't too bad (for now): a sort of stony jeep track, a mixture of stones and sand. It did however, require a degree of concentration, the small pothole-like dips and drops were numerous. I was having to watch my feet, as very often the sand would hide and cover a loose flat stone, that would, if stood on, slide away from under you.

I got overtaken by a couple of runners, one of whom was built like a brick shithouse - the type of bloke that would not look out of place on California's 'muscle beach', not running some Ultra-distance desert race!

Checkpoints 1 and 2 were reached in a fairly quick 'faff-free' time. At checkpoint 2 we were given some rather vague instructions. With a slight sweep of the arm, one of the race crew sort of indicated the general direction we should go to get to the next checkpoint. The route from here to the next checkpoint wasn't marked, it was entirely up to you how you got there!

At this sudden turn of events I switched on, and played for time. Two electrolyte drinks later the runner who had arrived a minute or two before me left. Now for my master plan: follow him at a very discreet distance and I would not let him out of my sight, let him lead the way (I know I know, it's just not cricket, but hey being a bit of a chicken I didn't want to get lost!)

Just as I was trying to justify my rather dubious tactics to myself, I got what I deserved: the runner ahead turned around and ran back towards me. Sensing that my master plan had been rumbled, I started to formulate my reason for running in the exact same direction. As he approached, we nodded and he ran past and back to the checkpoint. Now, a thought occurred - I bet that cheeky bastard had decided to follow me to the next checkpoint!

I did the only thing I could do. I carried on. Plodding along, desperately trying to work out in which direction the next checkpoint could be, whilst at the same time scouring the route ahead, I spotted a runner ahead, maybe a kilometre away.

Appreciating this stroke of luck, I attempted to speed up - more out of desperation - than ability, when the runner, who had run back to the last checkpoint, caught me up, explaining that he had left his hat behind and had to go back and get it.

Thank God for that. I hadn't been rumbled and my cheating ways hadn't been exposed. Now I could relax a bit and follow the 2 blokes in front!

Richard, with his recently-retrieved baseball cap slowly but surely pulled away from me but he was not so far ahead that I couldn't keep an eye on him.

Looking up ahead, occasionally I saw the runner in front of Richard running in all sorts of directions, left to right, back and forth and then Richard started to do the same - weaving from one side to the other, leaping and skipping, arms waving around. Then I spotted the reason for this seemingly odd behaviour - we were in what could be best described as a flood plain, there was water everywhere.

The 2 runners ahead were attempting to avoid the water but I could see that they were none-the-less having to splash their way through. I reasoned that one way or the other I was going to get wet feet, so I did the only thing I could - I took the shortest route possible straight through the middle, avoiding all the unnecessary weaving that I had seen the other 2 runners doing.

My tactical running (well all's fair in love and war!) was now paying dividends, I had saved myself a detour and saved a bit of effort. The wet feet were, I reasoned, a small price to pay!

This was, I decided, the only desert race I had ever raced where I wished I had bought a pair of wellies!

Once out of the 'lagoon' it was on to a sandy hill, then shortly after was checkpoint 3. It was at this checkpoint that you really appreciated the true value of the race crew. They were volunteers as were we but they were freezing cold and wet. Unlike us they had no real opportunity to get warm, they could quite feasibly be standing around for three or four hours waiting for a fleeting glimpse of a tired, knackered and possibly miserable runner to pass through, grab something, and shoot off.

And yet, when I approached the checkpoint it was filled with smiling faces, helpful, encouraging crew asking what they could do to help ie fill a water bottle, offer some electrolytes, even the words that are probably said to everyone "you're doing really well" help.

As I was busy topping up and refuelling, a runner came in. Kristinet was one of those people that was always smiling. Cold, wet, tired and slightly bedraggled, she arrived wearing the biggest smile, the sort of smile that makes those around her smile too.

I left - a minute later she followed and we struggled up the steep sandy hill which, thankfully, was wet, the wet sand made the going a lot easier and had this been the scorching hot desert conditions that it was supposed to be, this part of the run would have been a nightmare. Half an hour ago I was cursing the wet conditions and now I was grateful for those same conditions.

Kristinet slowly pulled away and I was having to work hard to keep her in sight. To make matters worse, she was stopping every so often to take pictures.

The sandy hill we were on was huge and fortunately we were not having to climb to the top: we were running along its side.

Eventually tufts of grass started to appear, these tufts became more numerous until eventually the amount of grass outnumbered the amount of sand. We were now in a field of grass.

The grassy ground made the going easier and I caught Kristinet up, not because I was getting faster but only because she was taking so many pictures.

We ran along together for a while and she explained that she had done this race last year and had loved it - however, she hadn't really trained properly and had suffered as a consequence - this year she had trained and was now enjoying herself a lot more.

We continued on and eventually spotted the end of the dune and it was only now that I realised that the 'dune' that we had been following, was in fact the 'Longest Dune in the World'.

We started our descent and could now see the end of the dune veering off to our right, then we spotted a 4x4 vehicle approaching us. As it got closer we both moved off the track. It stopped just in front of us and the driver got out, he explained that we were nearly there but was noticeably vague about how far was "nearly there".

We thanked him anyway and plodded on, the track took us to the end of the dune and a turning to the right. We both scoured the route ahead desperately looking for the checkpoint but nothing. Then up and to our right we spotted someone who looked out of place: he was clean and presentable, he saw us approaching then walked back to wherever it was that he had come from.

We carried on and then spotted the finishing flags and coaches - we made it in 10th and 11th place.

Day 3

After yet another sleepless night, in a still-damp tent, we were again up early for the race briefing.

The trick was to somehow make your way over to the race

briefing when half asleep, in the dark, whilst attempting to avoid the numerous puddles. No one really wanted to start the day's running with wet feet!

As usual, the briefing went in one ear and straight out of the other. A quick cup of coffee and it was onto the coaches for the drive to the start line. As we arrived at the start, it was good to get off the coaches: the damp, nervous bodies had again steamed up the windows and had made the air slightly less than fragrant!

Standing around in the damp clothes in the chilly early morning air had again made me shiver, and everyone just wanted to get going.

After some quick last-minute final instructions, we were given a countdown and allowed to go. The first part of today's route was much the same as yesterday: a sort of stony, rocky and sandy jeep track. The track seemed to climb ever so slightly, one of those climbs that was so slight that you really didn't notice it until you were half way up.

Moving along quite nicely, I noticed that after about 20 minutes the field was already very strung-out. The ground was tricky underfoot and I was again having to watch my feet, unfortunately that meant that I was not able to indulge in my usual 'sight-seeing'.

Eventually, I reached the turnaround point, a couple of the race crew were there showing us the way.

'The way' was a descent, the trouble was that owing to the loose stones, the descent was a lot harder than the assent, causing quads, feet and knees to complain. Following a couple of runners ahead kept me going, gave me something to focus on.

We were now between two big hills, eventually we passed the hills and the whole area opened up before us.

Looking ahead, I could see runners - running in every direction, left to right, right to left, running towards me and running away from me. Some had stopped and one was reading his course notes (a small notebook that we had all been issued with).

As I slowed down it became obvious that no-one had any idea which way to go, then just at that moment someone shouted that they could see the route marker.

We looked and followed. The marker flag could be seen, just, high up on a saddle (a dip between two hills). We all made our over to the marker, but before we reached it we needed to climb a short but steep hill. Getting to the top and reaching the flag had at last got me sweating, I was now warm for the first time.

I stood on the top for a few moments, one to get my breath back and two to take in the beauty of the place and again I realised how lucky I was to be here and to be able to take part in these types of races.

As is always the case with these races, the running was just one aspect!

I personally think that if you have entered one of these races purely to race, you miss out on so much. The beauty, the peace and quiet, tranquillity, the people, camaraderie all go to adding to the experience.

In some ways I am glad that I am not a competitive racer because if I was, my whole focus would undoubtedly be to race, head down, balls-to-the-wall racing.

I come to do the best I can, but I also come to experience: experience a part of the world most people never get the chance to see, meet the people - a diverse group of people from various parts of the world both racers and crew.

I'm not just talking about this race but in all the races that I have ever been lucky enough to take part in. As I stood by the flag, I spotted the next checkpoint way down below. I carefully made my way down, reached the checkpoint and grabbed a couple of electrolyte drinks, topped up my water bottle and moved off.

It was now getting warmer and the route was slowly going downhill. It did look as if finally the race was going to become a desert race:- the sun was at last promising to make its first appearance. Things were starting to look up, my clothes were now dry for the first time, the sun was out, I felt good and the route was relatively easy.

Eventually I spotted a building up ahead. I focused on it, hoping that it was the next checkpoint, it wasn't. A bit further on I saw a couple of the race crew, they were just showing the way and helping us to cross what appeared to be a main road. Once across the road, the trail seemed to get more sandy. The sun was now out and the temperature was on the rise.

The one problem with this was that I was now drinking a lot more than I thought. My water bottle was getting emptied at an alarming rate.

For the time being this was not a problem, I still had some electrolyte drink in my camelback. Though warm and unpleasant-tasting, it did mean that I wouldn't be dying of thirst just yet.

Moving along and sipping on my diminishing water supply, I scanned the horizon ahead, hoping to catch a glimpse of the next checkpoint, but nothing.

I now realised that I had grossly underestimated the distance between this next checkpoint and the last. I moved along and spotted a large and prominent mound of rock. I sort of speeded up, guessing that the checkpoint would be on the other side and out of sight, however, I was wrong - nothing.

Carrying on and cursing my complete inability to listen to race briefings, I took my last swig of water.

During the 'Augrabies Extreme' in 2010 I had run out of water and vowed there and then that I would never run out of water during a desert race again and here we are just one desert race later with no water!

I was taking small sips of my 'electrolyte drink' a drink that was warm and tasted like a rather unpleasant infusion, but hey, I hoped that it would, fingers crossed get me to the next checkpoint.

After about 45 minutes I spotted a white something, I couldn't make out what it was, but whatever it was, it was out of place in the desert landscape.

And, of course, I was willing it to be the checkpoint.

As I got nearer, I was able to see that it was indeed the next checkpoint. I started to speed up (again), attempting to make another one of my impressive entrances and look as though I knew what I was doing, instead of the shuffling wreck that was suffering from dehydration that was the unfortunate reality.

I sped up, raised my hand to the crew and promptly went arse over tit, tripping over my own feet. I felt a complete prat, but was too relieved to have arrived at the checkpoint to really care.

Fortunately for me, the crew were far too polite or professional to mention my comedy entrance. I gratefully took a bottle of water, took two big swigs then had a couple of electrolyte drinks, which were cooler and better-tasting than the luke-warm infusion in my camelback!

Just before leaving, I was told that there was only about 10km to go and most of that was on a fairly decent road. I thanked them and was on my way, wanting to get today over with.

Moving on down the trail, which had now become more sand than rock or stone, I noticed some large beach hut type huts. These were obviously some sort of holiday chalets.

Moving on through the huts and onto a dusty track led me onto the "fairly decent road" I had been told about.

From the road, you could see the minaret that was at the Soussveile lodge ie: the finish!

Running, or should I say shuffling along the road, one or two drivers waved. I waved back and, as I did so, noticed a runner behind. He seemed to be running better, by that I mean faster, so pride being what it is I sped up, just beating him across the finishing line.

It was good to finish and the fact that the sun was at last shining was a delightful bonus which in turn meant that we could get some stuff dry.

Stripping off my race kit and jumping into the shower was bliss but to step out into the sunshine was absolute bliss.

I set to work, sorting and drying out kit. Damp, musty sleeping bags, smelly, stale and musty tents opened and aired. Soon the whole campsite had been transformed from race HQ to refugee camp. Kit and shoes hung from every available hanging space - socks, shorts, knickers and shirts adorned every inch of fence. It looked like the day after a carnival day, multi-coloured bunting festooned the whole place.

Runners and crew were likewise sunning themselves. It seemed to be that we all assumed that the sunshine would not last and were consequently taking this opportunity to work on our tans.

For the first time, we were all able to mingle, up until now we had been virtual recluses, forced to hide away in our damp tents, hiding from the elements and each other!

Unfortunately for Nic, he became a medical emergency and was carted off to the nearest medical facility. He had kidney stones and was in absolute agony - they took him off, gave him a shedload of painkillers and told him to rest.

Day 4 - The Long Day

Today's route had again had some changes - owing to the flooding, large parts of the original route had been rendered impassable.

There had been no rain during the night and with yesterday's clothes drying session we were now, for the first time dressed in dry race kit.

The short walk to the start line made a pleasant change from the damp drive we had become used to.

After a quick few words and some last minute and up to date instructions, we were informed that it was forecast to be sunny and warm!

The track was well-used and ideal for running, as usual the racing snakes raced ahead and were out of sight within minutes.

We mediocre runners plodded along trying to get the pacing right - 58km was a long way and if the sun was out to do its worst we were in for a long day. It was not the day for 'cockups'.

I found myself running alongside a German runner, a runner I had not really seen but then owing to the self imposed 'hibernation' we had thus far enjoyed, it wasn't surprising. I'm sure a few more new faces would appear now that the relentless rain had stopped, which in turn had released us from our small damp and somewhat smelly - hideaways.

After about half an hour my running partner seemed to be getting slower, 20 minutes later I approached an 'unofficial checkpoint' a couple of the race crew were pointing us in the right direction.

After about 20 minutes we were negotiating our way across streams and little rivers then all of a sudden - checkpoint 1.

A quick top up of water, a clamber up a steep bank and back onto the trail proper. Running along, I was aware of a runner approaching from behind. When they drew level it was Richard, we plodded along together for a while, chatting and then we spotted checkpoint 2. Again, a quick top up and some instructions from the crew on how to proceed to the next checkpoint, which was basically to follow a main road and we would see it!

Leaving the checkpoint, Richard started to ever so slowly pull away. I tried to follow but failed miserably, deciding instead to keep him in sight. This road was long and monotonous, one of those that you could see for miles ahead and the horizon never seemed to alter - a bit like running on a treadmill, bloody frustrating.

It was only the fact that I had a runner ahead to focus on that kept me running, had Richard not been within sight I would in all likelihood have started walking, moaning and cursing my stupidity for once again signing up to do some stupid, pointless race.

These thoughts are common and frequent. I think every 'ultra' race I have done has been my last, "never again" is a recurring theme and at the time I'm usually suffering and in pain, but I am, at the time, deadly serious. As is the amount of checkpoints I have approached with the very genuine intention to stop upon arrival.

But for some reason I have yet to fathom, I leave the checkpoint promising that, at the next one, I'll stop.

I would like to think that it's pride but it is probably nearer the truth to say it's a mixture of cowardice and stupidity!

I am also fully aware that, no matter how painful the race is, it will stop, the pain will end. However, not finishing will be fucking painful and that pain will be permanent, always there, gnawing away!

So on I plod.

Following the road, which was now starting to get harder because of the fact that we were now climbing, Richard, who was probably 750 meters ahead, disappeared over the summit of the hill. Once I reached the summit I could just make out what I hoped was the next checkpoint.

I ran trying to keep the 'checkpoint' and Richard in sight and as I got nearer I was able to confirm that it was indeed the checkpoint.

I reached the checkpoint just as Richard was leaving. A quick couple of electrolyte drinks and I also left.

It was now getting hot and for the first time it actually felt like a desert race: clear blue skies, scorching hot sunshine and dunes, actual sand dunes. Though we were running on rocky tracks the dunes were just to our right and they were huge - the thought of actually having to climb one filled me with dread, these 'huge' dunes were nothing compared to the Monster dune 45 and Big Daddy the name of the dunes we were supposed to climb later.

As I ran along, I noticed that Richard had turned around a couple of times. Was he suffering, was he checking on me? I wasn't sure and besides, it didn't make a bit of difference. I was struggling, my legs were tired, so much so that I decided to walk for a minute or two. As I started walking, Richard turned around and then he also started walking - at that moment I realised that we were both using each other. He didn't want me to catch him and I didn't want to lose sight of him. We had, it seemed, reached a sort of understanding.

We carried on like this until the next checkpoint came into view. When I finally reached the checkpoint, Richard was still there, receiving instructions on how to proceed. I listened to the instructions, which were vague, to say the least. One of the crew sort of pointed over to his right and, with a generous sweep of his arm (which seemed to cover a 15 to 20 mile radius), explained that the road was over in that direction and we should hit the road and follow it along until the next checkpoint.

We left the checkpoint together, not because of any budding friendship or mutual respect but because I'm sure that, like me, Richard hadn't got a clue what he was on about - at least together we might just figure it out.

We ran side by side, trying to see footprints of the previous runners, but nothing.

This whole area had recently been flooded, silt and sand mixed together, the going was tricky and wet. Soft ground that required a degree of concentration lest you step onto an ankledeep extra-soft bit.

We carried on like this for some time, then way ahead movement, a reflection, a vehicle. We both saw it and realised that it was the sun shining off a windscreen.

Richard increased his speed. I tried and failed.

As we got nearer to where the reflection was seen, another one appeared and then, suddenly, just ahead of us was the road. I was glad Richard was ahead because if I had been here on my own, I would have had to have guessed: left or right (and I would have probably picked the wrong one!).

The road was in excellent condition and it was mighty tempting to run along it, but common sense prevailed and I started to run along the side. It was another one of those long, straight roads that was just demoralising. The only thing that helped break up the monotony was the sight of springbok and oryx and the fact that to our left were dunes - row after row of dunes. The knowledge that we were to climb to the top of one of them, but not just any one, the BIGGEST one, played heavily on my mind.

We ran along and the occasional car would speed past, then up ahead I spotted the checkpoint. Normally I would say finish line but this was a finish line with a difference. Once you crossed it you were given instructions to carry on and climb the worlds biggest dune, Dune 45, so named because of its position at 45 km along the road that connects Sesiem Gate to Sossusviel.

I reached the phantom finish line a couple of minutes behind Richard, who was now clambering up the side of the 170 meter monster, Dune 45.

I looked up and wished that I hadn't:- it was so steep that the summit was out of sight. I had a quick drink and started my ascent, after about two-thirds of the way up, Richard passed me on his way down, wearing a silly grin. He knew he was just about finished. I carried on, looked up, and realised that the last little bit had a severe kick in it - a really steep bit - on the top of which was a flag.

I reached the flag, grabbed a sticker of a smiley face (proof of reaching the summit), then I made my way back down.

I reached the bottom, handed in my sticker and grabbed the nearest chair. Sitting there, I noticed that a small crowd had gathered a few yards away from our checkpoint and a few of the guys seemed fascinated by what was going on, I moved closer to see for myself what the fascination was and, low and behold, there was a stunningly beautiful woman having her picture taken, she was dressed in the sexiest, skimpiest lingerie. A magazine photo shoot, using the desert dunes as a backdrop. It was, I decided, almost worth running the 58 km to study the photographer's art!

The Last Day

Woke up after an uncomfortable night.

Feeling not quite right, tired and with a slightly upset stomach. Nothing had happened - it just felt like that the moment I start to run, something unpleasant would happen. The situation was delicate to say the least. I tried to sort things out before I got to the start line but nothing.

The only thing I could do was to start today's run with plenty of toilet paper and a little prayer!

Whilst standing on the start line, listening to the race briefing, I got the distinct impression that the organisers had only a rough idea of how long and where the route would be: they seemed to be playing it very much by ear.

We finally boarded the coaches for the start of our last day, still not really knowing how far we would be running, but it was the last day.

Once we arrived we were given last minute final instructions.

The first 8 to 10 km were flat, normally a good thing. However, today I was looking for an escape route should an emergency arise and the upset stomach decided to give me what for.

There was nothing, nowhere to hide, the whole area was flat and featureless, small rocks and stones, dunes way off in the distance but nothing to hide behind. If the worst came to the worst, I would be on show, performing to all and sundry.

As the countdown began, we lined up, wished each other luck and then the 3 2 1 and we trotted off. I deliberately started slowly, just testing things out, after a couple of kms I felt confident enough to pick up the pace.

After a while, I had that uncomfortable bloated, I need to go feeling- was I flatulent or was I poorly? Do I or don't I? a terrible dilemma and one I'm sure we have all experienced at one time or other, should I or shouldn't I? Decision made and fortunately it was the right decision - flatulence and with it instant relief, I felt so much better and was consequently able to both relax and pick up the pace.

After about 10km the flat terrain came to an end right at the foot of a dune and then it was another monumental lung-bursting effort to clamber over the thing.

Once over the top, I could see the first checkpoint and Richard. We left the checkpoint together after being given a bit of advice. "Go around and not across, the dried up lake."

We were in some sort of basin and it was obvious that this basin had been flooded and full of water not long ago. Skirting around the thing took so much longer but looking at the footprints of a couple of the lead runners it was pretty obvious that they had tried the shortcut and failed, as the footprints had brought them back to the skirting around route.

We carried on around the edge and we were fully aware that the heat in this basin was magnified - it was incredibly hot and there was virtually nowhere to escape, it was a question of just getting out as quickly as possible.

As we plodded along we suddenly spotted one of the race crew, desperately trying to get some shade under a small bushy shrub. So small was it that it just about reached my knees, I couldn't blame her, the sun was relentless and where we were it was extremely exposed. Being in a bowl-like depression it seemed to bounce off the surface making it even hotter.

The poor girl was slowly cooking, but she smiled, said we were doing well and pointed us in the right direction.

The right direction just happened to be a very nasty-looking steep dune. We made our way over - on closer inspection it was worse than it had first appeared. The angle was such that you could not see the top. I plodded on, using my hands as much as I was using my feet - slow short steps, inch by lung-bursting inch we moved forward. Then we heard a voice telling us that we were nearly there, I couldn't even look up to see from where it was that the voice came. Then the top and the source of the mysterious voice: one of the race crew was on the top and giving directions whilst filming (you can see me and Richard descending the dune, on Youtube NDC 2012 In the dunes, Richard in blue me in white!), we followed his instructions, which were, fortunately, fairly simple - basically we were to descend this one climb the next one and follow the ridge line until we came across another member of the race crew who would then give us more directions to follow.

This continued until we came across a crew member who said that the finish line was just around the corner, and so it was 500 meters later that we crossed the finish line together.

I loved this race, with its static campsite, being fed and watered at the end of each day, power sockets and showers. A great first time desert race - well organised and worth every penny.

What next?

Here we go again. I was cold and my clothes were damp. Rain was forecast. I love desert races!

Coming off one of the world's biggest sand dunes, Dune 45,
I wasn't smiling on my way up!

THE WINTER 100 2012

What is it: A 100 mile trail race

When: November

Where: Starts from Streatley, Berkshire

Distance: 100 miles

It is: A race that consists of four out and back spurs

See: centurionrunning.com

This race was very much a part of my preparation for the 6633 Ultra, which was to take place in March.

I hadn't planned to race the Winter 100, but simply collect the miles and get myself 'match fit' for the 6633.

Unfortunately, for us, for a few days prior to the race it had rained, really rained, so much so that large parts of the country were flooded. Flood warnings were issued and the scheduled Winter 100 race course had not escaped.

Arriving at the hotel in Streatley-On-Thames the night before and the outlook did not look good - it was still raining and the forecast was more rain.

During the race briefing, we were informed that large parts of the original route had now been changed as most of it was under water and the bits that weren't would in, all likelihood, soon would be.

We were given new routes and new instructions, however,

there was a very real chance that these new changes could themselves be changed. In other words, no-one, even the race director, didn't really know what the final route would be.

Fortunately for Ultra-Distance Race organisers, ultra runners are a peculiar breed - all they really need is for someone to point them in the right direction and let them go. Not one runner complained, the very nature of the sport seems to attract the sort of personality that sees a problem or obstacle as simply that: a problem that needs to be solved or overcome.

With the talking finally over, it was time to don wet weather gear, Gortex trainers and sealskin gloves. A multi-coloured group of slightly apprehensive, damp runners stood on the start line, listening to the rhythmic slapping of raindrops hitting the fabric of the soon to be tested wet weather gear. I put my hood up, in the rather forlorn hope of keeping dry, but the noise of rain hitting the flimsy material was just amplified. I couldn't hear myself think let alone hear the countdown that was now taking place.

As the slow procession of anxious runners made their way through Streatley, nervous conversations took place. Previous races were spoken off and compared. After about twenty minutes or so the procession became a little strung out and the talking stopped.

Once we got out of Streatley the real racing snakes took off, us more mediocre runners plodded along the quagmire trying desperately trying to avoid the now churned-up, squelching, muddy route. Crossing fields and running through villages, then shortly before I got to the turnaround point, the lead runners were already heading toward me.

The return journey was a little worse than the initial outward run, the fields and narrow paths were now churned up and sticky underfoot. Horrible, heavy glue-like mud stuck to the underside of the shoes, slightly annoying but it did make for some rather interesting styles of locomotion. Hobbling, waddling, duck-like plodding could be seen, inching across what I guessed had once been a field, but now appeared to be more like a lagoon.

Arriving at the race HQ back in Streatley, I was pleased to have survived - everything was wet, even my super-duper, really expensive storm-proof wet weather gear couldn't cope with the onslaught of a real British downpour. Some of the other runners were not having a good time, there were a few sullen faces and shivering bloodied bodies. People had been slipping and sliding their way to the checkpoint, some were covered in scratches and grazes, the expressions etched on their faces encouraged me to get going. I was starting to get cold and I knew that if people started dropping out it could have a domino effect, at least if I got going I would warm up and not be witness (or get tempted to follow) to what I thought might happen (a mass exodus) and drop out.

I reluctantly left the warmth of race HQ and made my way out of Streatley, following, for several miles the same route that we had for the first loop - then a quick right hand turn, I slipped, moaned, carried on and promptly slipped again.

It was now dark, and with cloud-covered skies, was even darker: black as a witch's tit as they say. I followed the trail which led me into some trees, the relief was immediate - I was at last out of the wind.

My pace had slowed as self-preservation took over. I had to be cautious, being a cowardy-custard meant that I was being super careful.

The downside of having adopted a more sensible pace was that I was now getting cold. The terrain was tricky to follow but the sodden ground made things a whole lot worse and for the umpteenth time I went over. I was beginning not to enjoy myself. I have done races where I have been cold, tired, struggled with the terrain, not sure where I'm going, injured and in pain and on a couple of occasions I could have even cried but never have I been as fed up and pissed off as I was with the constant slipping over. What was preying on my mind was injury, I really could not afford to get injured. I could cope with the odd scratch, lumps and bumps but my main priority, and the only reason I was taking part in this race, was as part of my preparation for the 6633 Ultra, 15 weeks from now.

It was while I was mulling this over that I reached the Swyncombe farm checkpoint. I instantly felt more sorry for the crew, than I did myself. This checkpoint was, unfortunately, a tent. It was now just a sodden windblown excuse for a tent, for poor crew were bravely trying to help us, when the fact of the matter was they were as wet and quite possibly colder than us. At least we could get moving and warm up - they were static. I felt guilty for feeling sorry for myself, put on an extra top and left.

I later found out, that so horrendous were the conditions that two of the checkpoints, like so many of the runners, didn't survive the race. Swyncombe farm being one of them. They had been blown away and knocked down, reducing the crew to use their vehicles as impromptu checkpoints.

Though I was feeling okay and relatively strong, the slipping and tripping were again playing on my mind. I slowed down, watched every footfall, was ultra-cautious but the price I was having to pay was to be freezing.

My fear of injury was such that I had very little choice other than to be careful - it was sort of working - I was slipping less.

I plodded on and managed to reach the last checkpoint before Streatley. This checkpoint was inside a building, it was lovely to be out of the wind and rain. I took my time, had a hot drink and some food and gathered my thoughts.

When I could put it off no longer I, with great reluctance, left the checkpoint. Normally, I hate checkpoints and can't wait to leave them.

As I stepped out into the wind and rain, I tried to work how long it would take me to do the last two laps - no matter how quick I could do them, it would not be quick enough.

I approached the Streatley race HQ and decided to have a bit of a break and put some dry socks and shoes on, if only to cheer me up a bit. Two laps down, two to go.

I sat there eating and looking at the carnage around me.
As I was eating my third peanut butter, sandwich a runner
came limping in, blood running down one very wet shin, the
blood and rain mixture made the bleeding seem a whole lot
more dramatic. He grabbed a chair next to one guy who was
busy strapping up his foot, another runner that had earlier
withdrawn came hobbling past and then it happened:- my
bottle went. I knew I had pushed my luck but the chances of
me remaining injury-free were just too much of a concern. I
couldn't, wouldn't risk it.

The 6633 Ultra was my goal, it had taken me years to pluck
up the courage to have another go and I had spent a small
fortune, I erred on the side of caution and made a tactical
withdrawal. Decision made I walked over to the support
crew and informed them that I would be going no further.

The Winter 100 is organised by runners for runners, this
was the first time this particular race had been run and it
was a real shame that the weather was so awful but the way
the organisers and crew handled the last-minute changes
was impressive. I will be back - this race, like the 6633, is
unfinished business!

THE 6633 ULTRA 2013

The Rime of the Ancient Mariner

The ice was here,
The ice was there,
The ice was all around:
It cracked and growled, and roar'd and howl'd,
Like noises in a swound

Samuel Taylor Coleridge 1772 1834

What is it: Extreme Cold weather ultra distance race

When: March

Where: The Yukon region of Canada

Distance: Either 120 miles or 352 miles (193 kms or 566 kms)

It is: Tough (the statistics speak for themselves) a cold-weather extreme ultra-distance self-sufficient footrace

See: 6633ultra.com

Standing on the start line of the 6633 Ultra, memories came flooding back to five years ago, when I stood at this exact same spot.

2008

The year was 2008, I had raced in the Arctic twice before. In 2006 I had completed the Yukon Arctic Ultra 100 mile race and the following year had raced the 320 mile version and had somehow managed to be the first individual to finish, beaten only by a team of Italians.

Those two races had unfortunately given me, rightly or wrongly, confidence. I say unfortunately because, as I had finished my first two Arctic races, I figured that I had got the hang of racing in the Arctic. I had, after all, been racing some of the most extreme races on earth for 12 years never failed to finish and my positions were getting better with every race.

The 6633 was, I had decided, just another race that I could bullshit and boast about - all I had to do is what I always do, put one foot in front of the other until I reached the finishing line.

This race should, in theory, be easier than the Yukon Arctic Ultra because it is run along the Dempster Highway for the first 235 miles and then it switches onto a Ice Road all the way to the finish at Tuktoyaktuk on the Arctic Ocean. In other words, you are just walking along a very long road.

The Dempster Highway is predominately a gravel track and consequently the sledges we are required to have for our obligatory equipment have to have some sort of wheeled system without which the sledge would get worn down by the abrasive action of gravel on plastic.

It was this wheeled contraption that would give me so much trouble. I hadn't thought it through, I hadn't tested it. It was my rather cavalier attitude that would come back to haunt me.

As I stood on the start line, with my rather smug, 'just another race' attitude, I even thought about the possibility of winning!

However, the reality set in the moment we started, my sledge was giving me problems. It didn't feel right with just the two centrally-mounted wheels. Balancing the load was difficult, it was somehow front-heavy, the front of the sledge bounced, occasionally the front of the sledge would hit the ground and worse every bounce jarred my hips. It was like someone constantly prodding you - bloody annoying! I stopped, tried to re-balance the thing and as I was sorting out the load, I noticed that the front of the sledge was already being worn away.

The re-balancing act failed and the bouncing continued.

I am not a physically strong person, nor am I a member of MENSA and on this occasion my limited strength out-weighed my limited intelligence. I chose to ignore the blindingly obvious and continued to push and pull my way forward. It was, I'm afraid, a case of my limited brawn over my even more limited brain. Any sensible person would have stopped and sorted themselves out, but sensible and me have never really got on, so I quite literally ploughed on.

The effort was enormous, so much so that I had started to get a bad back. Each time the front of the sledge bounced it sent a shockwave up through my back, which was both annoying and painful. However, my stubbornness, or should I say, bloody-mindedness pushed me forward.

I arrived at the first checkpoint, tried again to sort my sledge out. It was now that I noticed the size of the hole that had been worn away by the constant bouncing - it was now collecting snow and gravel at an alarming rate. I cleared the snow and gravel, re-balanced the thing and, like a bloody idiot, continued on my way.

The effort required was too much, I was working hard, far harder than I should have been for a race of this distance. I continued on with my familiar slow, methodical 'autoplod', then suddenly I stopped. I had completed maybe 35 miles of a 352 mile race, less than one 10th of what I was supposed to do and yet out of nowhere, I realised the futility of what I was doing: there was absolutely no way I could finish this race - 12 years of racing Ultra-distance races and now for the first time, I withdrew, scratched, DNFd, whatever the term is I would not, could not, finish a race!

With the decision made, I vowed there and then that I would be back. I've done some tough races, races that I have had to dig deep for and races that have been bloody painful but nothing hurt like the pain of not finishing - never again will I have a race that I will not finish.

2013

It had taken 5 years to pluck up the courage to return but I was here, better prepared:- my sledge now had 4 wheels instead of 2, thus eliminating the balancing problem. And, crucially, I now had a healthy respect for the 6633 Ultra.

That healthy respect had manifested itself in a number of ways, one was the equipment - it was all tried and tested, no cutting corners, everything was thought through. Kit, including food, was well-considered and finally, training, normally I train to finish a race. I normally do enough training to get me to the finishing line. This time, however, I had trained hard and for the first time ever I trained to be competitive. Unfortunately, I can be a vindictive person - it's just one of the many flaws in my personality and five years ago the 6633 had beaten me. It had kicked my arse and sent me packing - this time it was my turn to kick arse. I would finish, no matter what.

As I stood on the start line, those memories of five years ago were uppermost in my thoughts. Things were different now, I was just confident as opposed to over-confident. The countdown began, my heart rate increased, I became extremely focused, gripped my trekking poles a little too tightly, 3, 2, 1, and we were off. I was oblivious to all that was happening around me, except for the one racer ahead, Kevin. He was already moving at an amazing speed, a speed I doubted he could maintain. (I was wrong, he managed to maintain more or less the same pace for the whole of his race!). I just focused on my own race - tempted though I was to chase, I remembered that 352 miles was a bloody long way. My strength has always been endurance. I can plod for a very long time. If I suddenly tried to use speed instead of endurance I would come a cropper. It's a cliché but it really was about the 'Hare and the Tortoise'.

I let Kevin go and was watching him disappear, when I was suddenly aware of someone beside me - Ben.

Ben and his partner were both doctors. He was here racing the 120 plus, this gave him the option of, once he had reached Fort McPherson, continuing all the way to Tuk. Kate was here as race medic but was doing the marathon distance to the first checkpoint.

Walking along together was enjoyable and it kept me in check. I'm sure that if I had been left to my own devices I would have tried to catch Kev.

We walked along until about the 20 mile mark and then I was on my own. I reached the checkpoint in 6 hours 10 minutes. The checkpoint is at 66 degrees and 33 minutes north, the official position of the Arctic Circle, hence the race name 6633. I topped up my small flask with hot water and left. I was in the checkpoint for a total of three minutes.

I gave myself a quick mental check and was pleased - everything felt good and there were no problems with equipment, feet felt good, no aches or pains, so unlike last time I was here.

As I left the checkpoint I could see Kev. Though I knew he was in the 120 mile race, I decided to keep him in sight, use his impressive pace to sort of drag me along. It might not be cricket, but it was, I decided, a bloody sensible thing to do and besides (I reasoned) he would never know!

During my 3 previous Arctic races I had learnt many things and one of those things was how to move for many hours without having to stop. This particular skill was now paying dividends because, even though our paces were similar, Kev's short regular stops to take drinks and things allowed me to gain some ground and before long we were walking together.

It was now late afternoon (I wasn't wearing a watch so had to guess) and we had covered around thirty-five miles. This part of the route is extremely exposed and has been affectionately nick-named 'Hurricane Alley' as it has a tendency to be at the mercy of some Katabatic winds. These hurricane-force winds are so strong that they have been known to blow over vehicles driving along the dempster, so any silly sod foolish enough to be walking along whilst pulling a sled would have very little chance. We were lucky the weather was beautiful, cold and crisp with lovely blue skies.

We walked along, occasionally talking bollocks, but more often than not we were just silently speeding along, both lost in thought, no doubt about our own races. It was early evening when Kev said that the unofficial Rock River checkpoint was not far ahead, this checkpoint was really just a place a place to sit down as nothing was supplied - not even water.

We continued on and to our right was a large disused shed, this shed had in the past been used as the checkpoint. The one we were looking at was three to four hundred meters further on.

We finally arrived at about 20:00. This improvised checkpoint was in fact a trailer, albeit a very nice trailer - spacious and warm. I think we were both surprised to see Mick, a fellow racer already in the trailer. He explained that he had been ill the night before and had got steadily worse as the day had progressed. He was left with no choice but to withdraw from the race, I could empathise with him, as it was more or less at the same point in the race that I'd had to withdraw, the last time I was here.

Kev left shortly after arriving. I decided to have a hot drink, a bit of food and a sit down. I still felt good, but was very aware of the enormous distance ahead I needed to be sensible. (A first for me!).

I left the Rock River checkpoint about 35 minutes after Kev. I felt refreshed and I felt strong. I pushed the pace a bit, knowing that my feeling good and strong was not likely to last, I had to take advantage of it while it was there.

Fortunately, not long after leaving the checkpoint was a climb. The Wright Pass is a long, strength-sapping, mind game. However, I like climbing and consequently got stuck into the thing with great gusto. After a while, I spotted up ahead the twin red flashing lights of Kevin - they at least gave me something to focus on. I tried to speed up but it really was just a token effort and didn't last long. I must have been moving well because I seemed to be gaining on Kev.

Eventually, we were once again walking along together and chatting. The evening was perfect - clear moonlit skies, so bright was the full moon that Kev hadn't bothered to put his headlight on. Mine was on only because the on/off switch was so small and fiddly that the only way I would have been able to switch it off would have been to remove the headlight and remove my gloves. In short, it wasn't worth the effort, so on it stayed.

As we carried on talking and walking, I caught sight of something up ahead and to my right - it was moving and it was moving toward us. Out here, miles from the nearest anything, meant that it could only be an animal and I just hoped that if it was an animal it had either eaten or was just curious. I gripped my walking poles just a little tighter, ready to use them as improvised weapons, should the need arise. Then the 'animal' spoke, it spoke with a very distinctive and very English middle-class accent. "Have you seen the northern lights?" We hadn't. So busy talking bollocks and pushing our way forward that we hadn't even noticed one of nature's most spectacular phenomenon.

The 'voice' belonged to Mark Hines, one of the support crew. Mark had decided to camp out on the Wright pass and had been watching our progress. We looked up and were indeed treated to the most spectacular light show on earth. I have seen the northern lights, or to give them their correct name, Aurora Borealis, a few times before and they always make me smile. They always fascinate me, so spectacular were they that they instantly reduced me and Kev into a couple of silent voyeurs.

Mark walked with us for a few yards before saying that it was just 6km to the summit.

We carried on silently. Kev broke the silence by pointing out a small Arctic fox. This fox was walking along beside us - it was maybe 8 to 10 feet away, happily walking along with us, curious and unconcerned. It stayed by our side for 15 to 20 minutes before finally crossing over in front of us, walked along for a few more minutes, got bored, and then disappeared into the snow.

Life, I decided, doesn't really get much better. I was in one of the most beautiful places on earth, I felt good and I felt strong. I was in a good position within the race, the northern lights were doing their best to impress, a curious Arctic fox was entertaining us and Kev was pleasant company. It is these small moments that make the lunatic sport of Ultra-distance running worthwhile. How many times have I been asked why, why do you do ultras? The answer was all around me. Unfortunately, most people will never get to see or experience the answer!

Kev seemed to be slightly stronger than me and was slowly inching his way ahead. I wasn't fussed or concerned, I was happy and comfortable with my own pace and was still very conscious of the 300 miles or so I had left. I watched Kev creeping ever further ahead.

Further and higher his lights went, before suddenly disappearing - the disappearing lights would, I hope, only mean one thing - the summit. It was not long before my summit theory was confirmed. The moment I reached it I was mesmerised, mesmerised by a dazzling display of lights. This mass of lights confused me:- was there a small town or village, was it the James Creek checkpoint? All I could remember about the top of the Wright pass was that it was the border between the Yukon and the Northern territories and the clocks went forward one hour. I desperately tried to remember the route details.

As I got closer to the mysterious lights I could see that they belonged to a huge lorry. One of the ice road truckers had parked up in the small parking area and his wagon was festooned with numerous headlights. Just behind the lorry I spotted Kev who was sitting down and having a tea break. I wandered over, had a quick chat, and though it was mighty tempting to have a rest, I really just wanted to get to the James Creek checkpoint so I could grab some sleep.

I left Kev and moved fast, the route had at last stopped climbing and allowed me to pick up the pace slightly. There was another added incentive and that was the fact that the checkpoint was only about 14/15 km away.

I hadn't got a clue what time it was and was busy trying to work out my plan of action once I got to the checkpoint, when a vehicle suddenly approached. It was Martin, the race director who informed me that the checkpoint was 13km away and they were expecting me.

I thanked him and moved off, desperately trying, and failing, to pick up the pace. After a while, another vehicle approached and this time it was Kate, the race doctor, who informed me that the checkpoint was 7km away, less than 5 miles. I again tried, and I again failed, to pick up the pace. Then, suddenly, turning a corner and slightly to my left was a wonderful sight of bright orange lights - never in the history of highway maintenance workshops has one looked so beautiful!

I pulled up outside, it was 05:53. I removed my sled bag and entered what was really just a vehicle workshop - the Hilton it was not. Smelly, dusty and noisy. However, it was warm and out of the cold. Sue, one of the race crew, beckoned me in, asked if I needed anything. Just hot water and a place to sleep was my reply.

The only other person there was Mick, the guy I had seen at the Rock River checkpoint, and he was asleep. Then, a few minutes after my arrival, the door opened and in came

Kev, annoyingly looking good and fairly fresh. I grabbed a small area of the floor, unrolled my sleeping bag and had a re-hydrated hot meal. Before I dozed off, Sue asked what I would need before I went and what time would I be leaving? I wanted to leave at 09:00 - it was now a little after 06:30 so I got my flasks out and said "I would like to fill these and if you could wake me up in a couple of hours so I could leave at nine?" Sue, like a mother hen, was fantastic and more than happy to kick me out at nine. I sort of fell asleep - it was a cross between dozing and napping. All too soon I was being woken, not by the gentle tones of the gentle female voice, but a fire extinguisher! Sue was busy boiling water for my flasks but the camping stove she was using was, to say the least, temperamental, so temperamental was it that it set fire to itself. A fire in a fume-filled, oil-stained vehicle workshop, was not great. Immediate action was required. Kev grabbed a fire extinguisher and was doing battle with the now flaming stove. Fine white powder and the smell of melted plastic now filled the air.

A few minutes later, Kev left. The time was about a quarter to eight. I tried to get back to sleep, failed miserably, so decided to get up and get going. I had a quick bite to eat and then started to pack. Sue, in the meantime, used the remaining two 'jetboil' stoves to heat water for my flasks. Just as I was about to leave, another racer, Ian, came in. His first question to me was "Are you leaving?" When I replied that I was, his next question was "How long have you been here?" I hadn't really noticed Ian prior to this - he seemed quietly composed, serious and organised - he finished getting himself sorted - I bade farewell, and left the James Creek checkpoint at 08:46.

The next checkpoint was Fort Mcpherson, some 47 miles away. I was glad to be on my way, I was feeling well fed and watered and it was another glorious sunny day - beautiful clear blue skies, cold, yes, but not quite the hostile Arctic weather I was expecting.

Shortly after leaving the checkpoint, the route passed through a gorge. The gorge was in shadow and was stunning; filled with broken ice and 'overflow' that needed to be avoided, beautiful aquamarine-coloured ice littered large parts. Such a visual feast was it, that your mind was somewhat distracted from the fact that you were actually climbing. The climb wasn't particularly steep but it was noticeable. As I neared the top of the gorge I could see that there was a right-hand turn and through the steep gorge walls the sun was shining and brilliant.

I was glad to reach the top - the effort to do so had left me nicely warm and once I got into the sun, I would no doubt, get warmer. I stopped, had a quick coffee and replaced my small down jacket with a gillet. Whilst I was doing this, I took in the stunning view. I could see for miles and scanned the route ahead for any sight of Kev - he must have been shifting because I could see nothing.

I moved off and, fortunately, the route was now descending, I decided to move fast, lest someone behind decided to scour the route looking for the runner ahead, me. I know it sounds petty and childish but I also know that if I see someone ahead it not only gives me a great boost to morale but it also gives me something to chase. In short, I didn't want someone using me even though I had used Kevin. Hypocrisy, another one of those flaws in my personality! (The sport of ultra-distance running really does have a knack of finding the strengths, weaknesses and flaws in your personality).

I moved quickly and still felt comfortable. After a while, I passed what appeared to be a campsite. It was now, however, snow covered and abandoned. Midway Lake, the sign post proudly stated. Midway between where and where, I wasn't sure. Then suddenly the road widened and another sign stated that this was an 'Emergency airstrip'. I continued along the annoying road, annoying because it was constantly undulating, small hill after small hill. You could never see further than the next small hill. It was when I was having a private moan to myself about yet another bloody hill that I realised a vehicle had drawn level with me. It was Martin

Like, the race director, he leaned out of the window offering words of encouragement and asked if I was racing Kev - I wasn't. Martin, I'm sure, seemed concerned that I was being a bit of a pillock. He didn't want me to blow my chances of completing the 352 miles to Tuk. I tried to reassure him but he didn't look convinced!

Shortly after Martin left, I spotted a 50km to Fort Mcpherson sign - roughly 30 miles.

At Fort Mcpherson I planned to have a good long break of at least six hours, so I was keen to crack on. I was eating and drinking regularly and felt surprisingly good. Even though I had not seen Kev since James Creek, it was knowing he was ahead of me that spurred me on. I always assumed that I would be able to spot him and maybe, just maybe, if he was resting, or had problems, would catch him.

I continued on with thoughts of catching Kev and not getting caught myself, when a sign proclaimed Peel River Ice crossing 2km ahead. Crossing the frozen Peel river and clambering up the other side another sign informed me that Fort Mcpherson was 11km away. I tried to hurry but my knackered old legs were having none of it. Then a vehicle approached, slowed down and turned around and stopped. It was one of the race vehicles coming to meet me. They said that Fort Mcpherson was just 5km away and they would guide me in because it was a bit tricky finding the school that the checkpoint was in.

I was grateful for that, as I know from bitter experience, that trying to find a checkpoint in a town, at night and when you're knackered, is never straightforward. (This was later confirmed when one of the runners left the school, but could not find the Dempster Highway and consequently spent an hour or so walking around fort Mcpherson until a race vehicle saw him and guided him out!).

I finally arrived at the Chief Julius School at 22:44, a little bit quicker than I was expecting. Kev had arrived a couple of hours ago and had managed to break the record for the distance by about four hours.

I went through my usual routine:- feet sorted out first, drinks and food, then told some exaggerated war stories and then a catch up on the latest news of other runners.

Once that was all done, it was a quick wash, teeth clean and bed. The school gym was the designated sleeping area. I was surprised by the amount of people there already. Each of them for whatever reason, had withdrawn. I felt, well, I don't know what I felt. Though most of them seemed to be awake, the gym lights were on and I could see and hear them fidgeting, farting, faffing, coughing and the odd snore. No-one spoke to me. I felt awkward, maybe they felt the same.

I got sorted, had more food and set my alarm. Just to make sure, I had asked Sue if she could wake me at 4:15 as I didn't want to oversleep. At a little before four I woke, lay there and a few minutes later the ever-reliable Sue came in and made sure I was awake. As I was packing up to leave, one of those deja vu moments - Ian walked in and again asked if I was leaving and what time did I get here!

Ian, I have to say, looked pretty good and I figured that he, if anyone, could win this race. I knew nothing about him, what races he had done (if any), his background, training - nothing except that he was on my tail and would be difficult to shake off. I put these thoughts to the back of my mind, as I had decided long ago that this was not a race for me, it was a challenge that I WOULD finish. If I got into a race my whole pace, strategy, plan, and way of thinking would be dictated by someone else. I knew what I had to do and I knew how to do it. In short, I had my plan and I was going to stick to it, come what may.

Leaving the Fort Mcpherson checkpoint at 05:14, I was in fact 46 minutes earlier than I had originally planned. However, it was my decision and had not been dictated by anyone else!

Once I found my way back onto to the Dempster, I suddenly realised how cold it was - so cold that I had to, for the first time, put on my big down jacket. I wanted to move fast on this section, it was one of the shorter sections at 38 miles. Thankfully the terrain was pretty good and allowed for speedy progress. After about three or four hours I had a quick drink of coffee. I carry a small flask on a hip belt - this allows me to have a hot drink whilst moving. With the snacks in my pockets and my camelbak, I have no real need to stop. I move constantly, eat and drink on the move, saving valuable time. I have seen racers in the past, stopping regularly to get something out of their sled or stop to eat or drink. It might only be for a minute or two but it is a minute or two lost!

The road was long and straight and you could, unfortunately, see for miles ahead. A vehicle would come past and you would spend the next twenty minutes, half an hour, watching it disappear into the distance. Consequently, I spent a large amount of this section with my head down, only ever looking at the few feet in front of me.

My mind began to wander. I'm often asked what I think about when I'm doing these things and I have to say that I think I have just about covered every subject under the sun, from who had a hit with that annoying tune I keep humming to myself, I should really learn to cook, I must finish that little landscaping project I started, I must knuckle down and train for the Norseman, I wish I had got one of those 'coldavenger' face masks, who was the woman who sang on the Flying Lizards, "Money that's what I want" single, I'm glad I went for the four wheels, and not two, and Cameron Diaz. Well, lets just say I think of all sorts of things. It helps if you have a great imagination, this is definitely not a sport for people with no imagination.

As I was lost in thought, a vehicle pulled up beside me - Martin. He explained that Tsiigehtchic was 13 kms away, and went on to explain how to get to it, as it was a bit of a maze. I thanked him and, as he pulled away, I tried to speed up - it didn't last long.

I drank the last of my lukewarm coffee and was busy shoving in a handful of Rolos, when I suddenly remembered the woman who sang with the Flying Lizards was called Deborah something!

As I got closer to Tsiigehtchic, which apparently translates to 'Mouth of the Iron River,' I again tried to speed up. Fortunately, the last little bit was downhill, unfortunately, however, it was taking me away from where I wanted to go. I tried to remember what Martin had said, something about having to go away from it before returning to it. I crossed my fingers and just followed the road. After a while and with Tsiigehtchic behind me I spotted the signpost that guided me in. Just as I was turning onto the frozen river crossing, a snowmachine came towards me and stopped. An elderly couple were on the thing - they introduced themselves and asked if I was okay. I replied that I was and I was just on my way to the Community Gymnasium. They asked where I had come from and then explained how to get to the Gymnasium. They then invited me to their house for some hot soup - tempting though it was, I explained that I was in a race and if I received any help I would be disqualified. I then went on to explain that the race had started at Eagle Plains and that I was now walking to Tuk.

They looked at me with a look that said "Of course you are."

I carried on along the river and on entering Tsiigehtchic, I saw coming towards me a couple of fellow racers that had kindly come to show me the way. Walking through the maze-like community I was thankful that they had come out, as I would never have found the thing.

I arrived at 17:26 and Shelly, one of the racers, asked if I would like a cup of tea. What is it about a good old cuppa? Even the offer is comforting. I hadn't planned to stay long, just long enough to have some food, a quick wash, clean my teeth, top up my flasks and go.

I left the checkpoint a couple of hours later at 19:35. I knew this next section at 51 miles was going to be tough, not just the distance but the long flat sections would be mentally challenging and I figured that if I could do most of it through the night, it would be a little easier.

As I was packing up to leave, Martin came over and gave me some directions and explained the route ahead. Unfortunately for the poor old racer, Martin suffers from a rare medical condition, so rare is it that it has yet to be named. There are medical terms for colour blindness (colour vision deficiency), word blindness (dyslexia) and even number blindness (dyscalculia) but hill blindness, or the complete inability to see or acknowledge the fact that when terrain ascends or climbs it, is called a hill.

Martin went on to explain that there was a slight hill three or four km away and after that the route is fairly flat. Martin saying that there is a 'slight hill' set off the alarm bells. I had already struggled to clamber up some of his flat sections, so I braced myself for a challenging slog, uphill climb.

With Martin's well-intentioned route description ringing in my ears, I left Tsiigehtchic. Once I dropped down onto the frozen river the wonderful world of silence returned. Lost in thought and plodding along the Dempster, a truck passed me, beeped his horn and waved. I smiled and gave him the thumbs up. The early evening dusk allowed me the opportunity to follow the truck's rear red lights for a few minutes as it made steady progress. It turned slightly right and then it started heading up into the night sky - the thing actually looked as if it was driving vertically, up and up it went before disappearing into the sky.

I carried on and then came face to face with the 'slight hill'. It looked awful, probably made worse by my over-active imagination. As I approached the thing, a thought occurred - I was walking on the left, they drive on the right, in other words, should a vehicle suddenly appear over the brow of the hill it would be on my side of the road and would not see me!

I went into self-preservation mode, crossed my fingers, removed my balaclava, so that I could at least hear any approaching vehicle. I watched the road ahead like a hawk and went hell for leather - speed and self-preservation far outweighed any idea of sensible pacing and besides, I could have a breather when and if I reached the safety of the summit. I just hoped that this small section of the Dempster would remain vehicle-free for the next few minutes!

I hugged the snowbank and hurried up all the time, keeping my eyes and ears peeled for any oncoming vehicles. I was lucky and reached the top in one slightly knackered piece.

Once on the top, I celebrated my good fortune with a handful of Haribos and a handful of Rolos. It was now dark and I was very aware that this section was "challenging" and I was extremely relieved that I could not see too far ahead. Feeling good, I pushed on at a reasonable pace, and then some time in the early hours, the 'sleepmonster' pounced. We had our usual tussle, but I have 'tussled' with the 'sleepmonster' enough to know when to back down and take a break and that time was now. Looking around, it was plainly obvious that there was nowhere to get off the road, with the metre high banks of rock hard, compact snow on either side, acting as a fence. I decided to have a picnic on the road.

Fortunately, the road being long and straight meant that any approaching vehicle could be seen for miles before it actually reached me.

I unharnessed, grabbed some food and coffee and, like the Mad Hatter, proceeded to have a little 'Tea Party', sitting on the Dempster eating Pringles crisps, shortbread biscuits, chocolate and jerky. As I sat there listening to the absolute silence, I looked around. Stillness and silence that's all there was, nothing, but nothing moved - it was as if I was sitting in a painting (well I told you I was tired!).

I continued on my way, the scenery and the terrain had not changed one bit. The road was long and straight, I was looking for any change just a little variety, anything to break the monotony. I was thankful it was dark, to do this section in the daylight would have been horrendous.

As the daylight appeared, I seemed to get a second wind. I drank more coffee, ate some Rolos and tried to put a spurt on. Then Martin made one of his welcome appearances, gave a few words of encouragement and disappeared.

I carried on and the terrain changed. There was a lot of overflow and large areas had been taped off - wet and slippery sections were everywhere and as I was carefully picking my way through, another vehicle approached. It was Murray, another one of the race crew. He explained that the Caribou checkpoint was 12 km ahead. I thanked him, and as he left, started to translate that into English 12 km = approx 8 miles.

I couldn't decide if that was good news or bad, but tried to hurry up anyway. I was still in the process of deciding, when I caught sight of one of the race vehicles parked up ahead and as I drew level, the occupants got out and said "Welcome to Caribou Creek". The time was 14:30.

I was mightily relieved, however, the two chalets that were being used were along a long narrow and soft snow-filled path. Looking at the soft-deep and uneven snow I was trying to work out how I was going to get my kit to the chalets when the guys who were now out of the race said they would bring my stuff in. Once again, the camaraderie of my fellow runners showed itself. I made my way along the path like an inebriated old drunk, tripping and slipping, occasionally one or other of my feet would disappear into knee-deep snow, as would one of my walking poles. Eventually I reached the chalets - one had a number of bunk-beds in and the other was being used for cooking, drying kit and as a sort of day room. I avoided the very tempting offer of a bed, tired as I was I didn't want to stay long: my plan had always been to have a good long sleep at the next checkpoint, Inuvik.

I once again went through my usual routine of checking and cleaning my feet, food and drinks, then once the personal admin was done I grabbed one of the three settees and got some sleep. I woke up at about 17:00 and got ready to leave, filled my flasks, had a bit more to eat and at 17:50 some 3 hours 20 minutes after arriving, I left.

I had no idea of how far behind or who it was in 2nd place but the fact that I was leaving checkpoints before they arrived was, I hoped, a good sign.

The next section was the second shortest at just 30 miles. Shortly after leaving Caribou Creek, I was treated to a small hill. Once on the top, the views opened up and were absolutely spectacular, the going was good and not too challenging. The short rest and sleep had recharged my batteries which had in turn enabled me to inject a bit of speed. It didn't last long and after about 4 or 5 hours I pulled over for a quick wee, something to eat and a cup of coffee. As I was drinking and eating, a vehicle approached and stopped - my first thought was that I had been caught "urinating in a public place". However, it was just a couple of the locals who asked if I was okay and did I need a lift? I replied that I was fine but my English accent must have thrown them, because they asked where I was from and what was I doing, out here at this time of night? I explained that I was in a race and that I was walking to Tuk. They humoured me but explained that the Ice Road was unusually slippery and I needed to be careful. I thanked them for stopping and moved off. A little time later another vehicle approached - it was Martin who stopped and informed me that Inuvik was 22km away. We had a little chat and he said that if I carried on at this rate I could break Mimi's record (Mimi Anderson Ultra-distance running legend holds the record for this race at 143:23 hours). This perked me up a bit, as he left he said that Kevin was coming out to meet me and would guide me in.

I carried on and again tried and again failed to pick up the pace but my mind was now, for the first time, beginning to think that I might actually finish the race and with Martin saying the record was a possibility, the thought that I could actually win this race occurred.

At home, when training and planning, I decided that my being able to finish would not be known until I had completed the massive 70 mile section from Inuvik to the Swimming point checkpoint - until then anything could happen.

As I was busy with thoughts of reaching Tuk, another vehicle approached. This time it was Kev, who explained how to get into Inuvik and that he would be waiting for me to guide me in. He confirmed that the chalet had a BED and a shower. I thanked him and watched him drive away.

It was, I decided, a perfect night. I could not only finish the race but I could, with a little luck, WIN and Martin had even said that the record was a possibility. On top of that, I was going to sleep in a bed for at least 6 hours and have a shower!

I spotted the orange lights and roadsigns. I was close, then I saw a sign that stated that Inuvik was 5km. I moved quickly and then spotted the headlights to Kev's car. He spotted me and flashed his lights. I drew level and he said that I was to follow him. I did. My eyes locked onto his rear red lights and they seemed to pull me along, then suddenly they stopped - we were here. The time was 03:35, it had taken me 9:45 to cover the 30 miles a little over 3 miles an hour, I was pleased with that.

Once in the chalet I was surprised to see so many people there, every inch of floor space was taken up with sleeping bodies and the only other bed had two bodies on it.

My first priority was a shower, then food. Then I sat on the bed sorting out my feet, before finally going to sleep. I had a great 5 hour sleep and woke at a little after 9:00. As I was getting ready, the guys who were no longer in the race were asking a 101 questions about kit, packing, pace and training. I was happy to answer and show them what I had, how it was packed, how I eat and drank whilst on the move, etc.

Once I had filled my flasks and finished packing it was time to go. I left the rather comfortable Arctic Chalets at 10:26.

Inuvik to Swimming Point - 70 miles

Lucky for me, a couple of the guys were going to take me down onto the Ice Road. Once on the frozen Mckenzie river, the temperature seemed to drop - it was bloody cold, so much so that less than an hour after starting, I had to stop and put on my warm overtrousers and an extra pair of gloves. Mick and Paul, the two guys that had showed me onto the Ice Road, now left. They were going for a cooked breakfast in a lovely warm hotel, BASTARDS. I could now get on and pick up the pace, I did this mainly to get warm and after a while I came to a wide left hand turn. The moment I turned into it, I was hit by a wind that I had not noticed until now. It was cold enough without the wind and now, with it, the windchill seemed to freeze my bones. Again I stopped and put on an extra layer, my super duper Norwegian windproof anorak. A quick cup of hot coffee, some jerky and I instantly felt better. However, that short stop to eat and drink had allowed the velcro fastening on my face mask to get 'iced up' making it difficult to close the thing. I moved off, aware that it was now starting to snow. I hoped it wouldn't last or if it did the wind would die out.

After about twenty minutes, my worst fears were confirmed: one of the locals that were driving towards me stopped and asked if I was okay and how far am I going? I explained that I was going to TUK, he looked concerned and asked if I knew there was a storm coming. I didn't and this was the first that I heard of it. I thanked him anyway and continued. Before long, another vehicle stopped and said that there was a lot of drifting up ahead and there were fifty mile an hour winds forecast. He then offered me some hot chocolate, a sandwich and an apple. I thanked him but explained that I was in a race and if I accepted any help (bloody tempting though it was) I would be disqualified. He wished me luck.

Not long after this, another vehicle, a 'highway maintence' vehicle approached me and told me that they were the last vehicle through, owing to the very heavy drifting and extremely high winds. Again, I thanked them.

I was now getting concerned (for concerned read scared!). It was getting dark and the road was disappearing. Another annoying problem was that the wheels on my sledge were happy to roll along the ice, but the drifting snowing was so soft that the wheels were not able to roll over the snow. Instead, the, pushed through which was a much less economical way of moving.

I ploughed on (sorry about that) but soon realised that the road had gone. There were no distinguishing marks, no trail markers, the metre high banks had gone. I was in a sea of snow, with no idea which way to go. I scanned the banks but even they had gone I turned around and could just about make out the outline of my sledge - so fast and thick was the snow that the tracks left by my sledge were instantly covered.

It was as if someone had thrown a rather large white sheet over me, a complete 'whiteout' - even my feet had disappeared. Though I had raced in heavy, freezing snow in the Yukon, this was different. The Yukon Arctic Ultra is on a well-defined trail and the only real way to get lost is by getting off the very obvious trail and then start pushing through trees. Or, if you are on a river or lake, the moment you step off the hard-packed trail you lose a leg in thigh-high soft snow.

I looked ahead, nothing, not a clue. Rather than waste energy by pushing on aimlessly I decided to do something that I very rarely do: bivi! I figured that I if I saved my energy, had a rest, ate and drank, I would be fresher and a little stronger to tackle the storm and if I was lucky - really lucky - the worst would blow over.

And so I got my bivi bag out, placed flashing lights on my

trekking poles and got into my snuggly, warm sleeping bag. One thing I always do when I'm doing these races is to put a bag of treats in my sleeping bag, because I know that by the time I decide to get in the thing I'm tired, fed up, slightly pissed off and usually wishing I was anywhere but here. But a little bag of goodies helps my rather low morale and the good thing is that I have usually forgotten it's there so to suddenly 'find' the bag in my sleeping bag cheers me up no end!

As I lay there like a child greedily eating sweets, I became aware of bright lights just outside. I unzipped my bag, popped my head out and there, parked not five feet away, was Martin Like, the race director, Martin had battled his way through to see for himself the conditions. I asked if he had any news about how long the storm was to last, he hadn't really, but thought that it might clear in the morning. After checking that I had all the kit required (should my bivi prove to be rather longer than planned), I assured him that I had, but hoped that I wouldn't have to use it.

He wished me luck and disappeared into the maelstrom. I returned to my sweetie bag and then got some much-needed sleep.

I woke after what I guessed was about four hours. The snowing hadn't stopped, but at least it hadn't got any worse.

I lay there for a few minutes, eating and drinking hot chocolate, then I decided it was time to go. I felt refreshed and I'd had a good sleep, eaten and rehydrated. This storm, I decided, could go on for a couple of days or a couple of hours. Me lying in a sleeping bag was achieving nothing. I would move while I felt good and if the storm did get worse, I could always bivi again.

Moving through a 'whiteout' in the dark is a bit like trying to walk in a straight line with your eyes closed: possible but bloody difficult. I moved slowly, hoping that I was at least moving slowly in the right direction. Eventually, the daylight appeared and slowly, very slowly, the snowing stopped and the wind died down so that by the afternoon, a calm had returned. This was confirmed by the fact that vehicles started to appear, which for me was an absolute Godsend, as it meant that I didn't have to concentrate so hard on route finding. I just jumped into the tire tracks they left behind.

I didn't know how much time I had lost but the one thing I did know was that any chance I may have had of getting the record was gone. I knew that to get the record, I would have had to maintain a fairly decent and consistent pace. The storm had put pay to that.

As I was plodding along, a vehicle came up behind me - Martin again, checking on us, to see if we were okay. He said that Ian had had a good night and was now only twelve km behind me. I thanked him for the update.

Once he left, I worked out that for Ian to have had a good night, he must have worked through the night, and worked hard, whereas I'd had a good sleep - this little nugget cheered me up no end.

It spurred me on and I pushed hard, setting a good and fairly fast pace and now that I could see for quite a distance, I was able to pick out various land marks and speed up until I reached a certain point. The chosen landmark might be a certain snowdrift, or even a vehicle that was approaching. I would speed up until it drew level, a sort of 'fartleking'.

Occasionally, a vehicle would stop and ask if I was okay - a couple of them asked if they could take a picture. I enjoyed these little distractions, as they relieved the boredom. It was now late afternoon, early evening. Another vehicle pulled up, only this time it was Scott and Mark, followed by another race vehicle containing Murray and welsh Mark, aka, Clanger! They were going on ahead to man the Swimming Point checkpoint. As they drove away I watched them and could still see them after about twenty minutes.

I tried to speed up and, as usual, failed miserably. Then

suddenly I spotted what appeared to be huge storage tanks, these tanks I hoped were part of the disused storage facility at Swimming Point.

I carried on then spotted a couple vehicles parked up. I tried to not get too excited, because, knowing my luck, they would be full of Japanese tourists taking pictures - it was only when one of the vehicles flashed its headlights did I realise that this was indeed the checkpoint. It was now about 20:30.

Approaching the two vehicles I was aware of a taped-off area, just in front of them. I grabbed my flasks and bag of food and First Aid kit. As I got into one of the vehicles I asked what the taped-off area was and was informed that it was where a lorry had recently broken through the ice and was now lying on the bottom of the Mckenzie river. (The driver had apparently managed to get out in one piece).

Clanger came over, grabbed my flasks and filled my dehydrated meal bags with hot water - at 6ft 4 inches and with knackered old stiff legs, the back of the car was not ideal, to say the least, but I was warm and out of the cold, I was also fed and watered and now I desperately tried to get some sleep. I had now been awake and constantly moving, for a little over twenty hours. Sleep proved elusive:- 1 - I couldn't get comfortable or stretch my legs and 2 - Scott snored.

I was fed and watered, but knackered. I gave up trying to sleep and decided to get going, reasoning that I could, if lucky, cover the last 47 or so miles in about 20 hours. So at 23:33 I left the warmth of the improvised Swimming Point checkpoint, to get back on to the Ice Road!

Swimming Point to Tuk - 47 miles

Leaving the warmth of the vehicles and stepping out on to the Ice Road was a bit of a shock and it wasn't long before I had to stop and put on my Arctic down jacket and an extra pair of gloves.

After a couple of hours, I caught sight of some lights coming toward me. It was one of the huge snowploughs clearing a path after the recent storm. These snowploughs are not like the snow ploughs at home - they are huge, the size of combine harvesters. I really hoped that the driver could see me.

I made sure that my headtorch was on full beam and kept moving it, to give the driver every opportunity to see me. It worked - he pulled up, opened his cab and asked the now familiar question:- "Are you okay?" I replied that I was, he then followed his line of questioning with:- "What are you doing?" I explained that I was in a race called the 6633 Ultra and there was a load of us and that we had started at Eagle Plains and were walking to Tuk. The silliness of this conversation was not lost on either of us. Here I was, an Englishman walking along a frozen Canadian river at 03:00 in the morning, telling a slightly bemused snowplough driver that I was trying to walk to Tuk! He replied by stating the bleeding obvious "You're crazy" and then offered me some hot coffee. When I replied that the race rules stated that I couldn't, it just seemed to confirm his "You're crazy" - theory, he wished me luck and informed me that Tuk was about 60 km away.

I carried on and he drove off. I was tired and could now feel the dreaded sleepmonster trying to make an appearance so I stopped, poured myself some coffee and ate some Rolos, Haribos and fruit pastilles, hoping the sugar rush would help me fend off the sleepmonster. I stood around for a few minutes longer than I normally would have, hoping that getting cold would also help keep me awake - stupid, I know, but desperate times call for desperate measures.

It worked, for now.

I finally moved off feeling a little better, but me and the sleepmonster are old adversaries and I knew from bitter experience that it would be back. For now, however, it was gone and if it could remain gone for the next couple of hours, it should be daylight. My mind started to wander, trying to remember Tuk and the hot showers and meals I would have when I got there, then bang - something hit me, a three foot wall of snow, a barrier. Some thoughtless bastard had placed a barrier of snow across the road, but who and why? I looked ahead and nothing, nothing but miles and miles of snow, the road was gone. As I turned to look around I noticed the road, then and only then did the penny drop. I had been sleepwalking and had somehow managed to make a perfect 90 degree turn and walked into the snowbank on the edge of the road.

Time for more coffee and at least it was now getting light. As I was drinking, a vehicle approached, waved and was gone. A few moments later, another appeared - the morning rush hour.

I kept moving, desperately willing the elusive Tuk into view, but nothing. Eventually, I spotted what could have been a tower, I didn't care what it was, it was something, something to focus on. I kept my eye on it, willing it to be Tuk. I had been watching it for a couple of hours and it just did not seem to get any closer, then heading toward me appeared a car full of teenagers. They slowed down, took some pictures and said that they had left Tuk and had been driving for half an hour. I thanked them and they wished me good luck. As they left, I tried to work out how far they would have driven in half an hour.

I never did work out how far they could have driven. I gave up when I realised it was a bloody long way!

I had now perfected my Ice Road shuffle and was putting it to good use, sort of scooting along the ice (a cross between sliding and running) then I realised that a vehicle was driving slowly along side me - a race vehicle. A few of the other racers were in it and cheered me on, some got out and proceeded to take pictures, pictures of a very desperate racer. Comments were made about the fact that I was STILL running, it wasn't strictly true, but it was better than limping, hobbling or crawling.

This little distraction cheered me up enormously. I watched them drive off, and followed their progress and again became disappointed at the distance I still had to do. After a while, I could make out buildings and movement, vehicles. I was close, but exactly how close I wasn't sure, 8 to 10 miles max, which could possibly translate in to 3 hours walking. I was tired and I was desperate, but I was also fed up and annoyed, annoyed that I seemed to be on a treadmill, walking hard but not actually making any progress. Tuk just never seemed to get any closer, then following the road around a bend I spotted a couple of the race vehicles driving toward me. Then another couple, a convoy. The cars full of support crew and racers had come to guide me in, the support was magnificent and very welcome. Slowly, like some slow procession of kerb crawlers, they drove by my side, some got out took more photos and walked with me. Kev, the winner of the 120 mile race walked with me for a while then a small, steep but mercifully short left-hand climb up on to terra firma. Tuk itself, through the small town and the finish line was in sight, right on the shoreline of the Arctic Ocean.

I had done it, it had taken me more than five years to reach the finish line of the 6633 Ultra, and by way of a bonus I had won the race.

The welcome and congratulations by the support crew and my fellow runners was fantastic and really appreciated.

The 6633 Ultra is a bloody tough race. The distance and hostility of the place commands the utmost respect - it doesn't matter who you are. Whether you are an elite, experienced Arctic/Ultra-distance athlete or first timer, it is do-able. Make sure that you are physically prepared, mentally prepared (it's more of a mental challenge than a physical one) and bloody well-organised and if I were to place those three things in order of importance, I would say mental, organised and physical.

Would I recommend it? YES, I would. Would I do it again? NO BLOODY CHANCE!

NOW WHAT NEXT!

The smile has returned - I've nearly finished.

And the winner is...

I've never won a race before and still couldn't quite believe it.

The other racers, who were generous with there help and support - a fantastic group of people.

Pete and Dean - who finished together.

The scenery - though beautiful - never changed. I felt very small.

One of those when will it ever end? moments - the slumped shoulders say it all.

The ice wall that I walked into after I had fallen asleep whilst walking!

FINALLY

*Be daring, be different, be impractical, be anything that
will assert integrity
of purpose and imaginative vision against the play-it-
safers, the creatures
of the commonplace, the slaves of the ordinary.*

Cecil Beaton: 1904-1980

As I sit here finishing off the book, I realise how very lucky I am. I have travelled all over the world, taken part in and survived some fantastic challenges, met some great and inspiring people - all because of that ten minute clip on TV.

Nothing would have been possible without the help and support of my 'slightly exasperated' wife. I am extremely grateful for her support and encouragement.

During many of the races I have taken part in, I have noticed that the people at the back of the field are without doubt the real heroes - their struggle, determination to finish and tenacious spirit commands respect from all - even the elite guys acknowledge this simple fact.

If you are thinking:- "Shall I have a go or is it a sport for a certain type of super fit athlete?" Let me assure you that yes, you might see the elite guys on TV or DVD flying around some desert, jungle, mountain or whatever, but the reality is so different. 90% of the field are battling away just to finish;

almost without fail, 90% or more have entered to see if they can reach the elusive finish line.

I have been beaten by older, retired people of both sexes, people with limbs missing, people with pacemakers fitted, hip replacements and cancer survivors. It doesn't matter, I enter to see if I can reach the elusive finish line and when I do, the pain goes away the smile returns and a feeling of absolute joy, relief, bliss, happiness. I haven't the words to explain the feeling of finishing a tough challenge.

Do you think you should have a go? You should. Will you finish? If you really want the finish line, you will.

Go on - you know you want to. It will hurt, the training will be boring and lonely but the feeling of achieving what is an extreme challenge is a feeling that will be with you forever.

Lastly a huge thank you to Andy Heading and Yann Besrest-Butler for some amazing photographs.

List of adventures;
Marathon distance and above

Marathon Des Sables 1996

London Marathon 1997

Himalayan 100 1998

London Marathon 1998

London Marathon 1999

Snowdon Marathon 1999

Isle of Wight Marathon 2000

Hi Tec Adventure Race 2000

Jordan Desert Cup 2001

Trailplus Adventure race 2002

Raid Amazonie 2003

Three Peaks Challenge 2003

Guadarun 2004

London Marathon 2004

Climbed Kilimanjaro 2004

Treadmill Challenge (100 miles in 24 hours) 2004

Paris Marathon 2005

7x7x7 (7 marathons 7 days 7 different ways) 2005

Jersey Challenge Adventure Race 2005

Yukon Arctic Ultra 100 mile 2006

West Wight Triathlon 2006

Dublin City Marathon 2006

Wight Challenge Adventure Race 2006

Yukon Arctic Ultra 320 mile 2007

Ironman UK 70.3 2007

Tough Guy 2007

6633 Ultra 2008 DNF

Atacama Crossing 2009

Norseman Extreme Triathlon 2010 DNF

Augrabies Extreme Marathon 2010

Yukon Arctic Ultra 430 mile 2011

Caesars Camp Endurance Run 2011 DNF

Centurion Running, NDW 50 2012

Centurion Running, Winter 100 2012 DNF

Namib Desert Challenge 2012

6633 Ultra 2013